China's Lessons for India: Volume II

Sangaralingam Ramesh

China's Lessons for India: Volume II

The Political Economy of Change

Sangaralingam Ramesh
University of Oxford
Oxford, UK

ISBN 978-3-319-58114-9   ISBN 978-3-319-58115-6   (eBook)
DOI 10.1007/978-3-319-58115-6

Library of Congress Control Number: 2017940624

Cover credit: Massonstock/iStock/Getty Images Plus

Printed on acid-free paper

This Palgrave Macmillan imprint is published by Springer Nature
The registered company is Springer International Publishing AG
The registered company address is: Gewerbestrasse 11, 6330 Cham, Switzerland

For my father and my mother,
Nallathamby Sangaralingam and Pathmarani Sangaralingam,
Inuvil and Karinagar, Ceylon.

Preface

Volume 1 focused on the analysis of the political economy of development of China and India. In this regard, it was found that the Indian economy is characterised by institutional rigidity and a lack of entrepreneurship at the microeconomic level. However, in the case of the Chinese economy, it was found that it is characterised by institutional flexibility and a high level of entrepreneurial activity.

Volume 2 of 'China's Lessons for India' focuses on the political economy of a change as it evaluates the nature of entrepreneurship in China and India as well as on the nature of innovation systems between the two countries. Another aspect of this study will be to establish how entrepreneurship and innovation have been responsible for economic change in India and China. Furthermore, in order to analyse the impact of the economic reforms on China's economy, a comparative case study, using propositions set out in Volume 1 is conducted in order to determine the impact of the reforms at a regional level.

China's economic reforms have had the effect of increasing China's internal and external markets, accompanied by high levels if economic growth. However, Britain's route to expanding its 'market' was to integrate more and more with the European Union through a customs union followed by the single market. The results for both countries have been different. A comparative study is presented in order to analyse the differences in economic growth between China and Britain from the 1970s to the present day. While the Chinese economy has experienced high levels of economic growth since the late 1970s, the British economy has not. This would indicate that in terms of increasing market size, effective integration is brought about through investment in infrastructure, incentivising innovation and entrepreneurship; and strengthening the institutional links between government, centres of innovation and commercial enterprises. This is in contrast to increasing market size as a result of a cumulative process of moving from a customs union to a single market and then to a union of a group of countries.

The book series would be of interest worldwide especially with regard to government for policy formulation, economists, NGO personnel, business professionals and also has general interest reading. The title suggests the context of the book is China's lessons for India. However, the policy findings of the book series are generally also applicable to countries in Europe, Africa and Latin America as well as Asia and North America. This is because the knowledge accumulated in the book series would be equally applicable not only to countries in Asia but also outside Asia. The material is timely, in view of Brexit, the rise of China and the potential of India. In this case the usefulness of the book series can be more than twenty years.

Oxford, UK   Sangaralingam Ramesh

Acknowledgements

The story of writing this book series is a long one. At its heart is the essence of a Ph.D. I completed at the School of Oriental and African Studies (SOAS), University of London in 2008. This Ph.D. started in October 2004 on a part-time basis, with the final year being 'full-time' although I was teaching at SOAS. I would like to thank Prof. Ben Fine for enrolling me, at the last minute, on the Ph.D. program at SOAS in October 2004. And I would also like to thank Dr. Dic Lo, Reader in Economics at SOAS for his generous support throughout and even beyond my studies. I would also like to thank Prof. Peter Nolan, Chong Hua Professor in Chinese Development, University of Cambridge and Prof. Christopher Cramer, Professor of the Political Economy of Development at SOAS, for their feedback following my Ph.D. Viva in October 2008. Anna Reeves of Palgrave Macmillan also gave me very useful advice with regard to the draft manuscript as did three anonymous reviewers. Finally, Lynda Cooper and Rachel Sangster, also with Palgrave Macmillan, helped with initiating the production process and I am also very grateful for their help.

While the main idea behind this book series was formulated during the time I was writing my Ph.D., the book series is an extension of the Ph.D. in many ways. These extensions include the applicability of China's economic success story to Indian economic development, the role of institutions as well as the role of entrepreneurship in facilitating economic development and economic growth in the context of China's economic reforms. For many years after the completion of the Ph.D. the ideas for this book series remained in my mind, but time could not be found to write them in words due to my teaching duties. Furthermore, while writing the book series began in 2012, it was sporadic and periodically interrupted. It was not until September 2015 when I started teaching at Kings College London on a part-time basis that time became more than sufficient for completing the writing of the series. Then following the completion of teaching at the University of Oxford's Summer School for Adults in early August 2016, I stayed at Keble College, Oxford and completed the writing of the draft manuscript at the Social Sciences Library, Manor Rd. Final amendments to the manuscript were completed at Bush House, Kings College London in my spare time.

Contents

List of Figures

List of Tables

1

Introduction

The purpose of Volume 2 of 'China's lessons for India' is to focus on the political economy of change in the context of China's economic reforms and the wider lessons which may be learnt from China's experience, building on the analysis in Volume 1, the political economy of development. The political economy of development in China and India is brought about by the nature of institutions, infrastructure investment and policy reorientation. However, at the heart of the political economy of change is the capacity for institutional change in order to support innovation, entrepreneurship and knowledge spillovers. This, in turn, will act to fuel sustainable economic growth.

There are essentially two models of innovation systems in a country, the National Innovation System (NIS) and the Triple Helix Model (THM). At the heart of the NIS is the Competence Block while the driving force of the NIS is the firm. On the other hand, the driving force of the THM is the strength of the university–industry–government linkage. Chapter 2 will focus on the evaluation of 'Knowledge Creation and Innovation Systems in China', and the NIS and the THM in particular. In this case, it will be established that the strength and the capability of national systems of innovation will depend on the

© The Author(s) 2017   **1**
S. Ramesh, *China's Lessons for India: Volume II*,
DOI 10.1007/978-3-319-58115-6_1

strengths of prevailing institutions such as education and research, the labour market and training opportunities, the strength and extent of development of the financial system, the nature of the tax regime as well as the strength of intellectual property rights. Moreover, Chap. 2 will establish that there are three different approaches to understanding why the structure and performance of innovation systems differs from country to country. These approaches include competition and entrepreneurship, competitive advantage of nations and a national system of innovation. Furthermore, this chapter will discuss specific reforms which incentivised entrepreneurship among researchers in institutes as well as the reorientation and reorganisation of research institutes with manufacturing firms. Components of China's innovative system in the context of telecommunications, the Internet, Corporate R&D, patents and scientific papers will also be evaluated.

The role of innovation systems in knowledge creation and the role of knowledge spillovers in the Chinese economy will be discussed in Chap. 3, where the focus will be on 'Knowledge Creation and Knowledge Spillovers: the aggregate economy'. This chapter will evaluate the nature of the NIS and the nature of the THM in the context of India and China. Moreover, this chapter will identify that the nature of the innovative system in India's case is more likely to be an NIS, while in China's case, the innovative system is more likely to be the THM. Chapter 4 will evaluate the nature of 'Entrepreneurship in China and India'. In this chapter, it will be established that the decollectivisation of agriculture in the 1980s was the cause of rising unemployment in the rural sector. This directly led to the rise of Town and Village Enterprises (TVE's). However, entrepreneurship was not viewed favourably by the government in the 1980s, and laws and regulations limited access to funds for entrepreneurs as well as a limitation on the number of workers which entrepreneurs could hire to a maximum of seven. Constraints on access to funding and on the hiring of workers had a negative impact on the growth of entrepreneurship in China. However, in the 1990s, the inefficiency of state-owned enterprises signalled a shift in government policy favouring private enterprises.

Chapter 5, a 'Comparative Study: Jiangsu, Hubei and Gansu 1949–2014', will analyse the impact of China's economic reforms on its Coastal, Central and Western regions by evaluating the case study propositions set out in Chap. 4, Modelling China's Economic Growth, in Volume 1. The case study will focus on a Coastal province, Jiangsu, a Central province, Hubei and a Western province, Gansu. Furthermore, the case study will encompass an analysis of infrastructural, knowledge creation and knowledge spillover factors which influence Chinese economic growth at the provincial level. These factors are associated with hard (e.g. roads, railways and freight), soft (e.g. education) infrastructure, manufacturing industry, S&T research parks and high-technology zones. Manufacturing industry has been included because it is associated with a concentration of infrastructure. Using the case study methodology specified in Chap. 4, Volume 1, the analysis will seek to answer the research questions set as well as addressing the research propositions specified. In this context, the analysis will find that Jiangsu is better endowed in terms of manufacturing and knowledge creation than is either Hubei or Gansu. Moreover, Jiangsu has a greater population density. With regard to knowledge creation, government grants to research institutions is bigger to Jiangsu Province. However, bank loans are more significant as a source of funds indicating a higher level of risk-taking, which is often associated with entrepreneurship. It would be reasonable to expect that entrepreneurship is higher in the Coastal region of China because of the reforms this region benefited first from the effects of open coastal cities, SEZs, NHTIDZs and Science and Technology Research Parks as well as the influx of FDI. Furthermore, the government reforms, facilitating horizontal linkages between research institutes, universities and firms enhanced entrepreneurial activity and stimulated knowledge spillovers, particularly in the Coastal region of the Chinese economy. Further, evidence that China's coastal region benefited disproportionately from the economic reforms can also be associated with changes in regional Total Fixed Investment in Fixed Assets (TFIFA). For example, after 1980, TFIFA in Jiangsu began to rise compared to either Hubei or Gansu, perhaps due to the development of SEZs. However, after 1995, TFIFA in Gansu was bigger than in either Hubei or Jiangsu. This may have been due to informal investment expenditure in the Western region prior to the formal implementation of the WDP in 1999. It is clear from the analysis that China is metamorphosing into its third stage of economic development, that of economic development through indigenous knowledge creation because of specific knowledge related reforms such as the '863' program, the Spark Program and Torch Program. This was accompanied by considerable decentralisation of economic control from central to local government.

There are two ways in which economic growth can be facilitated through the expansion of the market. The first is through regional integration facilitated by investment in infrastructure, free trade based on WTO rules and the use of supply side policies to facilitate free market forces and this entrepreneurship and innovation. This is the economic strategy China followed after and during the start of its economic reforms in 1978. On the other hand, another route a country can take to accommodate economic growth and market expansion is by following regional integration through the free trade area, customs union and single market scenario. This is the route which Britain has followed since joining the European Economic Community (EEC) in 1973. Chapter 6 will then evaluate Britain's attempted integration into the European Union as a means of regional integration and compare it with China's internal-regional integration since the start of its economic reforms in 1978. Britain started the European Free Trade Area with several other European states in 1960 just because it did not want to get involved with the European Community (EC) . This was because the basis of regional integration of that institution was through a customs union and the eventual denigration of national institutions at the expense of evolving supranational institutions such as the European Commission, the Council of Ministers and the EU Presidency. But in 1973, Britain decided to join the EEC, the forebear of the European Union (EU). In this case, it will be easy to see that the focus of the European regional integration project was not one of increasing market size and the enhancement of individual member states economic growth, but the formation of a United States of Europe. Therefore, the primary purpose of the European project was not an economic one, but rather a political project to form a supranational state—the United States of Europe (USE). Free movement, one of the four constructs of the European Union, has no economic sensibility about it. Its intention is to gradually erode national identity while creating a supranational European identity for the citizens of member states. In this way, over time there would be little opposition to the establishment of the USE. But the problem has been that this regional integration strategy has not produced the kind of economic growth for the member states of the EU which could have prevented the 'Leave' outcome of the British EU referendum on the 23rd June 2016. This is because high levels of economic growth would have prevented the widening disparities of income and lack of opportunity for many people in Britain. However, China's economic reforms, which started in 1978, has led to much higher economic growth than that experienced by either the EU or Britain since the period encompassing Britain's decision to join the EU and the commencement of China's economic reforms. While income disparity has increased between China's regions during the reform years, more people have been lifted out of poverty in China during the last 40 years than at any other time in human history. Furthermore, the Chinese government has put in place further plans to reduce these disparities by increased investment in infrastructure to aid further market expansion, notably the Karakoram highway and increased trade based on WTO rules. China is also actively investing in other countries infrastructure and at the same time expanding its maritime network by acquiring rights to own and operate sea ports in other countries. In this case, the lesson for India is that state-level institutions to some extent, especially over economic, regulatory and legal aspects, should have ascendancy over supranational institutions. It also follows from the findings of Chap. 5 that economic decentralisation enhances provincial and therefore national economic growth. This is very important in a country like India, which in many respects is similar to the European Union because it is a country of diverse nationalities and cultures, though united by one religion, which became politically united as one due to the power of the British Empire. Volume 2 will end with a 'Conclusion', which will bring together 'China's Lessons for India', political economy of development and political economy of change.

2

Knowledge Creation and Innovation Systems in China

The importance of the spatial proximity of the firms to maximise the effects of knowledge spillovers in knowledge-based activities has been highlighted in the literature (Ghio et al. 2015). However, the spatial proximity approach ignores the role of institutions which set the rules of innovation at a national level which, because of this, can be assumed to be fixed. On the other hand, the level of innovative capacity is not the same at each point on the spatial plain (Acs et al. 2016). There are two ways in which innovative capacity can be theoretically explained. Firstly, the role of the entrepreneur in the context of the innovative capacity of the economy falls under the umbrella of the national systems of entrepreneurship (Acs et al. 2014). Secondly, there is the national system of innovation (NSI) which depicts how innovative activities arise as a result of firms behaving within the national institutional context (Nelson 1993). According to the latter, the validity of the NSI depends on a number of assumptions. Firstly, countries differ in terms of economic performance. Secondly, the extent of the economic performance of a country depends on the level of development as well as the stability of institutions, such as a codified legal code, an effective judicial system and an effective form of government. The greater the extent of the development and stability of institutions in

© The Author(s) 2017
S. Ramesh, *China's Lessons for India: Volume II*,
DOI 10.1007/978-3-319-58115-6_2

a country, then the greater will be the positive impact on the country's technological and innovative capacity. Lastly, if a country is able to endear policies which favour technological development and innovation, then this will have a positive impact on the economic performance of a country. Furthermore, a knowledge economy is likely to facilitate greater entrepreneurial opportunities than is a non-knowledge based economy, (Acs et al. 2013). According to Hall et al. (2014), the framework of NSI depends upon a whole host of institutional factors which encompasses education and research, the labour market and training, the financial system, the tax regime as well as the strength of intellectual property rights. The major failing of NSI as a framework to analyse the nature of innovation in a national context arises from two different strands. Firstly, the nature and the role of entrepreneurship in innovating within the NSI framework are unclear. Secondly, the NSI is unable to account for the differences in the structure and the performance of innovative systems between emerging and developed economies (Acs et al. 2016). However, where countries do differ on the basis of the structure and the performance of the innovative systems, there are three approaches to understanding why this may be the case. The first approach is Competition and Entrepreneurship (Kirzner 1973). The second approach is the Competitive Advantage of Nations (Porter 1990). The third approach is the National System of Innovation (Nelson 1993). In the context of Competition and Entrepreneurship, there are two strands of thought which seek to explain how innovation, competition and economic growth may differ from country to country and from region to region. The Schumpeterian system, Schumpeter (1934), seeks to explain how the market mechanism evolves and innovates by changing the production function through a reallocation of resources. However, Kirznerian entrepreneurship, Kirzner (1973), suggests that economic activity takes place within the confines of the existing production function. If there is no change in the existing production function, then the implication is that there is no long-term improvement in national performance (Acs et al. 2016). The latter suggests that the reason why the production function changes according to the Schumpeterian system is that entrepreneurs are able to reallocate the factors of production by commercialising innovations by simply establishing new firms. However, according to NSI theory and Kirznerian entrepreneurship, the entrepreneur does not reallocate the factors of production, but commercialises innovations in the context of existing firms (Acs et al. 2016). The NSI framework, therefore, excludes the role of the Schumpeterian entrepreneur from the process of innovation and economic growth. But it does analyse country's economic performance from the perspective of differences in the quality, quantity and the nature of existing institutions. The NSI framework also excludes the role of governance in the formation of innovation systems. In the context of bioinformatics, it has been suggested that Chinese scientists lack the ability to set a research agenda, while the state lacks the expertise to form it (Salter et al. 2016). In a wider context, this assertion is not true as China has the largest number of domestic patent applications in the world. However, it can be asserted that the number of domestic patent applications is a dubious measure of innovative success because patents may have been filed by foreign MNCs. Furthermore, the quality of Chinese patent applications may be lower than that of other countries (Kennedy 2015). Nevertheless, it has also been found that increased government funding for university R&D will increase the quality of patents, while government subsidies for patenting will increase the quantity of patents but not necessarily the quality of the patents (Fisch et al. 2016). It is state funding that has enabled China to be at the frontier of stem cell research and China's spending on R&D is only second to the USA at a global level. In the case of India, which may lack a more formal and robust approach to innovation compared to China, it has been found that a culture of innovation at the firm level is important for the generation of new ideas (Jha et al. 2016). However, India has significant innovative capacity in software engineering with strong value chain links with the USA and Germany (Lema et al. 2015).

Modelling Innovative Systems

There are three major approaches to modelling innovative systems.[1] The first approach is that of Marshallian industrial districts. Marshall (1890) theorised that some economies are internal to a firm, while others are external to the firm. A spatial concentration of external economies can be achieved by concentrating small firms within a region. The application of special incentive policies such as low taxation of profits, no taxation on the imports of fixed assets and the retention by the exporting firm of foreign exchange earnings may be sufficient to persuade firms to concentrate themselves at a central point within the spatial plain. The theoretical logic behind SEZs and NHTIDZs emanates from the notion of Marshallian districts. Secondly, there is the concept of the innovative milieu approach or GREMI. In this approach, the presence or absence of a number of factors will influence innovative activity at a focal point within the spatial plain. These factors of innovation include qualified personnel to carry out R&D, freely available technical knowledge, the closeness of consumer markets, availability of local networking opportunities and availability of local inputs of production. The absence of one of these factors will increase costs associated with production or lower the return on the production of the goods. This school of thought also emphasises synergy of factors associated with collective learning, intensity of R&D and strategies for production among others. The third approach to modelling innovative systems is that of the regional innovation systems (RIS). This school of thought heralds the arrival of systems of innovation, which highlights the fact that the technological innovativeness and market competitiveness of firms are dependent on institutions within their local environment. Furthermore, innovation systems are classified on either a sector or geographical basis. The latter emphasises the fact that agents learn from each other and that knowledge is acquired from agents within firms and from agents between firms. The concept behind regional innovation systems is that national innovative performance is not dependent on just the innovativeness of individual firms but depends more on how firms interact to exchange R&D results as well as generating R&D results themselves. However, in a competitive environment, this exchange of R&D results is a naïve view, unless it is from an intermediate supplier firm to a producer firm. According to one definition,[2] the main features of a strong regional innovation system are strong linkages between centres of knowledge creation, firms who will use the knowledge to produce new technologically advanced products and institutions intermediating between the two. However, it is symptomatic that many regions do not have all the factors required to effectively form the linkages that an effective innovative system would need. This was the rationale for the Chinese government to institute policies to reform Chinese education and R&D. The reform policies strengthened knowledge creation and knowledge spillover effects. The intention of the reforms was to geographically proximate technological innovation, knowledge creation and final production within specific regions. For example, Zhongguancun in Beijing only became a RIS because it was, at the time that the reform policies were instituted, already an area of concentration of research facilities. The majority of enterprises sprang up in the area after the reform policies. Shenzhen only became an RIS in its own right because of the fact that high-tech producers from Hong Kong shifted manufacturing of goods from Hong Kong to Shenzhen to take advantage of low manufacturing costs. Moreover, research institutions in Beijing established branches in Shenzhen. These two examples indicate that while some geographical locations may not possess all or any of the factors required for generating the strong strategic alliances required of a strong RIS, the application of relevant policies will allow for alliances to form. Empirical analysis of the telecommunications industry in Shenzhen Hi-Tech Industrial Park has shown the varying levels of importance of cross-national, cross-regional and inter-regional connections to knowledge flows in Shenzhen (Wu 2016). According to the latter, cross-regional connections have a positive impact on-trade and non-trade interdependence, facilitating the exploitation of knowledge creation. On the other hand, inter-regional connections have a positive impact on on-trade interdependence and this enhances the exploitation of innovation. The importance of China's telecommunications industry to its national security has resulted in different levels of restrictions being imposed which has facilitated the flow of different levels of knowledge in Shenzhen (Wu 2016).

Another feature of an RIS which has not been identified in the RIS literature is the need for an efficient labour market and the promotion and development of entrepreneurial education in an economic and regulatory environment which is favourable to entrepreneurship (Bonnet 2016). While India and China may both have entrepreneurial education systems, India lacks an efficient and flexible labour market due to regulatory and legal burdens. Firms in India are also hampered by other legal and regulatory burdens as well as facing supply-side constraints such as the country's poor infrastructure. However, in the context of knowledge management support for innovation, it has been recognised in Indian entrepreneurial education that the best knowledge management support for education arises through the realisation that it is not an isolated process but one which best arises from the integration of the many activities of firms (Datta 2016). Recent developments within regional innovation policy suggest that governments have sought to expedite the diffusion of knowledge from universities to SMEs and from SMEs to larger corporations. The technological absorption and technological innovativeness of SMEs are being improved by improving networking opportunities among firms and the transfer of technology. There has also been a tendency for regional development and technology initiatives to converge in many countries.[3] A common strand in the regional innovation and development theoretical framework is that innovative agents have to be proximate in order to facilitate innovation. Proximate agents ensure good communication and networking opportunities. All three schools of thought have common aspects.[4] Firstly, there is a reduction in cost associated with 'neighbourly' communication and with learning and cooperation opportunities when firms are close together. Secondly, innovation systems are characterised by networking relationships among firms. Thirdly, there are interactions of an official and unofficial nature among firms in the proximity and an importance of domestic and global networking. Finally, in innovation systems, agglomeration economies occur due to the 'webs of local linkages and sub-contracting'. A number of theoretical models have also been developed in order to better understand the nature of economic systems. First and foremost, of these theoretical models, is the Triple Helix based upon which a number of variants have been developed. Variants of the Triple Helix Model include the Quadruple Helix and the Triple Helix Twins. According to the Triple Helix Model, the optimal conditions for fostering innovation result from effective interrelations between academia, government and industry (Cai and Liu 2015). The latter suggests that the Triple Helix Model represents a normative framework for understanding the linkages between economic actors involved in the innovation process. However, despite the positive view taken by many regarding the explanatory power of the Triple Helix Model, it has two main weaknesses (Cai and Liu 2015). Firstly, the model does not take into account differences between countries. Secondly, the model does not account for differences in social settings. The Triple Helix Model is essentially a theoretical model which results from the experiences of the evolution of innovation in developed countries. In the case of China, the geographical unit of an innovation system are the provinces (Chen and Guan 2011). These may be in contrast to other countries in which the units of innovation systems may be cities, for example. Due to provincial differences in R&D capability, the level of government support, the extent of academia, government and industry linkages, the development of innovative systems and the efficiency of innovation vary from one province to another (Cai and Liu 2015). According to the latter, in the case of China, the Triple Helix Model needs to be adapted because the extent of academia, industry and government linkages is dependent on 'top up' and 'bottom down' initiatives by central and local governments, respectively, with regard to innovation. Nevertheless, Cai and Liu (2015) studied the innovation process in the Tongji Knowledge Economic Zone in order to determine which factors impacted on the innovation process to the greatest extent. In this case, it was determined that there was inefficiency between 'top-down' and 'bottom-up' initiatives. This inefficiency was a result of the weak state of development of institutional mechanisms—legal and governance related which affected the extent to which 'bottom-up' initiatives could impact on the innovation process (Cai and Liu 2015). The latter also found that innovation in the Tongji Creative Cluster was based on knowledge-intensive services and this contributed more to the economic development of the Yangpu District than did high-tech manufacturing industries. The focus of the Tongji Creative Cluster was mainly due to the greater level of involvement of universities in the knowledge-intensive services compared to high-tech manufacturing. However, the university–industry link remains weak mainly because of the lack of protection and enforcement of intellectual property rights which have led to mutual mistrust (Cai and Liu 2015).

China's Innovation Systems

Innovation systems are necessary for the creation of knowledge, and their formation is facilitated by a concentration of infrastructure, good educational facilities and high R&D expenditure. The problem with China is that while a number of regional innovation systems coexist, mainly in the Coastal region of the country, a national innovation system has not yet formed. The three major economic systems in China include the Bo Hai Rim (BHR), the Pearl River Delta (PRD) and the Yangtze River Delta (YRD). Innovation systems have taken root mainly in the Coastal region for a number of reasons.[5] Firstly, central and local governments have provided the necessary resources for the establishment of scientific parks according to national science and technology programs. Secondly, the facilitation of FDI into China by the post-1979 reforms engineered a transfer of technology from developed countries. Specifically, FDI and its increasing technological content have tendered to favour the development of specialised operational clusters. It is the expectation of state policy makers that the production clusters formed in the three regions will evolve into technological clusters, which will in turn create an innovative climate in the whole country. Thirdly, the spontaneous development of industrial and technological clusters has facilitated the continuous development of innovation systems. Finally, education is stronger in these regions due to more funding opportunities, economic prosperity and the ease of delivery of education to end-users.

A feature of the clustering of centres of production in the Coastal regions of China has been the geographical concentration and subsequent agglomeration effects recognised by Krugman (1991) in his New Economic Geography. However, Sigurdson (2004) recognises that the spatial distributions of clusters will 'aside from a geographical concentration and also have to include sectoral or functional characteristics'. In these circumstances, Sigurdson (2004) suggests that 'functional proximity takes precedence over geographical closeness'. Furthermore, Sigurdson (2004) differentiates historically from the earlier stages of industrialisation in the nineteenth century and the nature of the industrialisation taking place in China today. He does this by suggesting that 'industrial plants as such are no longer the geographical concentration of complete production as was previously the case'. More relevant now to industrialisation and the formation of innovative high-tech clusters, especially in China, are the relevant knowledge linkages necessary to support production and a sufficient critical mass of business activities to activate a competence block. A competence block is the minimum set of competencies, which make up a functional innovation system, to profit and exploit from knowledge. Eliasson et al. (1996) define a competence block as,

> The total infrastructure needed to create (innovation), select (entrepreneurship), recognise (venture capital provision), diffuse (spillovers) and commercially exploit (receiver competence) new ideas in clusters of firms.

This definition suggests that education is the key to the formation of an innovation system. However, this definition does not recognise the importance of the role of government in facilitating innovation, entrepreneurship, the commercialising of innovation as well as the interlinking of the three at the same time. Both educational reform and reform of the research sector in China have created the environment in which innovative entrepreneurship can prosper. Reform of both sectors resulted in educated individuals engaging in innovative entrepreneurship. Many returning students from overseas have not only received Ph.Ds from American, European or ANZAC countries but also received further training. This has facilitated the transition of returning students, to China, into entrepreneurs. The Chinese government's reform of the research sector and associated benefits has proved to be fertile territory upon which the seeds of entrepreneurship have been sown. China has also made progress in its approach to modifying patent regulations in order to support emerging research in embryonic stem cells. For example, China has amended patent regulations so that more patents can be issued for embryonic stem cell downstream technology, although it can make its patent laws clearer (Peng 2016). On the other hand, while India has complied with Trade Related Intellectual Property Rights (TRIPS), the impact has been to divert innovation activity into other areas but it has had little impact on increasing India's export values (Bouet 2015).

China's Thirteenth Five-Year Plan (2016–2020) is indicative of the fact that the Chinese government will continue to encourage entrepreneurship by investing in new science and technology projects in the hope that it will lead to further innovation and the development of new technology Xinhua (2015). The latter suggests that the Thirteenth Five-Year Plan will focus on regulating the consumption of energy, water and construction land. Furthermore, there will be greater emphasis on investment in green energy and carbon emission regulations in energy-intense sectors such as power, steel, chemicals and building materials. At the socio-developmental level, there will be an emphasis on promoting health through the reform of the healthcare system and to lift more people out of poverty. The reform of the healthcare system will involve a government investment of 20 billion Yuan, as well as an estimated private sector investment of 40 billion Yuan, in 'precision medicine' in order to apply genome sequencing technology to fight chronic diseases such as diabetes, cancer and cardiovascular disease (Qionghui 2016). China's economy may have reached a 'tipping' point where there have been sufficient levels of capital accumulation in the economy such that the economy is transitioning from a focus on production to one based on innovation, whereas in the Indian economy this transition is taking time due to insufficient capital accumulation in the economy (Altenburg et al. 2008).

A competence block cannot be specifically designed[6] although, as in the case of China, the necessary policies, institutions and primary infrastructure can be created and applied to facilitate its formation. Sigurdson (2004) suggests that the creators of innovation do not have to be geographically concentrated in order to allow the competence block to function. Participants in the functions of the competence block could be part of a 'network that is dynamic and inventive in knowledge creation'.[7] Therefore, a competence block can exist primarily as a functional or sectoral cluster, and geographical location is of secondary importance. This feature is important because the availability of telecommunications and access to the Internet will make the formation of a competence block independent of its location. In order to trigger dynamic regional development and subsequent innovation-led growth, a number of factors are important. These factors include physical infrastructure, manufacturing, telecommunications infrastructure, science and technology research parks; and education. These factors allow not only regional development, urbanisation and the formation of cities but also the integration of regional innovation systems to form a national one. However, Sigurdson (2004) excludes the role of entrepreneurship in the process of innovation, the transition of knowledge into a usable product, service or solution. It has been shown in the context of the Indian crude oil industry that innovation is facilitated by entrepreneurial activity, resulting in new products and/or service which may be adopted by other firms in the sector (Iyer 2016). Moreover, in East Asian economies in which there has been little if any state involvement in the commercialisation of knowledge, resulting in innovation, it has been shown that entrepreneurial activity plays the role of a good substitute (Yoon et al. 2015). Furthermore, it has also been found that innovation in management practice is also important for efficiency in the Indian petrochemical industry. If senior management plays a leading role in the adoption of green technology, then this trend in the adoption of green technology will trickle down to the entire firm (Roy and Khastagir 2016).

The formation of cities caters for geographical closeness in two ways (Sigurdson 2004). Firstly, associated with cities is the territorial integrity with regard to the density of business services and population. Secondly, a city has the capacity to network with other cities which have similar characteristics. Sigurdson (2004) suggests that this two-dimensional geographical closeness attracts to cities, government and others, types of social and economic functions. However, with regard to industrialisation and urbanisation, China casts a picture very different from that painted by other countries going through a similar phase. In China, industrialisation accounts for 50% of GDP but only 30% of the population lives in urbanised centres. Regional development in China, especially in the Coastal regions, has given rise to four types of urban centres.[8] These are predominantly the pre-1949 foreign-led development of Coastal cities such as Shanghai, Tianjin, Wuhan and Guangzhou. These cities were only weakly linked to the interior hinterland, essentially because of a lack of transportation and communications infrastructure and deficient Social Capital. However, cities also formed in the interior or away from navigable waterways due to military or political reasons such as the need for balanced regional growth. These cities can be characterised by their less dynamic nature and inferior industrialisation. However, cities may also form because the area they are surrounded by has mineral resources. These include cities such as Tangshan, Datang and Ansghan which formed specifically because the areas surrounding them had mineral resources. The extraction of these mineral resources and the need for the transportation of these resources to centres of production were based on a desire to model the Chinese state in terms of the Soviet model. This led to the failed 'railways lead to prosperity' philosophy of 1949–1978. There were also cities which formed as a result of the 1978 economic reforms. These cities included Shenzhen, Dongguan, Wuxi, Suzhou, Yantai and Weihai. These cities formed due to the 1978 economic reforms, the subsequent influx of FDI and 'strong local support and new material and knowledge infrastructures'.[9]

The pre-1949 and post-1978 cities are those which have contributed significantly to the economic development of China. However, with regard to 'capturing' and maintaining comparative advantages in the production of goods and in the provision of services, the post-1978 cities have a greater role to play in the future economic development of China. Sigurdson (2004) suggests that:

> Capturing and keeping a comparative advantage will require specialisation. Technological clusters often play an important role and need a conducive environment that provides knowledge, supportive interaction and incentive structures to become successful.

Furthermore, in order to be successful, clusters of innovation require a well-educated workforce, R&D activity, transportation infrastructure and policy measures intended to increase the quality and quantity of labour and capital as well as encouraging the incubation of entrepreneurship.

Centres of Innovation

The foundation for manufacturing-led economic growth was laid, in China, in the late 1970s and 1980s. The foundations for innovation and technological growth in the Chinese economy were laid in the mid-1980s and the 1990s with the establishment of twenty-four New and High Technology Industry Development Zones (NHTIDZ) in 1991. The first high-technology park was set up in Zhongguancun, Beijing, in 1988. Zhongguancun benefited because of its proximity to a cluster of research institutes belonging to the Chinese Academy of Sciences (CAS) and centres of higher education such as Beijing University and Tsinghua University.[10] Furthermore, the closeness of central government and other related funding agencies meant that it was relatively easy for technological innovations to go from the drawing board to production. However, Sigurdson (2004) notes that the factors which favoured Zhongguancun are changing in three ways. Firstly, university researchers will often start up their own companies, independently from high-technology parks. Secondly, universities have moved away from enterprise creation to concentrate on teaching and their own independent research. Finally, the commercial incubation of discoveries is becoming increasingly institutionalised within universities rather than High Technology Parks. The NHTIDZs which followed were established using the Zhongguancun Technology Park in Beijing[11] as a model. A further twenty-seven NHTIDZs were set up in 1993 with an additional set up in 1997. Of the fifty-seven NHTIDZs, twenty-nine were established in the Coastal provinces, fourteen in the Central provinces and fourteen in the Western provinces. Guangdong, Shandong and Jiangsu are the provinces with the highest number of NHTIDZs, six, five and four, respectively. These provinces are all in the Coastal regions of China.

The transfer of technology and technological learning effects associated with spatial clusters in developing countries has tended to focus on the manufacturing and export sectors. However, a study by Zhou and Xin (2003) focuses on the dynamics of the interactions between multinational companies (MNCs) and domestic firms, with regard to technological transfer and learning effects in the ICT information communications technology (ICT) sector in Zhongguancun Technology Park in Beijing. Zhongguancun was originally the centre of technological research and education in Beijing. A number of renowned universities and research institutes were located in the area. This gave the cluster a rich concentration of scientific research expertise. However, this expertise served no purpose under the centrally planned economy because there was no need for product innovation. In the central planned economy, technological innovation and scientific research only served the needs of the military and the production process. Nevertheless, the post-1979 economic reforms unleashed forces of change, especially with regard to the funding of scientific research by central and local governments. This change in funding acted as a signal to scientists and researchers in universities and research institutions in clusters to become entrepreneurs and start up their own enterprises. Initially, these start-ups were engaged in the assembly and testing of parts as well as offering technological services. Nevertheless, they evolved into producing generic technological products for the Chinese language market.[12] Within the Zhongguancun Technology Park, there is a significant interaction between local firms and multinational companies in a hierarchical fashion. MNCs are 'top heavy' with regard to expertise and resources associated with management, technology and capital. However, the cultural, linguistic, low cost and local market knowledge difficulties often associated with MNCs operating in a foreign market have led the MNCs to follow a collaborative approach with local firms, fostering an atmosphere which facilitates the transfer of technology to and technological learning by local firms. The mechanism by which both are accomplished is through a division of labour between MNCs and local firms.[13] Indeed, at this time technological transfer and learning by local firms in the cluster were endogenous to that cluster as the resources required for technological innovation existed within the cluster. The growth of the technology market attracted MNCs to the Zhongguancun cluster which then went onto subcontract non-developmental work to local firms in order to comply with government regulations.[14] The move by the MNCs into the cluster disabled any incentive for local firms to technologically innovate. It is at this

point that the framework of analysis departs from the one used to analyse technological clusters in developed countries. This is because technological learning by and technological transfer to local firms changes
from an endogenous source to an exogenous one. However, this situation began to change in the 1990s when local firms began to make use
of the knowledge they had accumulated as the marketing agents of the
MNCs and develop their own products. One famous example of a local
firm which successfully did this was Lenovo. Domestic firms which 'in-
license' technology for use from foreign MNCs have been found to be
more innovative than domestic firms which rely on endogenous innovation (Li-Ying and Wang 2015).

It has been found that MNC R&D investment in China is market
oriented, while MNC R&D investment in India is resource (labour)
oriented while the upgrading of R&D investment tends to follow an
evolutionary pattern (Bruche 2009). Thus, in China, R&D investment
focuses on the commercialisation of knowledge, while in India the focus
of R&D investment is in education and training. MNCs can also be
expected to gain local market knowledge through forming joint ventures with local firms or by simply buying them outright (Thite et al.
2016). The market orientation of foreign MNC in China is exemplified
by the involvement of MNCs in China's energy industry. Both MNCs
and domestic firms have increased energy efficiency in China, but there
has been very little interaction between the two (Herrerias et al. 2016).

The bulk of the work undertaken by local Chinese firms in the
Zhongguancun cluster falls into software development, systems integration and consulting fields for Chinese ICT users. This is in addition
to sales and distribution services for the MNC's. The MNCs undertake high-end product development in Zhongguancun with a number,
including Lucent, Motorola, Sun, IBM and Oracle, opening research
centres in Beijing. Many Chinese employees gain experience with local
Chinese firms before leaving to join an MNC on better pay. However,
some may set up their own businesses. This brain drain slows down the
development and growth of local firms in the cluster. Zhou and Xin
(2003) chose Zhongguancun and the ICT sector to study the dynamics
and synergies associated with the technological transfer to and technological learning by local firms, specifically because of the unique ability

of this spatial cluster to accumulate and grasp the essence of exogenous technology and 'rewire' it for the Chinese market. The data for the study was collected by formal interviews with up to eighty senior executives of companies based in the Zhongguancun cluster. Questions asked in the interviews were related to company history, technological sources and development, interactions with MNC's, government bodies and research institutions, and the sub-contracting of technological work.

The evolutionary growth of the Chinese ICT sector as represented by firms in the Zhongguancun cluster has reached such a stage that companies are being forced by the needs of market specialisation to move from the basic business activities of installing systems and providing technical services to adding value-added activities. The interviews conducted by Zhou and Xin (2003) with senior executives of firms based in the Zhongguancun cluster illustrate this very point. For example, TongTech moved into the middleware sector for financial applications, directing its R&D research into this field. Legend shifted business strategy towards the manufacture of network equipment.[15] However, the Chinese purchasers of ICT equipment felt it safer to purchase ICT equipment from MNC's based on the reputation for the quality of their products, despite the fact that Chinese companies such as TongTech prided itself for producing ICT equipment which took into account the uneven infrastructure in China in product design. Nevertheless, MNCs had also begun to take into account the differences needed in product design and manufacture in order to take into account the differences between countries in the levels of infrastructure development as well as government policy. In order to achieve this, foreign MNCs had established local R&D centres.[16]

Zhou and Xin (2003) also suggest that indigenous R&D factors within the Zhongguancun cluster, such as the availability of science and technology research expertise, have also helped local firms to develop and deviate from the standard products of MNC's. Furthermore, the workforce in the cluster is not only highly educated, but also mobile and entrepreneurial mirroring the economic requirements of a market economy. This is in stark contrast to the immobility of labour and its non-entrepreneurial nature in the state-owned enterprises. Education, mobility and entrepreneurship facilitated the efficiency of the diffusion of information in the Silicon Valley cluster in the USA.[17] A further advantage favouring the diffusion of information and innovation for the Zhongguancun cluster is that the cluster is located in Beijing, a city which hosts a large number of international conferences and trade shows.[18] With regard to government policy, a shift occurred in 1999 when the administration of the Zhongguancun cluster changed from coming under urban district level to the municipal government. This gave firms based on the cluster access to the State Council with benefits flowing from the relationship including increased funding for universities based in the cluster and improvements in infrastructure. Furthermore, there was a shift by the government from directly managing state-owned ICTs to promoting and regulating the ICT market under free market conditions.

Elements of Centres of Innovation

Telecommunications Infrastructure Pre-1978

The Ministry of Posts and Telecommunications (MPT) was formed in 1949. The Directorate General of Telecommunications (DGT) was set up as a section of the MPT in 1950. The DGT had responsibility for regulation, supply services, financial and human resource management of all aspects of telecommunications in China. However, in the latter part of 1950, all these separate activities of the DGT were handed to separate departments within the MPT. The DGT was left in sole charge of the operations of the telecommunications network. Posts and Telecommunications Administrations (PTAs) were handed the responsibility of administering the edicts of the MPT at the provincial level. This form of organisation was seen as bureaucratic as each department of the MPT was reflected in the PTA. Decisions which were made at the provincial level were always referred up to the MPT.[19] As a result of the Great Leap Forward, all activities of the MPT except management of the Beijing and national trunk networks were handed over to local and provincial governments. However, towards the end of 1959 control of budgeting, planning and supply reverted to the MPT. This was due to the chaos, which had resulted from provincial and local government management of these activities during the Great Leap. In 1962, control of all telecommunications activity became centralised with control directly held by the MPT. Further developments did not take place until 1969 when the MPT was dismantled and the DGT was put under the jurisdiction of the military. In China after 1949, telecommunications were seen as a national security concern.[20] Therefore, little thought had been given to telecommunications as a service sector industry and an accessory to knowledge creation. Profits from the postal service, which had been amalgamated with the railways, were used to subsidise telecommunications deficits. The latter arose because the telecommunications sector was not profit driven and heavily subsidised by the state. Due to financial difficulties sustained over the years by the telecommunications sector, the MPT was re-established in 1973. At the same time, the PTAs were established under the dual control of both provincial and MPT administrations. Any profits made by the PTAs were handed directly to the provincial governments. However, the telecommunications sector lacked any market orientation. The development of telecommunications in China was subject to the requirements of the state and the military. The objective of both was the same—that of maintaining control of the general population. Moreover, the residential telephone was a luxury made available to only senior politicians and military officers.[21] Furthermore, prior to the 1978 reforms, there was no incentive for enterprise in China's telecommunications sector, and due to central planning, operating efficiency and profits were not relevant sector/firm objectives. The political disturbances of the Great Leap Forward and the Cultural Revolution contributed to the Chinese telecommunications sector operating inefficiently. Thus, the Chinese telecommunications sector suffered operating losses from 1966 to 1978. During this period, only 38% of the population had a fixed line telephone.[22]

Telecommunications Infrastructure Post-1978

Following the 'Four Modernisations' program of Deng Xiaoping in 1978, the telecommunications infrastructure was seen as integral to the economic development of China. Without access to 'instant communication' to local and foreign destinations, and in the absence of a multimoded transport network, multinational companies would be reluctant to take advantage of the opportunities offered by China's post-1978 economic reforms. Furthermore, the restricted availability of telecommunications to the general population made the dissemination of knowledge and its creation difficult. This argument ensured that the telecommunications sector in China became recognised as an industry in its own right in 1979. At this time, control of all aspects of telecommunications development was handed to the MPT. Moreover, directive 165 issued in 1979 stipulated that the post and telecommunications sectors should be separated and each sector should be administered separately. Nevertheless, this separation did not formally occur until 1998. Further reform of the Chinese telecommunications sector was necessitated because of the realisation that there was a lack of contractual obligations between the administrative units of the MPT and other institutions in the sector. This led the Chinese government to introduce three substantial changes to the administration of the telecommunications sector.[23] Firstly, the performance of the telecoms sector was delegated to enterprise management. Secondly, MPT administrative authority was handed to the lower levels of provincial governments. Finally, incentive schemes were introduced.

In 1980, Chinese government policy on telecoms was directed towards the development of intra-city telephone networks. Local PTEs were given authority over all locally collected revenue and the price setting of telephone installation fees. In 1984, the 90% rule was adopted. The implications of this move were threefold. Firstly, 90% of all government investment in the telecoms sector was to be considered as non-payable loans. Secondly, 90% of all foreign exchange revenue was to be retained by the MPT. Thirdly, 90% of all earnings were to be retained by the MPT. In 1988, the State Council adopted a policy document, which encapsulated four principles regarding the development of telecommunications infrastructure in China. Firstly, the MPT should coordinate all planning and development. Secondly, resources for infrastructure construction should be drawn from diverse sources. Thirdly, each administration level should have its' responsibilities clearly defined. Finally, government administration of the telecoms sector should be coordinated with that at the local level. In return, the MPT gave its departments more autonomy and set up two separate posts for the Director General of Telecommunications and Director General of Posts. The following year provincial-level regulatory bodies were set up. However, joint ventures between Chinese firms and foreign firms remained restricted, and in 1992, the MPT stipulated that all such ventures were forbidden. This was restated much more strongly the following year and excluded all foreign investment or management of broadcasting networks or wireless networks in China. Nevertheless, China Telecom became a recognised legal enterprise when the MPTs DGT registered it as such with the government in 1995. In the same year, the State Council lifted the embargo on foreign investment in China's telecom sector. This raised the prospect of much needed foreign investment into China's telecom sector which would bring not only new technology into the sector but also the opportunity for Chinese workers to acquire new technical skills. Forty-nine per cent of China Telecom floated on the Hong Kong stock market in 1997, and in the latter part of the 1990s, China Unicom was formed combining forty-five joint ventures. However, the Ministry of Information Industry [MII] decreed that this was illegal. In early 1999, the MII stated that China Unicom should unwind all its joint venture contracts with foreign firms. China Unicom was rewarded later on in the year when the State Council stipulated that China Unicom should gain a bigger share of the mobile network and that it should be the sole operator of the CDMA mobile system, in competition with China Telecoms GSM system. At the same time, China Netcom was approved as China's third major telecom company. Consideration was also given for the separation of China Telecom into four separate divisions: fixed line, satellite, paging and mobile communications. In mid-July 1999, China Unicom's plan to build long-distance networks in China was approved by the Ministry of Information

Services, and the number of China Telecoms fixed line users exceeded 100 million for the first time.

The first authorised foreign venture occurred when AT&T was allowed to own and operate an IP network in Pudong, Shanghai, in May 1999. This was seen as an offering to the USA to persuade it that it would be better to let China accede to the WTO. The number of mobile subscriptions in China did not begin to go up noticeably until after the year 1999. By signing the WTO agreement, China accepted that eventually there would have to be 49% foreign ownership of Chinese telecoms companies. In the first half of 2000, China Mobile was formed through the separation of China Telecom (HK) from China Telecom. The company expanded through the purchase of provincial mobile networks covering Beijing, Tianjin, Shanghai, Liaoning, Hebei, Shandong and Guangxi.[24] In September 2000, China Telecom started to divest itself of non-core businesses in order for it to become cost-efficient so that it could become an internationally competitive company. For the first time, China had 65 million mobile phone users which exceeded the 51 million mobile phone users in Japan. In July 2001, the number of mobile phone users in China reached 120.6 million exceeding the 120.1 mobile phone users in the USA.[25] This represents an 85% increase in approximately 11 months. Nevertheless, by July 2006 the number of mobile phone users in China had increased to 431 million. However, at this time there were approximately 376 million landline connections in China. By 2013, the number of mobile phone subscribers in China had increased to over 1.2 billion, while the number of fixed-line subscribers had fallen to 266 million. These figures suggest that mobile phone utilisation is almost universal in China. However, some people may have more than one mobile phone. So, care needs to be exercised in drawing any conclusions regarding mobile phone utilisation among the population. Nevertheless, it is clear that mobile phone telephony is allowing China to jump technologies. For example, instead of establishing branches in remote regions, banks can facilitate banking transaction through mobile applications. Moreover, the figures indicate the knowledge trajectory on which the Chinese economy is heading. The regional distribution of mobile phone subscriptions in China in 2013 suggests that the Coastal region of China has the largest number of mobile phone subscribers compared to either the Central or the Western regions of China. Nevertheless, the discrepancy between these two regions with regard to the number of mobile phone subscribers is much smaller in comparison with that between them each and the Coastal region.[26]

In the latter half of 2001, China Telecom was split into two companies, one servicing Northern China, which merged with China Netcom, and the other Southern China. A number of foreign ventures and contracts were entered into at this time. Motorola won a contract to upgrade and expand China Mobile's GPRS packet network and Alcatel took control of its Shanghai joint venture. In December 2001, China finally acceded to the WTO. Following China's accession to the WTO, there followed a number of foreign investments in the Chinese telecommunications sector.[27] For example, AT&T launched telephony services in Shanghai through a joint venture with Shanghai Telecom. Then, Alcatel Shanghai Bell was launched in Shanghai as a manufacturing centre. In August 2002, projects for the construction of a seventeen-city broadband network with foreign participants were announced. And in January 2003 UTStarcom won a deal for China Telecoms PHS network in Shaanxi.

3G and 4G Mobile Networks

3G technologies began to be deployed around the world in 2000 in order to meet the increasing bandwidth demands of multimedia applications (Dekleva et al. 2007). However, it was not until the beginning of 2009 that the Chinese government began to award 3G licenses to mobile phone operators in China (Jing and Xiong-Jian 2011). It is interesting to see that India and China adopted different 3G standards strategies (Liu and Jayakar 2016). While India allowed mobile phone operators to select any standard, China invested heavily in a domestic standard, the Time Division Synchronous Code Division Multiple Access Standard. China was probably being more entrepreneurial than India by specifying its own standards for mobile phone operators to use. The 2008 reforms provided the pathway to the issuing of 3G licenses (Xia 2011). In the 3G era according to the latter, at the end of 2008, China Mobile maintained a market share of 73.6%, albeit under stiff competition. It was in 2008 that the number of industry players in the provision of telecommunications services fell from six to three due to the combined effects of government reforms and industry consolidation (Xia 2011). The three remaining telecoms operators China Mobile, China Unicom and China Telecom were issued with different 3G licenses as well as retaining a 2G network upgraded to the technical capacity of a 2.5G network. According to Xia (2011), the government reforms resulted in the establishment of the Ministry of Industry and Information Technology (MIIT) to regulate not only the telecommunications sector but also the defence and the tobacco industry. Before 2004, the MII was in charge of the regulation of the sector, and it was much stronger than the SASAC.[28] However, after the industry was politically separated from the MII to the SASAC, a conflict of objectives arose. This was because MII was more motivated to increasing competition in the industry, while SASAC was not due to its protective role. This conflict of objectives remained until the latter half of 2008 when the government merged the MII into the MIIT.[29] After this, the MII was focused on the regulation of the technical aspects of the industry, while the SASAC was now focused on promoting competition in the industry (Xia 2012). The issuing of 3G licenses took place in the backdrop of rushed reforms, industry consolidation and an immature technological framework (Xia 2011). However, this has to be viewed from the perspective that at the time China and the global economy was engulfed in the aftermath of the Global Financial Crisis of 2008. Faced with rapidly declining exports, the Chinese government instigated a $580 billion dollar fiscal expansion through increased lending to state-owned enterprises and increased infrastructure building. In this context, the 3G investment could have been seen as stimulating the economic growth which is much needed for China (Xia 2011). However, the latter suggests that while 3G commercialisation faces a number of constraints, these constraints may be rapidly overcome by the adoption of 4G technologies which could catapult China into a lead over developed countries with regard to mobile phone telephony. The constraints to 3G commercialisation include the following factors.[30] Firstly, the lack of technological adoption due to switching costs, the substitution effect and technological barriers. Switching costs relate to the costs associated with the adoption of 3G compatible handsets. The substitution effect relates to the reluctance to switch from 2.5G to 3G services due to the similar data capacity of both. And technological barriers are those associated with the lack of information about 3G to potential adopters. Secondly, the efficacy of the integration of merged parties with regard to structural, cultural and organisation integration. Thirdly, the effectiveness of the convergence of telecommunications, the Internet and cable networks as proposed by the government. Lastly, institutional and regulatory uncertainty may act as a constraint to the full commercialisation of 3G due to the lack of investment by firms. However, to some extent, this last constraint is diminished because the three main mobile telephony providers are state owned. The effectiveness of the constraint to 3G commercialisation is reflected in the relatively low percentage of 3G users compared to the total number of mobile phone users at a national level. In June 2010, the total number of 3G users in China was only 3% of the total number of mobile phone users in China, while the global average represented 14% (Xia 2011).

It was in 1999 that China put forward a proposal for an indigenous air interface standard, the TD-SCDMA, for 3G mobile telephony to the International Telecommunications Union as an alternative to other 3G standards which were being developed by European–Japanese and US–Korean consortia (Stewart et al. 2011). However, the TD-SCDMA standard took 10 years to be implemented, and by this time, other 3G standards such as the UMTS/WCDMA and the CDMA 2000 had already been widely implemented and in use. Moreover, other global mobile phone operators were also starting to deploy 4G mobile broadband technology (Stewart et al. 2011). The development and the implementation of the TD-SCDMA 3G mobile telephony standard are an example of how Chinese government requirements have influenced technology knowledge spillovers from foreign MNCs to Chinese firms, resulting in indigenous technological innovation. Without collaborating with indigenous Chinese firms through joint ventures in order to satisfy Chinese government requirements, foreign MNCs would be unable to gain access to the profits which could be made in the potentially huge Chinese market. This may explain the entry of foreign MNCs such as Alcatel, Ericson and Siemens into the Chinese telecoms markets as well as the emergence of indigenous Chinese telephony firms such as Huawei and ZTE (Stewart et al. 2011). In this case, in order to develop the TD-SCDMA mobile telephony standard, software and chipsets, the Chinese government instigated the establishment of the TD-SCDMA Industry Alliance in October 2002. The Alliance was composed of firms such as Datang Mobile, Soutec, Holloy, Huawei, Lenovo, ZTE, CEC and Potevio. This was part of an informal strategy to promote indigenous innovation which became formal in 2006 with the unveiling of the 'National Guideline on Medium- and Long-Term Program for Science and Technology Development' covering the period 2006–2020. At the heart of this policy was the formulation of technology standards as a part of national science and technology programs within industry, universities and research institutes (Stewart et al. 2011). According to the latter, the development of the TD-SCDMA 3G standard involved the transfer of Siemens TD-CDMA intellectual property to a Siemens–Huawei joint venture with continued investment by Siemens. Moreover, in order to integrate TD-SCDMA technology into Alcatel's mobile technology, Datong Mobile worked with the joint venture between Alcatel and PIIC, Shanghai Bell (Stewart et al. 2011). The latter maintains that it was Chinese government strategy regarding the implementation of the TD-SCDMA technological standard which ensured that foreign mobile phone MNCs worked with relatively recently established Chinese counterparts in order to maintain access to the Chinese market. Chinese government intervention in the standardisation process has illustrated that the government, in place of the market, 'can act as a project founder, risk undertaker, interest moderator, collaboration facilitator and process monitor'.[31] Nevertheless, despite government intervention, the levels of 3G commercialisation in China fell short of government projections, due to commercialisation constraints which have been previously discussed, and by January 2011, the level of 3G penetration in China only amounted to 50 million subscriptions.[32] However, once the TD-SCDMA technology standard had been implemented in 2009, the Chinese government set its sights on post-3G standards and the development of the TD-LTE technological standard as a proposal to the International Telecoms Union as a 4G specification.[33]

Internet Development

The Internet and the computer are valuable tools not only for the transfer of knowledge but also for its creation. Research can be conducted through the World Wide Web, and people with innovative thoughts and ideas can explore the originality of their idea before expanding on it. Software packages accessible with computers can make the creation of knowledge a faster process. Such packages allow innovative thoughts and ideas to be written down, re-thought, researched and edited. In effect, research becomes more productive, and knowledge creation is enhanced in research institutions. Furthermore, the Internet, computers and software enhance Social Capital by strengthening the interactions between people.

In China, the Institute of High-Energy Physics was the first institution to access the Internet by dialling mode in 1987. More scientific personnel became the first users of the Internet when in 1994 a TCP/IP Internet connection was established. In 1994–1995, the growth of Internet access spread to educational and research sites, when the China Science and Technology Network and the China Education and Research Network were established. Following the establishment of these two networks, a national Internet campaign was launched, and initiatives such as the 'Inter-networking a Hundred Institutes' and 'Inter-networking a Hundred Colleges' were established.[34] In 1995 and 1996, two further commercial Internet applications were established: the China Public Internet and the China Golden Bridge Network. In 1996, the four networks became interconnected. Xiongjian and Xu (2001) suggest that the number of Internet users in China was 4.6 million in 1999 and breached the 10 million mark in September 2000. By 2003, the total number of Internet users in China had reached 63.2 million, and in 2000, the ownership of personal computers had reached 15.9 million. In 2007, there were 210 million Internet users which mean that 84% of China's population is still not online. However, by

2012, there were 564 million Internet users in China. These figures represent an indicator of the Chinese economy's knowledge creation trajectory. This view is supported by the fact that by the end of June 2015, the number of Internet users in China had risen to 668 million.[35]

The Internet in China

In 1997, the State Council announced that the China Internet Network Information Centre and the four major inter-connecting networks in China would be responsible for collecting statistical data on the development of the Internet by conducting user surveys. The first such survey was conducted in October 1997 and in subsequent years in January and July. The data collected and definitions used in the first survey were refined in subsequent surveys. The detail of the data and the additional data presented in subsequent surveys by CINIC can only result in better conclusions being drawn from the demographical, educational, income and usage factors governing the development of the Internet in China since 1997. However, data redefinition, specifically with regard to changing and expanded categories, has presented some difficulty in compiling data tables for analysis. Nevertheless, it has been possible to determine that the number of Chinese Internet users was 137 million in 2006. However, this figure had increased to 564 million by 2012. This represents an increase in the number of Chinese Internet users from 2006 to 2012 of 312%. The number of Internet users in China in 2012 represents 41.75% of the total population. Clearly, in order to take better advantage of the 'knowledge'-based economy offered by the Internet, its use by the general population should be expanded significantly. However, Internet utilisation in China is growing. But, in 2011, approximately fifty-six out of every hundred Internet users in China were male. However, by January 2012, this figure had stayed around the same level. The data also suggests that the Internet in China is still relatively a male preoccupation. However, the gender gap in Internet usage has had a tendency to equalise over the period 1999–2005. Furthermore, since the first Internet user survey in 1997 to the one in January 2005, on average seventy-three out of every one hundred users of the Internet in China have been aged thirty or below. The only other age group which has seen any substantial growth in percentage usage over the sample period has been the 3640, moving from four out of every one hundred users in 1997 to nearly eight out of every one hundred users in January 2005. Nevertheless, Internet usage by age has not remained in ascendancy among those aged thirty or below. Internet usage by other age groups has also increased significantly from 2005 to 2011/2012. As younger people become old, Internet usage is a growing trend, perhaps facilitated by rising incomes and increased accessibility of technology. Moreover, in 2005, it was those mainly with a high school education and a bachelor's degree used the Internet in China. However, this may be due to the fact that the survey was biased because a significant proportion of those surveyed had a bachelor's degree or at least a high school education. Nevertheless, the observation may be attributable to the fact that the majority of those using the Internet in China are either or have been enrolled in high school or below or enrolled on an undergraduate degree. This feature clearly establishes a link between the Internet, its use and the facilitation of knowledge diffusion and knowledge creation. Nevertheless, the Internet usage remains a predominant pastime of those still in high school in 2012. However, the number of Internet users in university and above seems to have been fallen, comparing 2012 to 2005.

Furthermore, data based on the average monthly income of Internet users in China suggests that in the early part of 2005, forty-seven out of every one hundred Internet users in China earned fewer than one thousand Yuan.[36] This is in contrast to data suggesting that six out of every one hundred Internet users in China had no income. Due to the fact that there is no unemployment benefit in China, it is therefore highly likely that those with no income accessing the Internet in China are dependents of income earners. Thus, there may be double counting included in the income-based data of Internet users in China. A surprising feature of the income-based data on Internet users in China is that fifty-three out of every one hundred users are accounted for by middle- and high-income earners, while the latter (above 4000 Yuan) account for only five out of every one hundred users.[37] The data presents a contradiction as it is intuitive to expect that high-income earners would represent the greater number of Internet users as it is expensive to pay for computers and connection services to third-party vendors. However, this does not seem to be the case, and therefore, one has to conclude that the contradiction can be accounted for the fact that students and children are accessing the Internet from campuses, Internet cafes or the parental home. However, by 2012, Internet usage by income group had begun to increase in higher income bands. On the other hand from data[38] relating to the regional distribution of Internet users in China from October 1997 to January 2005, it can be seen that Beijing and Shanghai started off with a high proportion of users, Sichuan and Hebei with a low percentage of users, Guangdong, Shandong, Jiangsu, Zhejiang with a medium percentage of users but through time these provinces have lost percentage share (Jiangsu, Hubei, Shanghai, Beijing, Hebei) to other provinces or stayed at relatively the same level.[39] Another distinct feature of the data[40] is that Coastal provinces (Guangdong, Shandong, Jiangsu, Zhejiang) and well-developed municipalities (Beijing and Shanghai) have a relatively high percentage of the total number of Internet users in China, while any growth in the number of Internet users in Western provinces such as Yunnan, Gansu and Xinjiang has remained almost static. This suggests that the Internet facilitates knowledge creation mainly in the Coastal region and in well-developed urban centres nearer to the sea than the Western and Central regions of China. The data[41] for the regional distribution of Internet usage in China up to 2012 suggests that even in 2012, Internet usage remained a predominant activity of the Coastal or East China in comparison with Central China and Western China. The static or low growth of Internet users in Western China may be due to income effects, power supply constraints and low levels of educational attainment. The post-1978 reform policies have facilitated the development of the Coastal regions and some of the certain municipalities of China. The economic prosperity associated with the Coastal regions has aided in the spread of Internet use by males, students and dependents of income earners, those with a high school/lower or undergraduate degree education and those aged under thirty. Further, it may seem that the provision of the infrastructure associated with the Internet is more easily facilitated in more urbanised areas. This contention is supported by the trend in the urban–rural penetration rate data.[42] However, while Internet usage has remained the preserve of the urban sector, the growth in its usage has increased from 2008 to 2012 for both urban residents and rural residents. This may suggest that incomes may be increasing at the same time that infrastructure is also improving.

In China, the Internet has become a medium by which knowledge is being desseminated to students studying online courses. According to available data,[43] a variety of courses and subjects are studied using the Internet as a method of delivery. The most popular of these courses in terms of total enrolments is Management. The Internet would be an ideal medium to deliver education to the interior hinterland, where the geographical features of the land mean that the delivery of education by conventional methods is difficult compared to its delivery to the Coastal regions. The Internet can thus act as a facilitator of knowledge creation in the interior of China. This aspect of the delivery of education in China is identified because, due to its geography, the delivery of education to sparsely populated Gansu is difficult. The use of a technology such as the Internet in delivering education will assist in eliminating the income disparities between China's interior hinterland and the prosperous Coastal region, by facilitating innovation and economic growth. However, the problem most often associated with a freely available Internet resource is that it may be used to stir political dissent within the country. It is perhaps for this reason that the Internet in China is tightly regulated by the government.

In June 2007, the number of Internet users in rural China had reached 37.41 million out of a total rural population of 737 million.[44] However, in urban areas, the number of Internet users numbered 125 million, representing an urban penetration rate of 21.6%.[45] The ownership of computers among rural and urban residents is also a similar story. In December 2006, while only 2.7% of the rural population owned computers, this figure was 21.6% in urban areas. The year-on-year increases in computer ownership were only 0.6% for rural areas, while for urban areas this figure was 5.7%. Nevertheless, by 2012, the Internet penetration rate in urban China had increased to 48.7%, while the Internet penetration rate in rural China had only increased to 23.7% of the rural population, as shown in Table 3.8. This may be due to the lack of technical infrastructure in rural areas to facilitate Internet usage or perhaps because people's lifestyles have developed no need for Internet usage as of yet. Moreover, people living in rural areas may lack the skills as well as the educational level to be able to access and use the Internet. Nevertheless, the main characteristics of rural Internet users are that they are predominantly male, below the age of thirty with at least a senior high school education.[46] The first two characteristics are borne out by the analysis above, but not the latter. This may be because the data has not been analysed in terms of rural or urban sectors, but at an aggregate level by region. But, the findings in the analysis above and the findings of the CINIC (2007) report suggest that more investment needs to take place in both the education of the rural population and in the Internet infrastructure in these areas.

Research Institutes and Corporate R&D

The reform efforts of the Chinese government with regard to research institutes since 1978 have been geared towards increasing the spillover of knowledge creation into the productive sector of the economy so that economic growth in China will be dominated by innovation and invention. Indeed, five industries were earmarked by the Chinese government for strategic development.[47] These industries include bio-technology, e-business and knowledge-based services, software, design of integrated circuits and clean coal. The growth of these sectors requires a high level of innovation and invention in order to be internationally competitive. The ratio of corporate R&D increased by 50% over the 1990s (NBS 2002). This is significant, and the implication is that R&D spending by enterprises has overtaken R&D spending by the government. However, the increase in R&D spending by enterprises has been the backdrop to a shortage of core and advanced technology.[48] The government attempted to resolve the issue by transforming the nature of research institutes at the end of the 1990s.

After 1949, all research work was carried out in a number of institutions and all funding was provided by the central government. Such funding was provided for research carried out by sections of various ministries, the Chinese Academy of Sciences, universities, research carried out by central government departments and S&T research carried out by local government. Before the 1978 reforms, most state-owned enterprises had attached research units. However, all research activity was geared towards the innovation and invention of production techniques and processes as opposed to product innovation and invention. This was a direct consequence of central planning and a lack of competition amongst state-owned enterprises. There was no need for product invention or innovation because there was 'no consumer'. However, as a result of the 1978 economic reforms, two important changes were introduced with regard to science and technology and research institutes in China. These changes included the science and research responsibility system and the contract on charge system. The implication of these two changes was that research was carried out only on those projects with an NPV greater than zero, and individuals carrying out the research could benefit economically from their research. The next major reform with regard to research came in 1985 when the State Council offered a 'Decision on the S&T System'.[49] The implications of this reform were threefold. Firstly, for the first time, the government stipulated that the results of research should be used for profit. Secondly, institutes which exploited technology were encouraged to join forces with manufacturing factories or spin-off into manufacturing units themselves. Thirdly, the government encouraged the importation of technology to improve existing productive capital or the implementation and use of new productive capital. As Kong (2003) notes, the major impact of the 'Decision on the S&T System' was that research became profit orientated and central government could no longer be relied on for funding the research work of institutes. The impact of this reform was to incentivise entrepreneurship and knowledge spillovers. The next major reform of research work in China came in 1992 following the inauguration of the socialist market economy in China. In order to take advantage of the earlier reforms of the research institutes, the government expected the institutes to implement organisational innovations. In order to encourage the research institutes to implement these organisational innovations, the government instituted the 'S&T Progress Law of PRC' and the 'Climbing Programme'.[50] As a result of the implementation of laws and programmes by the government, a number of changes to R&D activity in China occurred. Firstly, state-owned research institutes implemented the rent responsibility system. This allowed researchers to monetarily benefit from the activities of their own research efforts. Secondly, research institutes became commercialised in nature, but their legal status only changed in 1999. Thirdly, one hundred research institutes were granted S&T import and export rights and the right to engage in foreign trade. Finally, central government encouraged the development of technological industry zones and private new technology enterprises.

The next major reform of research institutes in China occurred in 1995 when the government introduced the 'Decision on Accelerating S&T Progress' and the 'Decision on Profound S&T System Reform'.[51] These reforms were designed to endow the research environment in China with structure and incentives to innovate. For example, it was proposed that all research activity in China should be organised around a core of universities and institutions. The new reforms were also intended to ingrain economic awareness into all research activity. Moreover, it was intended that the focus of research activity was to be on the development of innovations with a high-technology content and the commercialisation of all research activity. In 1999, the 'Bayh–Dole Act' came into effect in China; its effect was that Chinese institutes conducting research using Chinese government funding could patent the research results. This led to more collaboration between research institutes and enterprises through joint venture vehicles (Boeing et al. 2016). In 1999, research institutes could be categorised by those which exploited technology and those which carried out research with a public orientation. Kong (2003) notes that the main changes made to the institutes were with regard to organisation, system and structure. As a result of these reforms, 242 research institutes had been transformed into enterprises by the end of 2000. Following the successful transformation of the first group of research institutes, the government began the transformation of a further one hundred and thirty-four institutes in the latter half of 2000. The government saw the need for the transformation of the institutes as a way to accelerate the flow of research results into the productive sector of the economy. In this way, economic growth in China could take place through knowledge creation, rather than imitation. However, although economic indicators such as total income and profits of research institutes increased, salaries of researchers and taxes paid by the transformed institutes to the central government increased disproportionately, Kong (2003) suggests that the innovative and inventive capabilities of the research institutes suffered as a result of the transformation of research institutes organisation, system and culture due to reform. This may be due to the increased competition between institutes to produce research which would impact on the Chinese economy through the productive and manufacturing process. Furthermore, the competition for funding of projects, following the loss of central government funding, meant that the number of possible research projects fell to those with a positive NPV. After China joined the WTO in 2001, there was a surge in R&D investment, primarily because Chinese firms could capture more market share abroad through product and process innovation. The latest reform of China's R&D and innovation policy by the state was the 'Medium- to Long-Term Plan for Science and Technology Development' from 2006 to 2020. This specific reform brought considerable changes to China's innovation policy with the aim of improving the Chinese economy's technological sovereignty (Boeing et al. 2016). Furthermore, the objective of the 'Medium- to Long-Term Plan for Science and Technology Development' (MLTPSTD) is to shift the burden of promoting economic growth from investment to innovation (OECD 2014). However, the MLTPSTD is not a policy in isolation. It runs congruently with the 'State Medium- to Long-Term Human Resource Development Program' (2010–2020) and the 'State Medium- to Long-Term Educational Reform and Development Program' (2010–2020). The three congruent and integrated programs represent a mechanism for integrated innovation which will allow China to become a powerhouse in innovation through the improved management of the development of human resources, an increase in the number of skilled personnel and scientific projects which result in innovation (Angang et al. 2014). China's R&D reforms and innovation policy as ensured that China is the number one economy in the world with regard to the total number of patent applications received annually by the domestic patents office.

This has been the case since 2011 (Boeing et al. 2016). At the moment, China is second only after the USA in terms of value in monetary terms with regard to national R&D expenditure.

Kong (2003) finds that the number of LMEs undertaking S&T research activity has fallen since 1991. LMEs instead focused on things like customer service rather than improving the technology of their business. This implies that research activity was contracted out to universities and research-oriented enterprises. This may explain why the revenue from the sale of new products by LMEs between 1991 and 2001 increased by only 6.41 times.[52] Nevertheless, Kong (2003) finds that in the ten-year period 1991–2001, enterprises themselves funded their own S&T research work, while the funding of research projects by central government and bank loans decreased. However, it is because enterprises have had to fund their own research that Kong (2003) finds that research activity by LMEs has fallen since 1991. Thus, while overall corporate R&D in China has increased since the commencement of reforms, this has been against the backdrop of decreased research activity by LMEs themselves.

Despite the reforms, data[53] suggests that government funds and enterprise funds account for the major funding sources for science & technology (S&T) activity in China. It can also be ascertained that while government funds account for the second largest source of all S&T funding in Western China, enterprise funds account for the foremost source of all S&T funding in Coastal China. This suggests that an entrepreneurial motive for the creation of knowledge and its commercialisation is greatest in Coastal China. Empirical work suggests that differences in the networking activity of entrepreneurial firms are a good determinant of inter-regional growth differences within a country (Huggins and Thompson 2015). An analysis of available data[54] suggests that the Eastern/Coastal China has the greatest number of scientists and engineers, and institutions of all three types [institutes of higher education, LMEs and independent research] employ the largest number of scientists and engineers in the East, with large and medium enterprises accounting for the largest employment of scientists and engineers. With regard to the number of scientific and technical personnel in state-owned and collective enterprises and institutions by region, the data[55] suggests that the Coastal region dominates in the employment of scientific and technical personnel in all sectors except in the agricultural sector, in which the Western region dominates. This could be because agriculture dominates manufacturing in the Western region and there is less inclination there towards the tertiary or knowledge-based sector. However, in all three regions, the number of scientific and technical personnel employed is greatest in teaching, whereas scientific research employs the least. This may be because scientific research requires more qualified scientists and engineers, whereas scientific and technical personnel are less qualified technicians, which is why they are so plentiful. Moreover, according to the data,[56] it is clear that the Coastal, Central and Western regions of China have the greatest number of the full-time equivalent of R&D personnel in descending order, respectively. Similarly, in that order, the R&D personnel in the Coastal region are more focused on experimental development which tends to be more practical than the other types of research indicated. This focus could be due to the fact that there is more focus on manufacturing in the Coastal region. On the other hand, the full-time equivalent of R&D personnel involved in either applied research or basic research is the lowest for all three regions in descending order.

Invention in Geographical Space

Patents

Figure 4.8, Chapter 4, Vol. 1, shows that innovation and technology are the key driving force of an economy which is at its PPF. Such an economy cannot grow any further through the greatly reduced impacts of externalities brought about by improved transportation infrastructure. It was discussed in Chap. 4, Vol. 1, that in a developed economy markets are less fragmented and therefore the impacts of externalities and spill-over effects brought about by improved transportation infrastructure would not have the same impact on economic growth that they would have in a country like China which is characterised by fragmented markets. In China, externalities generated by infrastructure investment will tend to merge fragmented markets.

The interpretation of the role of knowledge creation on economic growth varies according to which school of thought is followed. In Chap. 3, Vol. 1, both the neoclassical and endogenous strands of growth theory were evaluated. The effects of technology and innovation have for many years been downplayed because of the pre-eminence of neoclassical growth theory which considers technology to be a public good requiring neither capital nor labour for its formation. Economic growth due to knowledge creation remains a black box according to this approach, suggesting that there is no role for government in this regard. However, the advent of endogenous growth theory caters for the dynamic effects of technology and innovation on economic growth, thus assigning government a key role in its facilitation and economic development.

A key measure of innovation and technological progress is the number of patents which are granted by the Chinese patent office. In the case of China, the distribution, number, types and regional distribution of patents can be seen as a sign of regional development. The patent system in China is organised in such a way that it encourages the diffusion of technologies.[57] Furthermore, Sun (2003) has carried out three sets of regression analysis using 'Patents in the US', 'Chinese IMPORTS' and 'DISTANCE' of the patent registering country from China as the dependent variables, regressed against 'Total Patents', 'Inventions' and 'Utility & Design Patents'. The results of the regression analysis suggest that demand quantities such as imports rather than FDI are important determinants of foreign patent registration in China. However, in his regression analysis, Sun (2003) has left out FDI as an independent variable because used with 'IMPORTS' data it would have caused multicollinearity problems and consequently made the results misleading. It is because Sun (2003) has not sought to use data on FDI in his analysis that his conclusions are open to question. Another empirical study has found that foreign ownership of a domestic Chinese firm has a strong effect on the volume of patent registrations by that firm (Choi et al. 2011).

In China, for statistical reasons, patents are classed under three headings. Firstly, patents may be classed as invention patents, which include new products or methods. Secondly, patents may be classed as utility patents, which include new shapes or new structures of products. Finally, patents may be classed as design patents, which include new shape, design or colour of a product. Clearly, the first type of patent, as an indicator of innovation, has a bigger impact on the economic growth of a country than the second or third categories. The literature is suggestive of the fact that in China there is a geographical concentration of patents in two types of provinces.[58] The first type includes the Coastal provinces such as Guangdong, Fujian, Zhejiang, Jiangsu, Shandong and Beijing municipality. The second type of province includes populous provinces such as Sichuan, Hunan, Hubei and Liaoning. The distribution of patents between East, West and Central China is shown in Fig. 4.9, Chapter 4, Vol. 1, which illustrates aggregate data on domestic invention patents granted by region. At the aggregate level, it is clear that centre of invention is East China. This may be reflected by the three innovation systems within that region. Nevertheless, the problem with aggregate data is that it excludes provincial effects at the microlevel. Furthermore, aggregating data misses out fine points such as that the populous Coastal provinces are the regions of innovation. The implication is that a large population base allows for an increased number of human–human interactions and an increased frequency for the exchange of ideas, leading to increased innovation and invention. However, although the population is useful in considering human interactions, the population density is more relevant for this purpose.

Sun (2000) has carried out an analysis on the spatial distribution of patents in China using data on demand-pull and technical infrastructure. He defines the latter has a network of firms which provide business services, technical knowledge and R&D. The definition suggests that a clustering of these activities facilitates invention in both products and methods of production. Moreover, Sun (2000) suggests that the location of business services within an innovative cluster is critical for the functioning of that centre of innovation in commercial terms because of the need for the marketing of new products, technologies and methods. Therefore, the clustering of demand and supply factors creates agglomeration effects, economies of scale and an environment in which agents interact frequently. Thus, Sun (2000) suggests that the distribution of patents implies that invention and innovation are urban processes. This view is in contrast to Sigurdson (2004) who suggests that invention and innovation are processes that do not depend on the notion of geographical distance or the concept of urbanisation, but rather clustered more on functionality and by sector. This paradox can be resolved by recalling a number of facts. Firstly, government policy in the 1980s and 1990s favoured the commercialisation of research results with funding for projects being determined by the practicability of research results. Secondly, in the East of China, the majority of the funding for S&T projects comes from enterprise funds (LMEs), and the East of China is much more prosperous than Central or Western China, presenting more funding opportunities for S&T projects. Finally, most of the new technology parks were set up in urbanised provinces and municipalities. These three factors account for the finding by Sun (2000) that urbanised areas are centres of innovation. Sigurdson (2004) on the other hand looks at innovation from a global perspective, where clusters of knowledge creation and innovation do not have to reside close to clusters of manufacturing in geographic space.

Intuitively, this can be explained by the ready availability of telecommunications and Internet access, which ensures that R&D can be geographically independent of centres of manufacturing. Clusters of manufacturing exist in geographic space to allow firms to take advantage of agglomeration economies, the division of labour and specialised production. However, the creation of new products, e.g. a bioengineered drug, may involve an expensive investment over a lengthy period of time with no definite chance of success. Table 2.1 extrapolates the differences between manufacturing and research.

Sun (2002) has also analysed the sources of innovation in China's manufacturing sector. In his analysis, Sun (2002) uses three measures of innovation. These include patent certifications, new product sales and product applications. These measures were the dependent variables in the three sets of regression analyses carried out by Sun (2002). The dependent variables were regressed on a number of independent variables including the number of enterprises by region, number of

Table 2.1 Differences between manufacturing and research

Feature	Manufacturing	Research
Type of labour	Unskilled	Highly qualified
Productivity	Large	Low
Cost	Low	High
Probability of success	High	Uncertain
Duration	Short	Long
Economies of scale	Specialisation/Division of labour	Similar projects/Knowledge gained reapplied

Source Author

employees, total sales of enterprises, new product sales, patent applications and patent certifications. The major independent variables were the number of enterprises with in-house R&D, expenditure on technology absorption, expenditure on domestic technology markets and gross transactions value in local technology markets. New product sales are an important indicator of the effective commercialisation of the invention and thus, contribute to GDP. The results of Sun (2002) indicate that creativity in Chinese industry, as measured by granted patents, is accounted for by the in-house R&D activity of Chinese enterprises rather than by spending on imported technologies. Furthermore, Sun (2002) argues that the innovation in China is fragmented, ineffective and prone to regional variation because of the expenditure on the absorption of imported technologies. This conclusion supports the argument that while China may have a number of regional innovation systems, in the Coastal regions, it lacks a national innovation system. Sun (2002) makes policy recommendations on the integration of research. Nevertheless, despite the findings of Sun (2002), in China the data[59] suggests that there is a great emphasis on R&D activities and new product development in high technology industry. The focus of this strategy is on electronic and communication equipment, medical and pharmaceutical products, electronic computers and office equipment and electronic components. However, the adoption of new technology by consumers, such as 3D printing, is not dependent on the level of education but is dependent on age as absorptive capacity begins to decline as age increases (Wang et al. 2016). Furthermore, according to the Wang et al. (2016), design-oriented consumers are more likely to adopt 3D technology despite their level of education.

Scientific Papers

While the number of patents granted by region is an important indicator of invention and innovation with direct relevance to the commercial world, the publication of scientific papers is an equally important indicator of regional and institutional knowledge creation often neglected in the literature. Furthermore, data relating to the publication of scientific papers in China has not been subjected to rigorous analysis, perhaps in the same way as patent data.

The regional distribution of scientific papers taken by the major referencing system based on discipline is another indicator of knowledge-intensive activities. According to the data,[60] it can clearly be seen that the Coastal region leads in all three types of paper (ISTP, EI and SCI)[61] taken up by the major referencing system. Furthermore, a detailed analysis of the data[62] associated with scientific papers published by discipline and by type of institution clearly shows that the centres of knowledge creation in all disciplines except astronomy, earth sciences and medical care are universities. If it is now assumed that universities are responsible for a disproportionate amount of knowledge creation and that greater student enrolments/numbers of regular institutions of higher education occur in the Coastal region of the country, then it is safe to refute the argument that knowledge creation is only due to the activities of MNC's in that part of the country. In the context of the number of schools and students in undergraduate or specialised courses in institutions of higher education by region in 2010, the data[63] confirms the view that knowledge creation is embedded in the Coastal region because this region has the highest number of degrees conferred, graduates with degrees or diplomas, enrolments and entrants into educational institutions as well as the highest number of schools. In this context, the Coastal region is followed by the Central and Western regions in descending order.

The findings, which have been established, contradict the literature to an extent. In its' current mode of economic development, the Chinese economy has moved from an economy manufacturing low-technology exports to one manufacturing high-technology exports through the transfer of technology from foreign MNC's, either through joint ventures or the reemployment of trained Chinese personnel from foreign MNCs to domestic companies. However, endogenous Chinese innovation seems to be taking place only in manufactured goods with low-technology content.

Jakobson (2007) writes 'in 2005, 88% of China's high-tech exports were produced by foreign corporations. So globally China is a borrower, not a creator of technology. An innovation system needs to be built that can transfer innovation into economic growth and welfare'. Physical [roads, railways, telecommunications] and soft infrastructure [Education] are key factors in the development of innovation systems and the development of both forms of infrastructure goes hand in hand with government policy towards creating an innovative economy. Kroeber (2007) notes that China is not yet a high-tech powerhouse. This is due to three reasons. Firstly, the process of production encompasses the final assembly of low-value goods. Secondly, foreign MNCs dominate the economic landscape. Finally, innovation in the Chinese economy is limited. Figure 2.1, above, shows the inter-linkage between Social Capital, infrastructure, knowledge creation and knowledge spillovers in contributing to overall economic growth in China.

It would be useful at this point to surmise some of the key points which have been established in this chapter. Innovation systems, according to theory, can be categorised as Marshallian industrial districts, GREMI or regional innovation systems which rely on location on the spatial plain. A common theme with regard to innovation systems is that innovative agents have to be proximate in order to facilitate innovation. A classic example is Zhongguancun in Beijing. Regional innovations systems in China number three. These include the Bo Hai Rim, Pearl River Delta and the Yangtze River Delta. Nevertheless, an argument that innovation is geographically independent has been countered by an argument which says that it is. However, the key to understanding innovation systems is the concept of the competence block. A

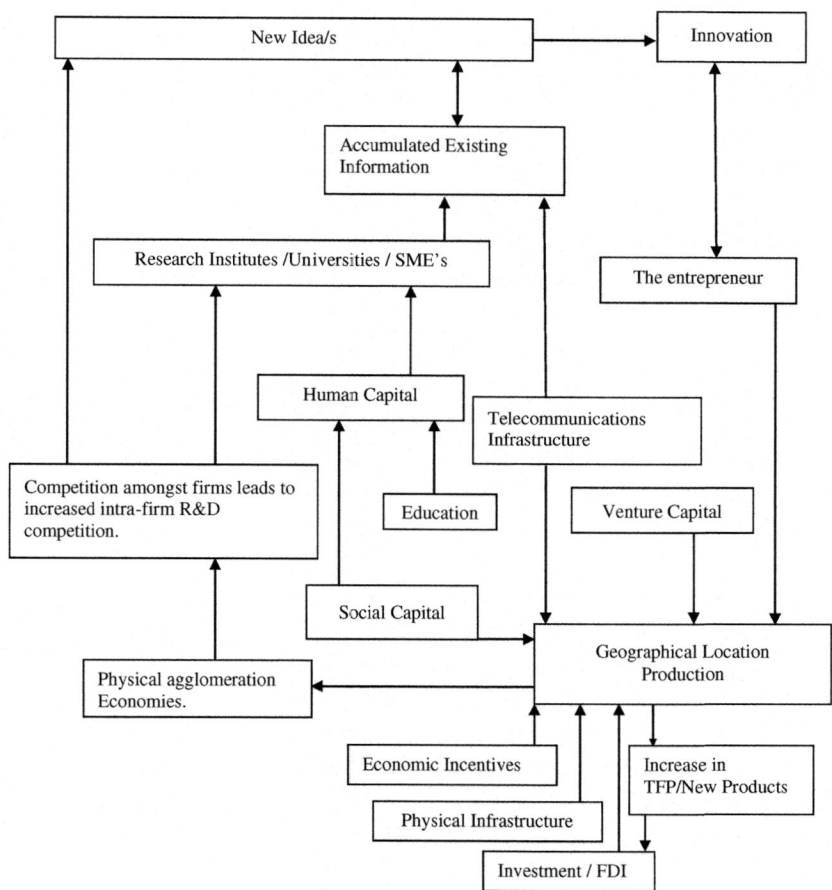

Fig. 2.1 Invention, innovation, knowledge and economic growth. *Source* Author

competence block has key factors associated with it. In this regard the role of telecommunications, the Internet and R&D in innovation in China was evaluated. Telecommunication, pre-1978, was not a profit-oriented sector acting as a civil population control mechanism as well as being restricted to military personnel and party cadre. Post-1978, the importance of telecommunications to commerce was realised and the necessary reforms put in place. The Internet is still very much an urban phenomenon; its use is being restricted to the Coastal region of the country. The rural uptake of the Internet and computers is constrained by the lack of skills of the rural population as well as a lack of ICT infrastructure in the rural economy. With regard to R&D, the government focused reforms on maximising the spillover of research in institutions to commercial enterprises. The way in which this was to be done was to encourage entrepreneurship among academia. Finally, it has been recognised that infrastructure is essential for the development of innovation systems. In China's case, a lack of a nationally integrated infrastructure network has prevented the development of a national innovation system. The following chapter will evaluate government policy with regard to education and other institutions which have impacted on knowledge creation and spillovers at the aggregate level with specific reference to innovation systems and the competence block.

Notes

1. Turpin, T & Mohannak, K (2002), 'Contemporary Perspectives and Debates' in 'Innovation, Technological Policy and Regional Development', Turpin, T (Eds), Edward Elgar, Cheltenham, UK.
2. Cooke, P (1996), 'Regional Innovation Systems: Concepts, Analysis and Typology', RESTPOR Conference.
3. Hassink, R (1999), 'Towards Regionally Embedded Innovation Support Systems in South Korea? Case Studies from Kyong-Taegu and Kyonggi', 16th Pacific Regional Science Conference, Seoul.
4. Kavoos, M & Turpin, T (2002), 'Contemporary Perspectives & Debates' in 'Innovation, Technological Policy and Regional Development', Turpin, T (Eds), Edward Elgar, Cheltenham, UK.
5. Sigurdson (2004), 'Regional Innovation Systems in China (RIS) in China', EIJS Working Paper No. 195.
6. Sigurdson (2004), 'Regional Innovation Systems in China (RIS) in China', EIJS Working Paper No. 195.
7. Ibid.
8. Ibid.
9. Sigurdson (2004), 'Regional Innovation Systems in China (RIS) in China', EIJS Working Paper No. 195.

10. Ibid.
11. Ibid.
12. Zhou, Y and Xin, T (2003), 'An Innovative Region in China: Interaction between Multinational Corporations and Local Firms in a High-Tech Cluster in Beijing', Economic Geography 79(2), 129–152.
13. Ibid.
14. Ibid.
15. Zhou, Y and Xin, T (2003), 'An Innovative Region in China: Interaction between Multinational Corporations and Local Firms in a High-Tech Cluster in Beijing', Economic Geography 79(2), 129–152.
16. Ibid.
17. Angel, D (2000), 'High-technology agglomeration and the labour market: The Case of Silicon Valley', in 'Understanding Silicon Valley: The anatomy of an entrepreneurial region', Kenney, M (Ed), SUP.
18. Zhou, Y and Xin, T (2003), 'An Innovative Region in China: Interaction between Multinational Corporations and Local Firms in a High- Tech Cluster in Beijing', Economic Geography 79(2), 129–152.
19. Yan, X and Pitt, D (2002), 'Chinese Telecommunications Policy', Artech House, London.
20. Ibid.
21. Ibid.
22. Ibid.
23. Ibid.
24. Lu, D and Wong, C.K (2004), 'China's Telecommunications Market: Entering a New Competitive Age', Edward Elgar, Cheltenham, UK.
25. Ibid.
26. China Statistical Datasheet 2014, National Bureau of Statistics, PRC.
27. Ibid.
28. Xia, J. (2012), Competition and regulation in China's 3G/4G mobile communications industry—Institutions, governance and telecom SOE's, Telecommunications Policy, 36, pp. 503–521.
29. Ibid.
30. Xia, J. (2011), The third-generation-mobile (3G) policy and deployment in China: Current Status, challenges and prospects, Telecommunications Policy, 35, pp. 51–63.
31. Gao, P., Yu, J., and Lyytinen, K. (2014), Government in standardisation in the catching-up context: case of China's Mobile System, Telecommunications Policy, 38, pp. 200–209.

32. Stewart, J., Shen, X., Wang, C., and Graham, I. (2011), From 3G to 4G: Standards and the development of mobile broadband in China, Technology Analysis and Strategic Management, Vol. 23, No. 7, pp. 773–788.
33. Ibid.
34. Xiongjian, L & Xu, Y. 'Networks' in 'Telecommunications in China: Developments and Prospects', Eds (Jintong, L, Xiongjian, L and Yan, W), Nova Science Publishers, 2001.
35. CINIC (2015), 'The 36th Statistical Report on Internet Development in China', http://www.apira.org/data/upload/The36thSurveyReport_oTmyiO.pdf.
36. China Internet Information Centre, Statistical Report of the Development of Chinese Internet, Various Years.
37. Ibid.
38. China Internet Information Centre, Statistical Report of the Development of Chinese Internet, Various Years.
39. Ibid.
40. Ibid.
41. Statistical Report on Internet Development in China 2013.
42. Statistical Report on Internet Development in China 2013.
43. China Statistical Yearbook 2011, Number of Students Enrolled in Internet-based Courses by Field of Study (2010), Table 20–16.
44. CINIC (2007), 'Survey on Internet Development in Rural China'.
45. Ibid.
46. Ibid.
47. Zhang, X (2003), 'Policies for Developing High-Tech Industries in China' in 'Conference on China's New Knowledge Systems and Their Global Interaction: Summary of Papers', Sigurdson, J (Ed), VINNOVA.
48. Kong, X (2003), 'Corporate R&D in China: The Role of Research Institutes' in 'Conference on China's New Knowledge Systems and Their Global Interaction: Summary of Papers', Sigurdson, J (Ed), VINNOVA.
49. Ibid.
50. Ibid.
51. Ibid.
52. Ibid
53. National Bureau of Statistics, China Statistical Yearbook 2011.

54. National Bureau of Statistics, China Statistical Yearbook on Science and Technology 2008.
55. National Bureau of Statistics, China Statistical Yearbook, 2011, Table 20–64.
56. National Bureau of Statistics, China Statistical Yearbook, 2011, Table 20–80.
57. Sun, Y (2003), 'Determinants of Foreign Patents in China', World Patent Information 25.
58. Sun, Y (2000), 'Spatial Distribution of Patents in China', Regional Studies, Vol. 34.5.
59. National Bureau of Statistics, China Statistical Yearbook, 2011, Table 20–55.
60. National Bureau of Statistics, China Statistical Yearbook on Science and Technology 2008.
61. SCI = Science Citation Index, EI = Engineering Index, ISTP = Index to Scientific and Technical Proceedings.
62. National Bureau of Statistics, China Statistical Yearbook on Science and Technology 2008.
63. National Bureau of Statistics, China Statistical Yearbook 2011, Table 20–27.

References

Acs, Z. J., Audretsch, D. B., & Lehmann, E. E. (2013). The knowledge spillover theory of entrepreneurship. *Small Business Economics, 41*, 757–774. doi:10.1007/s11187-013-9505-9.

Acs, Z. J., Autio, E., & Szerb, L. (2014). National systems of entrepreneurship: Measurement issues and policy implications. *Research Policy, 43*, 476–494. doi:10.1016/j.respol.2013.08.016.

Acs, Z. J., Audretsch, D. B., Lehmann, E. E., & Licht, G. (2016). National systems of entrepreneurship. *Small Business Economics, 46*(4), 527–535. doi:10.1007/s11187-016-9705-1.

Altenburg, T., Schmitz, H., & Stamm, A. (2008). Breakthrough? China's and India's transition from production to innovation. *World Development, 36*(2), 325–344.

Angang, H., Yilong, Y., & Wei, X. (2014). *China 2030*. Berlin: Springer.

Angel, D. (2000). High-technology agglomeration and the labour market: The case of Silicon Valley. In M. Kenney (Ed.), *Understanding Silicon Valley: The anatomy of an entrepreneurial region*. Stanford: SUP.

Boeing, P., Mueller, E., & Sandner, P. (2016). China's R&D explosion—Analysing productivity effects across ownership types and over time. *Research Policy, 45,* 159–176.

Bonnet, J. (2016). *From knowledge to innovation economy: Developing education and creating entrepreneurial ecosystems, WP 2016–02, UFR SEGGAT*. France: University of Caen Normandie.

Bouet, D. (2015). A study of intellectual property protection policies and innovation in the Indian pharmaceutical industry and beyond. *Technovation, 38,* 31–41.

Bruche, G. (2009). The emergence of China and India as new competitors in MNC's innovation networks. *Competition & Change, 13*(3), 267.

Cai, Y., & Liu, C. (2015). The role of universities in fostering knowledge-intensive clusters in Chinese regional innovation systems. *Science and Public Policy, 42,* 15–29.

Chen, K., & Guan, J. (2011). Mapping the functionality of China's regional innovation systems: A structural approach. *China Economic Review, 22,* 11–27.

Choi, S., Lee, S., & Williams, C. (2011). Ownership and firm innovation in a transition economy: Evidence from China. *Research Policy, 40,* 441–452.

CINIC. (2007). Survey on internet development in rural China.

CINIC. (2015). The 36th Statistical Report on Internet Development in China. http://www.apira.org/data/upload/The36thSurveyReport_oTmyiO.pdf.

Cooke, P. (1996). *Regional innovation systems: Concepts, analysis and typology*. RESTPOR Conference.

Datta, P. (2016). *An innovative executive education model for Indian manufacturing*. ISPIM Innovation Forum Presentation, www.ispim.org.

Dekleva, S., Shim, J. P., Varshney, U., & Knoerzer, G. (2007). Evolution and emerging issues in mobile wireless networks. *Communications of the ACM, 50*(6), 38–43.

Eliasson, G. & Eliasson, A. (1996). The biotechnical competence bloc. Revue d'Economie Industrielle, 78–4 Trimestre.

Fisch, C., Block, J., & Sandner, P. (2016). Chinese university patents, quantity, quality and the role of subsidy programs. *Journal of Technology Transfer, 41,* 60–84.

Gao, P., Yu, J., & Lyytinen, K. (2014). Government in standardisation in the catching-up context: Case of China's mobile system. *Telecommunications Policy, 38,* 200–209.

Ghio, N., Guerini, M., Lehmann, E. E., & Rossi-Lamastra, C. (2015). The emergence of the knowledge spillover theory of entrepreneurship. *Small Business Economics, 44*(1), 1–18. doi:10.1007/s11187-014-9588-y.

Hall, M. J., Layson, S. K., & Link, A. N. (2014). The returns to R&D: Division of policy research and analysis at the National Science Foundation. *Science and Public Policy, 41*(4), 458–463. doi:10.1093/scipol/sct055.

Hassink, R. (1999). Towards regionally embedded innovation support systems in South Korea? Case-Studies from Kyong-Taegu and Kyonggi. In *16th Pacific Regional Science Conference,* Seoul.

Herrerias, M., Cuadros, A., & Luo, D. (2016). Foreign versus indigenous innovation and energy intensity: Further research across Chinese regions. *Applied Energy, 162,* 1374–1384.

Huggins, R., & Thompson, P. (2015). Entrepreneurship, innovation and regional growth: A network theory. *Small Business Economics, 45,* 103–128.

Iyer, C. (2016). Impact of entrepreneur on the sectoral system of innovation: Case study of the Indian crude oil refining industry. *Technological Forecasting and Social Change, 102,* 102–111.

Jakobson, L. (2007). *Introduction in innovation with Chinese characteristics: High tech research in China.* London: Palgrave.

Jha, A., Bose, I., & Ngai, E. (2016). Platform based innovation: The case of Bosch India. *International Journal of Production Economics, 171,* 250–265.

Jing, Z., & Xiong-Jian, L. (2011). Business ecosystem strategies of mobile network operators in the 3G era: The case of China mobile. *Telecommunications Policy, 35,* 136–171.

Kavoos, M., & Turpin, T, (2002), *Contemporary perspectives & debates in innovation, technological policy and regional development.* In Turpin, T. (Eds.), Cheltenham, UK: Edward Elgar.

Kennedy, A. (2015). Powerhouses or pretenders? Debating China and India's emergence as technological powers. *The Pacific Review, 28*(2), 282–302.

Kirzner, I. M. (1973). *Competition & entrepreneurship.* Chicago: University of Chicago Press.

Kong, X. (2003). Corporate R&D in China: The Role of Research Institutes in Conference on China's New Knowledge Systems and Their Global Interaction: Summary of Papers. J. Sigurdson (Ed.), INNOVA.

Kroeber, A. (2007). China's push to innovate in information technology. In *Innovation with Chinese characteristics*. High Tech Research in China

Krugman, P. (1991). Increasing returns and economic geography. *The Journal of Political Economy, 99*(3), 483–499.

Lema, R., Quadros, R., & Schmitz, H. (2015). Reorganising global value chains and building innovation capabilities in Brazil and India. *Research Policy, 44*, 1376–1386.

Li-Ying, J., & Wang, Y. (2015). Find them home or abroad? The relative contribution of international technology in-licensing to indigenous innovation in China. *Long Range Planning, 48*, 123–134.

Liu, C., & Jayakar, K. (2016). Globalisation, indigenous innovation and national strategy: Comparing China and India's wireless standardisation. *Technology and Strategic Management, 28*(1), 76–95.

Lu, D., & Wong, C. K. (2004). *China's telecommunications market: Entering a new competitive age*. Cheltenham, UK: Edward Elgar.

Marshall, A. (1890). *Principles of economics*. Reprinted by Palgrave Macmillan in 2013.

NBS. (2002). *Chinese S&T statistical yearbook for 2002*. Chinese National Bureau of Statistics

Nelson, R. R. (1993). *National systems of innovation: A comparative analysis*. Oxford: Oxford University Press.

OECD. (2014). *OECD science, technology and industry outlook 2014*. OECD.

Peng, Y. (2016). The patentability of human embryonic stem cell technology in China. *Nature Biotechnology, 34*(1), 37.

Porter, M. E. (1990). *The competitive advantage of nations*. Cambridge: Harvard University Press.

Qionghui, W. (2016). Banking on gene power for precision medicine. http://english.caixin.com/2016-01-05/100896127.html.

Roy, M., & Khastagir, D. (2016). Exploring role of green management in enhancing organisational efficiency in petro-chemical industry in India. *Journal of Cleaner Production, 121*, 109–115.

Salter, B., Zhou, Y., Satta, S., & Salter, C. (2016). Bioinformatics and the politics of innovation in the life sciences: Science and the state in the United Kingdom, China and India, Science, Technology & Human Values, (pp. 1–34). Sage.

Schumpeter, J. A. (1911/1934). *The theory of economic development: An inquiry into profits, capital, credit, interest, and the business cycle*. New Brunswick: Transaction Publishers.

Sigurdson, J. (2004). *Regional innovation systems in China (RIS) in China* (EIJS Working Paper No. 195).

Stewart, J., Shen, X., Wang, C., & Graham, I. (2011). From 3G to 4G: Standards and the development of mobile broadband in China. *Technology Analysis & Strategic Management, 23*(7), 773–788.

Sun, Y. (2000). Spatial distribution of patents in China. *Regional Studies, 34,* 5.

Sun, Y. (2002). Sources of innovation in China's manufacturing sector: Imported or developed in-house?*Environment and Planning A, 34,* 1059–1072.

Sun, Y. (2003). Determinants of foreign patents in China, World Patent Information 25.

Thite, M., Wilikinson, A., Budhwar, P., & Matthews, J. (2016). Internalisation of emerging Indian multinationals: Linkage, Leverage and Learning (LLL) perspective. *International Business Review, 25,* 435–443.

Turpin, T., & Mohannak, K. (2002). In T. Turpin (Ed.), *Contemporary perspectives and debates in innovation, technological policy and regional development.* Cheltenham, UK: Edward Elgar.

Wang, Q., Sun, X., Cobb, S., Lawson, G., & Sharples, S. (2016). 3D printing system: An innovation for small-scale manufacturing in home settings?— Early adopters of 3D printing systems in China. *International Journal of Production Research.* doi:10.1080/00207543.2016.1154211.

Wu, Chi-Han. (2016). Benefiting from external knowledge? A study of telecommunications industry cluster in Shenzhen, China. *Industrial Management & Data Systems, 116*(4), 622–645.

Xia, J. (2011). The third-generation-mobile (3G) policy and deployment in China: Current Status, challenges and prospects. *Telecommunications Policy, 35,* 51–63.

Xia, J. (2012). Competition and regulation in China's 3G/4G mobile communications industry—Institutions, governance and telecom SOE's. *Telecommunications Policy, 36,* 503–521.

Xinhua. (2015). China unveils proposal for formulating Thirteenth Five Year Plan. http://news.xinhuanet.com/english/2015-11/03/c_134780352.htm.

Xiongjian, L., & Xu, Y. (2001). In L. Jintong, L. Xiongjian, & W. Yan (Eds.), *Networks in telecommunications in china: Developments and prospects.* New York: Nova Science Publishers.

Yan, X., & Pitt, D. (2002). *Chinese telecommunications policy.* London: Artech House.

Yoon, H., Yun, S., Lee, J., & Phillips, F. (2015). Entrepreneurship in East Asian regional innovation systems: Role of social capital. *Technological Forecasting and Social Change, 100,* 83–95.

Zhang, X. (2003). Policies for developing high-tech industries in China in conference on China's new knowledge systems and their global interaction: Summary of Papers. J. Sigurdson, (Ed.), VINNOVA.

Zhou, Y., & Xin, T. (2003). An innovative region in China: Interaction between multinational corporations and local firms in a high-tech cluster in Beijing. *Economic Geography, 79*(2), 129–152.

3

Knowledge Creation and Knowledge Spillovers: China's Aggregate Economy

China's emerging innovative economy is in an ascendancy, for a number of reasons.[1] The New Economic Geography (NEG) allows for an analysis of the distribution of economic activity in spatial locations. The framework of the NEG model assumes that it is because transport costs are associated with a proportion of the value or quantity of goods produced that increasing returns to scale in transportation causes consumers and firms to agglomerate at a point in space.[2] In this regard, transport costs are assumed to be fixed in the short run and cannot be adjusted by firms to lower costs. Nevertheless, in the long run, transport costs can be adjusted for by building transport routes or by firms relocating sites of manufacturing to regions where transport costs are lower. However, with regard to innovation, the ease of availability of telecommunications and Internet access essentially ensures that knowledge creation and knowledge spillovers can take place with negligible transport costs, particularly due to its geographically independent nature. The availability of telecommunications and the Internet means that knowledge creation and knowledge spillover activities become dimensionless phenomena. The greater are these assets in the Chinese economy,

© The Author(s) 2017
S. Ramesh, *China's Lessons for India: Volume II*,
DOI 10.1007/978-3-319-58115-6_3

then the greater will be the likelihood that a national innovation system (NIS) will emerge. However, in order for such an innovation system to take root, it is essential to have effective national policies in place with regard to education and the formation of institutions which facilitate knowledge creation and knowledge transfer. In this context, this chapter will evaluate the nature of innovation systems education and the role of institutions which act as centres of research and research commercialisation.

Innovation Systems

Innovation Systems in China

The concept of Innovations Systems entered the literature in the 1990s as economists developed a systematic framework with which to analyse the technological innovation of firms in a region.[3] There are generally two models of innovation.[4] The first is the national innovation system (NIS), the heart of which is the 'Competence Block' and the Triple Helix Model, which highlights the university (U)–industry (I)–government (G) linkage. The driving force for innovation in the NIS model is the firm, but in the Triple Helix Model it is the strength of the UIG linkage.[5] One of the main features of policies for innovation in China is that they have been regional, favouring the Coastal region rather than policies tailored to the national level. However, these policies have facilitated the formation of regional innovation systems as opposed to a national one. Empirical analysis has found that while in the technologically advanced Coastal regions of China, domestic R&D has a bigger impact on regional economic growth, in the less technologically advanced regions of China such as the Western region, learning by doing is much more important for regional economic growth and development.[6] This may explain why greater emphasis for technology-led reforms was placed in developed urban centres such as Beijing or China's Coastal regions. Furthermore, interregional technological diffusion is found to be more important for regional economic growth than is FDI, and this effect is stronger, the closer is a region to its production possibility frontier (Li et al. 2013). However, the latter also finds that R&D is important for both the assimilation of foreign technology in advanced regions and interregional technological transfer. But in less technologically developed regions such as the Western region, learning by doing has a bigger effect on the assimilation of interregional technological transfers.

Case studies of Liuzhou (Guangxi), Quanzhou (Fujian) and Ningxia (AR) provide evidence of local innovation systems with independent, individual and unique characteristics.[7] These case studies indicate that despite a single national policy driving innovation, each local innovation system is structurally differentiated from the other. Ningxia is an autonomous province in the North-West of China, and the local innovation system has a number of notable features.[8] The typical firm structure in the province is represented by SoEs, and within the province, there is a shortage of S&T resources. Reform policies have little impact on the local industrial base, and there is no networking among firms, universities and S&T institutes. Despite its lack of S&T resources, local government has implemented fiscal measures to stimulate innovation. These measures include a venture fund, to provide finance for technology entrepreneurs and a rule that firms should spend 1% of their sales receipts on R&D. Moreover, the local government has embraced the central government's policy of the horizontal integration of S&T by pushing S&T institutes towards achieving full firm status to ensure the diffusion of R&D benefits into the commercial world. Nevertheless, R&D expenditure, patents and export value of high-tech products in Ningxia are lower than that in Zhejiang, Shandong and Guangdong. The high disparity in innovation between Ningxia and other prosperous parts of China has led to the exodus of qualified S&T personnel from Ningxia. The lack of a typical rudimentary innovation system in Ningxia has led to the establishment of a knowledge/resource innovation strategy to take advantage of Ningxia's comparative advantage in natural resources. This strategy has led the province to focus its innovation on sectors such as biotechnology, new materials technology, medicine, water conservation and environmental industries. An example of this strategy would be Ning Guangxia, a floppy disk manufacturer from Shenzhen, which sets up Ephedra production facilities in Ningxia and applied technology and management skills to boost production for export. Ning Guangxia has also set up a research office in the Zhongguancun S&T Research Park in Beijing.

Quanzhou City is located in Fujian Province on the Coastal region of China; its local innovation system has a number of features.[9] The main geographical feature of Fujian Province is that its surface is 90% covered by hills and mountains. During the pre-reform period, the central government did not invest in SoEs in the province due to the tense political situation with Taiwan. Therefore, on the advent of the reforms, the provincial economy became populated with non-state enterprises (NoEs) which spearheaded the local innovation system. In comparison with Ningxia, the factors of production tended to be more efficiently used. Most of the NoEs in the province precipitated from cooperatives and TVEs, and these NoEs benefited from the flood of FDI and foreign trade which resulted from the post-1979 reform policies. Once the NoEs were fully exposed to open markets, they had to technologically innovate in order to survive, expanding secondary and tertiary industries in the process. The main drivers of innovation were the directors of the firms (in-house research), customers, foreign distributors and expatriate personnel employed by the firms. There is a lack of formal S&T institutions in the county and difficulty for firms to network with each other and facilitate interactive learning. However, local government established an S&T system, expert consultant group and a Mayoral steering group to manage government planning schemes to formalise the innovation process. In Quanzhou, businesses have a number of funding opportunities available to them including banks, the SMEC Tech Dev Fund and an S&T loan system. However, FDI has had a limited role in the development of Quanzhou's local innovation system, restricting itself more to the establishment of primary industries within the province. Thus, FDI has facilitated the development of labour-intensive industries in Quanzhou. These labour-intensive industries further depended on more FDI to increase exports without the need for technological innovation. Most of the firms established in Quanzhou are SMEs, and no large-scale enterprises have been established in the City. The essence of the Quanzhou innovation system is that Quanzhou firms have managed to divorce management of the firms from associations with formal government institutions without losing the benefits of those associations. However, the only problem is that family-run firms will seek to maintain family tradition by producing the same products and will not therefore see the benefits of product innovation.

Liuzhou City is in Guangxi autonomous region. Like both Ningxia and Quanzhou, Liuzhou's local innovation system has a number of features.[10] State-owned enterprises (SoEs) populate the economic landscape with firm's innovation processes and local innovation system characterised by entrepreneurship. This is a characteristic which Liuzhou shares with Ningxia. Due to the fact that both Ningxia and Liuzhou are populated by SoEs it may be construed that the local innovation system is less efficient that in Quanzhou. Although Guangxi is a target for investment by state S&T programs, the region has low innovative and R&D activity. However, Liuzhou has seen intensification in the development of its traditional industries rather than technologically innovative activity. The post-reform management culture of firms in Liuzhou was the key to the transformation of inefficient and unprofitable SoEs into SoEs with a culture associated with technological innovation. This post-reform management culture was characterised by access to entrepreneurial management courses and an appreciation of the benefits of networking with other firms, regionally, nationally and globally. It is a post-reform business culture which has encouraged the transformation of SoEs, in order to internalise R&D activity within firms. Liuzhou SoEs have found it easier to adapt to the risk-taking environment through technological innovation facilitated by 'Socialist Market Economics' from the technologically innovative inertness dictated by 'Central

Planning'. A feature of this kind of behaviour has been the appointment of technologically oriented personnel to determine and manage projects of innovative importance. Within, Liuzhou industrial innovation is concentrated in five pillar industries. These include automobiles, machinery, metallurgy, paper and chemical products. While traditional industries are still prominent, high-technology industries are still at an 'infant' industry stage within the region. In order to facilitate technologically innovative entrepreneurial activity, the municipal government of Liuzhou has put in place a number of policy initiatives, and funding for R&D was available in the 1995–1998 period from both public and enterprise sources. However, the latter has been the greatest source of funding consistently exceeding 85% over the 4-year time span. For coordination and support of the local innovation system, the local government sets up a number of services and agencies. In Liuzhou, human capital formation suitable for R&D purposes is low. Therefore, how has innovative activity occurred within the former SoEs? The answer is that Liuzhou SoEs have endogenised the R&D activities of entities in other regions by forming strategic and collaborative alliances. These alliances have been formed between enterprises, universities and academics in a two-way process using a number of methods including consultation, joint ventures, training and collaborative research projects. Innovative firms within Liuzhou include Liugong Loader Truck, Wuling Mini Car, OVM Anchor Series and Liangmianzhen Toothpaste. The incremental innovative activity within these innovative SoEs has led to complementary innovation among their suppliers.

The case studies of the local innovation systems of Ningxia, Quanzhou and Liuzhou make it possible to generalise the features which an ideal innovation system should have whether at the national level or at the local level. Firstly, networking between firms in regions where S&T and educational facilities are lacking is of paramount importance. Secondly, the entrepreneur features strongly in embracing opportunities for technological innovation. Thirdly, innovation systems tend to form much more quickly when entrepreneurs are supported by public funds. Finally, formal bodies to facilitate the exchange of information between entrepreneurs and general technological activities provide a mechanism to minimise duplication of entrepreneurial activity. However, Chang and Shih (2004) categorise the roles of six institutions which are required for an effective innovation system to form. These include policy formulation (government), performing R&D (universities, research institutes, firms), financing R&D (government, firms, or both), the promotion of human resource development (government, national educational sector), technology upgrading (universities, research institutes, firms, government) and promotion of technological entrepreneurship (government, research institutes, firms). Furthermore, these six institutions which comprise an innovation system interact in four ways in the context of an innovation system.[11] The different types of interactions include networking, personnel mobility from one firm to another, R&D collaboration and the permeability of technology from one firm to another. The six institutions which comprise an innovation system and the four interactions among the institutions are a more detailed schema of the four points outlined immediately before. Now that the desirable features of an innovation system have been considered, it is necessary to consider the notion of a competence block.

The Competence Block

In analysing the agglomeration economies which arise due to knowledge creation, the concept of a competence block is a useful one. According to Sigurdson (2004), a competence block is a prerequisite for an innovative system. A competence block cannot be specifically designed although, as in the case of China, the necessary policies, ideology, institutions and primary infrastructure have existed and are being augmented to facilitate the formation of a competence block.[12] Individuals or as Sigurdson (2004) calls them 'agents' do not have to be geographically concentrated in order to allow the competence block to function. Participants in the functions of the competence block could be part of a 'network that is dynamic and inventive in knowledge creation'.[13] Therefore, a competence block can exist primarily as a functional or sectoral cluster, and geographical location is of secondary importance. This is in contrast to the NEG of Krugman (1991) where the centralised location of manufacturing activity is pivotal to the formation of agglomeration activities. SEZs act as a focus for manufacturing. The SEZ program in China has resulted in an increase in FDI which has not crowded out domestic investment.[14] Due to dense investment in them, the SEZs accomplish agglomeration economies (Wang 2013). According to the latter, the impact of SEZs is different in different regions. For example, provinces in which SEZs are established later in the reform era experience fewer economic benefits than provinces in which the SEZs were established earlier in the reform era. Furthermore, provinces with multiple SEZs experienced greater economic benefits than did provinces with only one SEZ.

The locational independence of a competence block tends to be greater the availability of telecommunications and access to the Internet. Therefore, it is evident that such a geographical de-clustering with regard to knowledge creation cannot be accounted for by the framework of the NEG. In order to trigger dynamic regional development, subsequent innovation-led growth and the formation of a NIS, a number of factors are important. These factors include education, labour force participation, manufacturing, Science & Technology Research Parks, Universities & High-Tech Zones, returning students and physical infrastructure. It is intuitive to see that transportation and communications infrastructure lowers the cost of knowledge and information exchange as well as the costs of the transport of goods from and resources to sites of production. The economic benefit of localised telecommunications and transport infrastructure can be seen from the spectacular contribution to China's economic growth of SEZs and NHTIDZs. Therefore, by investing in transportation and telecommunications infrastructure in rural areas the effects of urbanisation can be simulated through spatially dependent clustering (manufacturing) and spatially independent clustering (knowledge-intensive activities). The mechanism by which infrastructure simulates urbanisation is by increasing the population and thus the economic density of space. In so doing, infrastructure investment acts to reduce the income disparities between the booming Coastal provinces of China and its interior hinterland.

Components of a Competence Block Education

The history of education in China can be split into three periods:

(a) The Mao Zedong period: 1949–1976,
(b) The Deng Xiaoping period: 1977–1997,
(c) The Jiang Zemin period: 1997–2002,
(d) The Hu Jintao period: 2002–2012 and
(e) The Xi Jinping period: 2012–present.

The Mao Zedong Period: 1949–1976

Once Mao Zedong declared China a Republic in 1949, the educational system was to be designed to serve two masters:[15]

(a) The political needs of the Chinese Communist Party and
(b) The economic development of the new Republic.

In order to achieve the above two objectives, the educational system of the Soviet Union was embraced and applied to the Chinese educational system so that it could supply the needs of a planned economy. With this in mind, the initial reforms advocated a reduction in the number of universities in the country, more emphasis on an increase in the number of colleges dedicated to teaching applied subjects as well as a shift of universities from the Coastal regions to the interior hinterland in order to balance the quality and quantity of teaching in the country.[16] These initial reforms led to the diversification of the Chinese educational system as well as to its' centralisation, setting the trend for its future development and role in supporting the development of the Chinese planned economy. However, because education was seen as the tool to support the development of the planned economy, there was little emphasis on facilitating the development of student's creative skills. Furthermore, there was little incentive in the planned economy for innovative research as there were no economic benefits for those carrying out the research.

The Soviet educational model lasted until 1958 when Mao Zedong felt that the Soviet system did not suit the needs of the Chinese worker who needed to accumulate sufficient knowledge through education. The latter was required for two reasons: firstly, to modernise working practices and secondly, to build the advanced tools needed for production. Moreover, the Soviet system was seen as one benefiting the ablest student at the expense of the less able one. Therefore, there was a need to implement an educational model which benefited all students and left none behind. It was in 1958 that the 'walking on two legs' policy was applied to the Chinese educational system. This led to the establishment of community-sponsored schools as well as state-sponsored ones.[17] Government policy at this time also encouraged the establishment of work-study colleges as well as the established formal full-time schools. The purpose of the educational reforms at this time can be seen as serving three purposes:

(a) Reinforcement of the party doctrine on the masses,
(b) Formalising vocational education and allowing the masses to acquire the skills to become engaged in productive labour and
(c) Encouraging knowledge transfer by engaging educational institutions in managing farms and factories and vice versa.

The next phase in the development of the educational system in China began with the advent of the Cultural Revolution in 1966. The educational system was seen to have failed the ideological and political aspirations of the Chinese Communist Party. Therefore, it was seen that the educated themselves had to be ideologically re-educated. Thus, economic development was supplanted by the perceived need to reinforce party rule. As a result of the Cultural Revolution, all educational establishments were effectively closed down for a few years.

The Deng Xiaoping Period: 1977–1997

The death of Mao Zedong in 1976 saw the political rehabilitation of Deng Xiaoping who took the Chinese educational system back to its pre-1966 structure. At the same time, the educational system was given a new philosophy of the 'three orientations'—modernisation, the world and the future. China's reformers realised from an early stage that the change from a planned economy to a socialist market economy required the nation to develop its human capital due to the innate differences between the two economic systems. This difference is nicely surmised by Agelasto and Adamson (1998):

> In a planned economy, critical economic processes are largely determined not by market forces, but by a central economic planning body which implements society's major economic goals. A market economy, on the other hand, manifests extensive private ownership of capital and allocates goods and services by the price mechanism with government supervision, in the absence of omnipresent government intervention.

Thus, there are differences between the type of human capital which are actively engaged in productive activity in a planned economy and a socialist market economy. In a planned economy, there is no need for workers to use their initiative, be innovative or be creative. However, in a market economy, there is a need for such skills because firms compete with each to meet the needs of the consumer. Moreover, in a market economy, there is a need for multi-skilled and technically apt workers as employment is not guaranteed. However, in a planned economy, students graduating from institutes of higher learning were assigned jobs in work units as production targets needed to be met. Nevertheless, due to economic growth, the demand for graduates increased, and many graduates ended up finding themselves jobs rather than being allocated to one. Modernisers of the Chinese economy realised that the transition of the Chinese economy from a planned to a market mechanism must be reflected by reform of the Chinese educational system. This parallel transformation of the Chinese economy and the Chinese educational system is evidenced by the results of Deng Xiaoping's Open Door policy on Chinese education. Firstly, foreign teachers were brought into Chinese schools. Secondly, thousands of Chinese students were given the opportunity to study in foreign universities for higher degrees.[18] Many of those who returned became entrepreneurs or academics. Another key driver of the reform of the Chinese educational system is that in order to allow the economy to grow at a sufficient pace, the educational system should produce an educated workforce to meet the employment requirements of Chinese firms. Therefore, the focus of the reform of the Chinese educational system was to allow it to deliver quality education, offering relevant courses and producing a healthy quantity of educated workers to meet the needs of economic development. At the same time, the educational system was expected to increase educational opportunity for all. The reform of the Chinese educational system can be broken down into a number of phases. In the first phase, the educational system, which had been virtually dismantled and made obsolete during the Cultural Revolution between 1966 and 1977, was reinstated. The focus of the educational system at this time was to deliver the kind of human capital needed to meet the rapid economic growth of the Chinese economy engineered by the post-1978 economic reforms and allow the country to meet the goals of the 'Four Modernisations'. It was also allied with the reform of existing educational structures as well as the reallocation of administrative responsibilities within the educational sectors.[19] Other features of educational reform in the first phase encompassed funding and degree status. In 1980, a clear demarcation was established between provincial and central government control of educational expenditures and incomes. Furthermore, the degree system was re-established in 1981, thirty-two years after the establishment of the People's Republic of China. The implication of this is that no degrees were conferred before 1981. It has been noted in the literature[20] that has economic reforms progressed the job requirements of the manufacturing and service sectors became more knowledge and technology intensive in nature. As discussed previously the NEG does not account for the fact that knowledge can be created. The second phase of educational reforms was in 1985.

The second phase was initiated because of a perception by Chinese reformers that the educational system as it was would not be able to sustain the demand for educated workers which was being fuelled by China's economic growth which was increasingly becoming knowledge and technological intensive in nature. By late 2007, it was becoming apparent that the Chinese economy was increasingly short of skilled professionals. Unless this shortfall in knowledge-intensive labour is addressed, then China's continued economic growth on a knowledge trajectory may be put in jeopardy. A number of areas were identified in which development was needed: [21]

(a)   The vocational educational sector,
(b)   The educational system so that it would facilitate the development of skills such as creative thinking in students,
(c)   Moving away from the centralisation in the administration of educational institutions and
(d)   Focusing on teaching subjects to students who would then better match available jobs.

A number of reforms were introduced into the Chinese educational system as a result of the 'Decision of 1985'.[22] Firstly, a requirement for nine years of compulsory education for all students was introduced. Secondly, the role of vocational education in secondary education became more prominent. Thirdly, decentralisation of the control of higher education administration was facilitated. A consequence of this part of the reform was that institutions began to become localised. Finally, despite the fact that central government paid teachers wages and fixed costs, educational institutions were encouraged to diversify their sources of funding.

Furthermore, during the reform period, self-funded students from outside the state plan were allowed to be admitted by institutions of higher learning. As Kai-Ming (1998) points out, this encouraged affluent students, who may not have matriculated, to study. However, in 1995, a reform was introduced to match the requirements of admissions criteria and fees for students admitted to institutions of higher learning from both within the plan and outside it. This was an attempt to stop rich students who were less academically minded from being admitted to institutions of higher learning. Moreover, there were a number of other features of financial reform of the educational sector following on from the decision of 1985. Firstly, in 1987 student subsidies were stopped and replaced by scholarships and other financial incentives for students to encourage them to study in a less developed area of the country. Secondly, in 1989 institutes of higher learning were allowed to charge fees for accommodation and other maintenance costs. Thirdly, this was followed by a pilot project in 1993 where thirty institutions were allowed to charge admitted students' full fees. By 1997, all institutions of higher learning had started charging fees to admitted students. Finally, in 1994 a clearly defined system of taxation was established so that both central and provincial governments could easily identify sources of income.

The Jiang Zemin Period: 1997–2002

Under the guidance of Jiang Zemin, the focus of reform turned to manifest itself in a policy of using China's educational system to develop the country by science and technology, the foci for reform being on:

(a) Increasing the cost-effectiveness of the delivery of education by squeezing economies of scale out of the existing educational system,
(b) Raising the quality of education and
(c) Matching the economic and social development of China by the reform of its educational system.

In order to meet these objectives, there was a need for even deeper reforms. Thus, policy makers indicated that government spending on higher education was to be increased to greater than 4% of GDP. This is quite significant when it is considered that China's economy is expanding at over 9% every year. The realisation that even deeper reforms to the educational sector were needed meant that a number of goals to be achieved by 2010 were put into place. Firstly, in order to facilitate the diversity of opportunities open to parents and students in higher education, private schools have to be encouraged. Secondly, more educational opportunities have to be offered in rural and urban areas. In urban areas, more community education was to be offered in the form of pilot projects to entrench the economic and social capital developed since the start of the economic reforms in 1978. In rural areas, there was to be an optimisation of the coordination of adult, basic and vocational education in order to extract efficiency gains in the delivery of education.

Thirdly, the legal status of every educational institution has to be enshrined in the law, and national educational policies were to be provided to all educational institutions by the central government to ensure the consistency of education throughout China. Finally, each institution has to aspire towards a three-in-one model in which the needs of students, the economy and the community are met. In addition, institutions should facilitate the development of student's skills to analyse and solve problems through creative thinking.

Disparities between rural and urban education have become marked over the reform years. This disparity has been caused mainly by changes in the way in which higher education is funded. The urban population and provincial administration in the prosperous Coastal regions of China are better able to fund educational activities than the rural population and hinterland provincial governments can. The way in which a unified and nationally consistent educational system can be put in place is by following the principle of the two basics—eradicating illiteracy and implementing the policy of giving every child 9 years of compulsory schooling. Moreover, by giving teaching staff opportunities to develop; and increasing the staff/student ratio then efficiencies could be realised, resulting in an increase in the quality of education delivered. The latter would also be effected by institutionalising national education standards, policies on research and the instigation of national inspection policies. It was hoped that such elaborate reform policies would facilitate the formation of a national innovation system which China is currently lacking.

The Hu Jintao Period[23]: 2002–2012

The Tenth Five-Year Plan ran from 2001 to 2005. In the context of science, technology and education, the objective of the Tenth Five-Year Plan was to speed up the development of these areas.[24]

The Compulsory Education Law (CEL) has been in force since the mid-1980s (Fan 2006). The objective of the law was to ensure that each child received nine years of basic education. This would encompass primary and junior middle school (Chakrabarti 2014). However, the CEL was only ever implemented in the urban areas of developed regions, leaving rural areas and less developed regions wanting. Furthermore, girls in rural areas were denied some level of at least basic education. So, under the Eleventh Five-Year Plan, the objective was set to increase the average educational attainment of the population from 8.5 years to 9 years. The Twelfth Five Year Plan ran from 2011 to 2015. Its educational objectives were as follows:[25]

(a)   Increase the capacity for technology and innovation,
(b)   Workers education should be improved,
(c)   The children of migrant workers should have the same access to compulsory education as the children of urban residents as well as progression from middle school to high school,
(d)   The children of rural residents were entitled to 9 years of free compulsory education,
(e)   Rural residents were also given access to secondary level vocational education, free of charge as were urban residents who were experiencing financial difficulties and
(f)   Educational opportunities were to be extended to the disadvantaged with subsidies to cover the costs of education being given to the poor, orphans and the disabled.

Thus, it can be seen from the preceding discussion that both the Eleventh Five-Year Plan and the Twelfth Five-Year Plan aimed to make access to education a universal opportunity: firstly, by aiming to achieve the objective of 9 years of compulsory education for all children and secondly, by ensuring that educational opportunities were not restricted because of a lack of financial resources.

In 2011, President Hu Jintao delivered a speech at Tsinghua University in which he reiterated the purpose of China's universities as that of guiding the nations' social and economic development (Rhoads et al. 2014). Furthermore, according to the latter, it could not be felt any longer that China was learning from the world but rather the time had come for the world to learn from China. Chinese universities were to be seen as the driving force behind China's transformation from an economy based on manufacturing to one that was based on innovation and technology

(Mok 2013). However, the problem is in the heterogeneity of the quality of education provided by Chinese universities from one province to another (Wenbin 2012). According to the latter, there is a serious misallocation of resources among Chinese universities, with universities in the underdeveloped regions, such as the Western region, receiving fewer resources than do universities in the more developed regions of China, such as its Coastal region. In the context of university education in China, there is now a call for quality rather than quantity.[26] Nevertheless, even at the school level, the economic reforms have had a pronounced impact on the quality of education being provided (Liu and Dunne 2009). In the 1980s, fiscal decentralisation meant that the burden of funding education at the provincial level was shifted from the central government to the provincial government, and schools had to compete for a limited pool of funding. Richer provinces in China's Coastal regions were able to offer more funding to all schools while this was not the case for schools in the poorer provinces in China's Western region. However, some empirical evidence contradicts this by suggesting that as the educational system expands in China the level of spatial interaction between neighbouring provinces increases thus reducing the differences in educational levels between the provinces (Gu 2012). This could happen if one province produces more graduates than does a neighbouring province, then limited job opportunities may mean that the province producing more graduates 'exports' these graduates to a neighbouring province where they may be able to find jobs as teachers as the educational system expands (Gu 2012). In the 1990s, there was a shift towards improving the quality of education in Chinese schools by moving away from the rote learning methodology. However, this shift was constrained by the focus of China's pre-university education system on the Gaokao, the results of which will determine the university that would be attended by a student (Liu and Dunne 2009). Higher education research institutes, which emerged after 1978, provided scholarly analysis of China's ever-expanding educational sector for policy makers to make informed decisions (Wang and Liu 2014).

Increased competition among Chinese universities, for funding based on the extent of innovation, would help transform the economy into a more innovative one. Increased competition among Chinese universities can only be achieved if they are able to make a transition from the public sector to the private sector either as a whole or as a part through a hybrid form of the two. Table 3.1, above, shows that the private percentage of total higher education enrolment for both China (19.9%) and India (30.7%) are much lower compared to technologically, economically and socially advanced countries such as Japan (77.4%), South Korea (80%) and Taiwan (71.9%). Furthermore, while in China the private percentage of total universities is 0%, as of 2008, but in Japan, South Korea and Taiwan it is 76.7, 84.8 and 64.1%, respectively.

Xi Jinping Period: 2012–2020

At the heart of President Xi's economic strategy is a movement away from the allocation of basic resources by the state with a stronger role for market forces (Kroeber 2013). However, the state will still maintain a part ownership of the country's productive assets, in conjunction with the private sector, through SoEs.[27] Increased marketisation of China's economy but with the presence of a strong state was the message from the Third Plenum of the Communist Party which was held in November 2013. The Third Plenum was also the stage from which China launched the 'Decision on Several Major Questions about Deepening Reform'. This represents an agenda of 336 reforms, under 16 headings, which encompass 'the economy, society and political system and institutions'.[28] The reforms were scheduled into three phases (Wong 2016). Phase 1 would focus on reforms associated with the financial management of public services and management of the central government's budget. Phase 2, commencing in 2015, would focus on the reform of the tax system, and Phase 3, commencing in 2016, would focus on the reform of financing between the provincial government and central government. However, in the context of education and the Third Plenum's deepening reforms initiative, the focus was on the following:[29]

(a) Open the educational sector to foreign investment,
(b) Introduce a subsidy scheme for households finding it difficult to finance their child's education,

Table 3.1 Private and public higher education shares—2001 to 2008—Asia

Country	Private % of total HE enrolment	Year	Private % of total HEIs	Year	Private % of total Univ. enrolment	Year	Private % of total Univ.	Year
Bangladesh	14.4	2003/2004	48.6	2005/2006	44.2	2005	71.6	2005
China	19.9	2008	28.3	2008	0	2008	0	2008
Hong Kong, China	59	2007/2008	54.5	2007/2008	59.4	2007/2008	22.2	2007/2008
India	30.7	2005/2006	42.9	2005/2006	–	–	–	–
Indonesia	71	2007	95.5	2007	–	–	89	2007
Japan	77.4	2007	89.6	2007	73.2	2007	76.7	2007
South Korea	80	2006	87	2002	78.4	2004	84.8	2004
Taiwan	71.9	2004	65.8	2004	66.8	2004	64.1	2004
Thailand	9.9	2007	46.9	2007	16.8	2001	28.3	2003
Vietnam	10.4	2005	12.6	2005	–	–	–	–

Source Compiled by author using data from 'The Program for Research on Private Higher Education'
http://www.prophe.org/en/data-laws/international-databases/

(c) Ensure that educational provision is standardised across China and that it is a meritocracy,

(d) Lifelong continuous education, special education and preschool education should be developed and reformed,

(e) Make sure that students have more developmental time by reducing school workload,

(f) Reform examination-oriented university admission system so that one examination does not determine one's whole life,

(g) Reduce the number of subjects examined in the nationwide uniform examination,

(h) Higher middle school, pre-university students, should face standardised tests,

(i) Separate educational management function from student appraisal,

(j) Broaden the powers of provincial governments to plan education in their jurisdiction and

(k) Increase the autonomy of schools to be able to run courses.

From the above, it can be seen that the drive towards educational reform in China to 2020 is to increase access to education as well as to increase the quality of education in the context of student performance and teaching standards.

Impacts of Educational Reforms

After 1949, the educational system served to support the planned economy and politically educate the masses. During the Great Leap Forward, the number of universities in China increased by 267%, although by 1963 the number of universities had dropped by 50%. Furthermore, during the Cultural Revolution, the only educational reform applied to the Chinese educational systems was to shut down the universities and send the teachers, professors and students into the countryside to be politically re-educated. This meant that a generation of workers were denied a formal education depriving the planned economy of the skilled manpower required to meet production targets. Moreover, fewer subjects were taught, universities moved into rural areas, and from 1970, only those students recommended by workers, peasants or soldiers could be admitted to universities. The lack of competition in the higher educational sector during the Cultural Revolution meant that the brightest students were not getting into university. The only credentials required of students to get into university at this time were that they had to be politically correct. However, the impacts of educational reforms after 1977 were substantial.[30] According to Kang (2004), the purpose of higher education in China has been redefined:

> Higher education is not only the teaching centre, but also an important scientific research community, the centre of technological innovation, and an opportunity to create in different kinds of culture. The most important function of higher education is to increase the quality of the Chinese national identity and to develop the Chinese personality.

As a result of the reforms, the educational system became more structured, international in orientation, diverse and was seen to add value to society at large.

The international orientation of the Chinese educational system ensured the transfer of teaching methodology and practices to diffuse in. The need for the educational system to facilitate creative thinking was paramount. However, the educational reforms have had the unintended externality of contributing towards increasing disparities in income between the Coastal regions of China and the interior hinterland. This has been due to the fact that the reforms resulted in:

(a) The shift in funding of students from the state to the students themselves and
(b) The shift in managing and sponsoring institutions of higher learning from the central government to the provincial governments.

The reason for this is that due to the economic reforms applied to the Chinese economy since 1978, the Coastal regions of China have urbanised greater and prospered more than the interior hinterland. The structure of the education system in China is shown in Fig. 3.1.

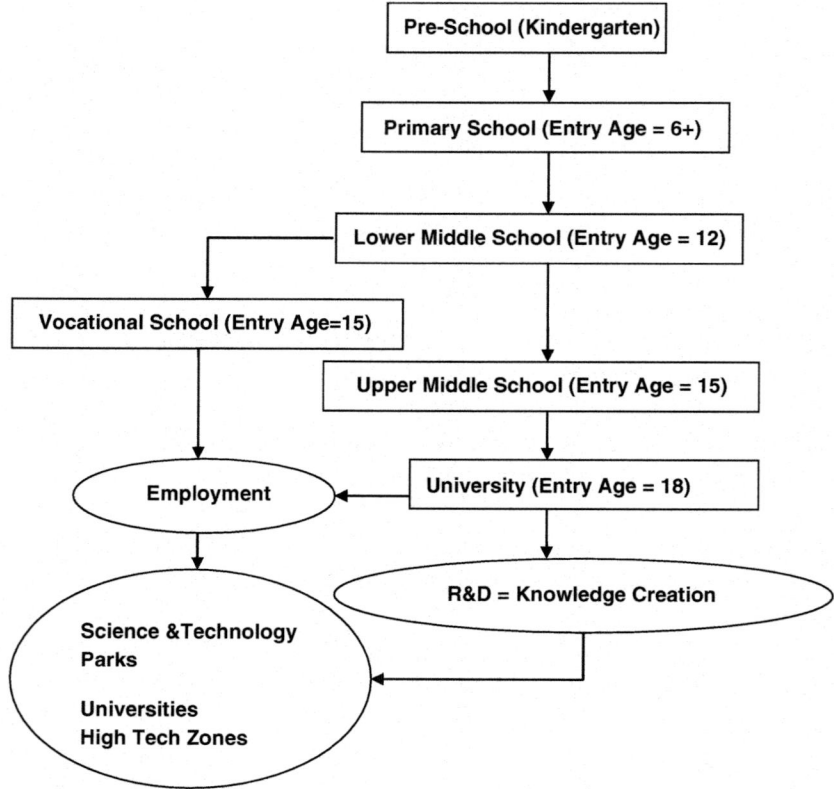

Fig. 3.1 The Chinese educational system. *Source* The Author

During the reform era, universities have gained economies of scale by amalgamating with each other in order to become recognised as one of the one hundred universities in China to be 'First Class' in the world. The status of a first-class university would attract preferential treatment and funding from the central authorities. Furthermore, the change in the administration of the universities from departments of education of the local governments to the central education department has prompted the amalgamation of universities aligned with the former to those aligned to the latter.

Centres of Research and Research Commercialisation

Functions of Universities

Universities play a leading role in the economic and social development of the region where they are located and according to Jing (2000) universities have a number of functions. Universities have traditionally been centres of knowledge creation and innovative thinking, offering lifelong learning for the local catchment area and opportunities for social development through an alumni network. Moreover, due to the expertise of academic staff at universities, universities also act as diffusers of technical information to the rest of society. The main ways in which this is achieved include selling directly to the consumer, joint ventures based on an education—production—research relationship and the popularisation of technology through the mass media. It is through commercialising the results of technological innovation by transfer to manufacture and establishing joint ventures with industry that universities act as promoters of technology transfer. While in developed countries, with a well-established innovation system, firms of an appropriate size may have their own R&D departments solely focusing on developing new products and processes by improving technology, this may not be the case in an emerging economy such as China (Kafouros et al. 2015). Therefore, it is important that firms in an emerging economy like China form mutually beneficial collaborations with researchers based at Chinese universities and research institutes.[31] Nevertheless, the extent to which Chinese firms may benefit from such collaboration differs across China's regions. This regional heterogeneity of institutional development in China exists primarily for three reasons (Kafouros et al. 2015). Firstly, the extent of the enforceability of Intellectual Property Rights varies between different Chinese provinces. This may be due to differences in the strength of legal institutions as well as to the extent of provincial differences in the levels of influence of the central government over the provincial government. Secondly, the level of international openness will vary between one province and another. Coastal provinces like Jiangsu are most likely to be more internationally open than are Western provinces such as Gansu due to having better hard infrastructure (roads, telecommunications, airports, etc.) and soft infrastructure (skilled workers, researchers who are more qualified, etc.). Thirdly, due to variations in soft infrastructure, the quality of research produced will vary between institutions in different provinces. Furthermore, in the context of the Triple Helix Model of innovation, based on the strength of university–industry–government (UIG) linkages, it has been found that UIG linkages are stronger in Singapore, South Korea and Taiwan than they are in China (Singh et al. 2015). But they are stronger in China than in India. Nevertheless, according to Singh et al. (2015), in contrast to developed economies, the total volume and the quality of IP in the newly industrialised emerging economies of Singapore, Hong Kong, South Korea, Taiwan and China tends to be lower. In China's case, the universities also tend to play a smaller role in the level of national research output in comparison with countries such as Singapore, Hong Kong, South Korea and Taiwan.[32] However, citation rates for universities in Hong Kong and Singapore tend to be the highest in the context of the five emerging industrialised economies (Singh et al. 2015). In contrast to these five newly emerging industrialised economies, in the USA universities were bound by the Bayh–Dole Act of 1980 to commercialise any intellectual property which was a direct result of federally funded research (Leydesdorff and Etzkowitz 1998).

It is often the case that university academics work on a consultancy basis with industry, and therefore, universities supply industry with skilled personnel who have up-to-date technical and management skills. Furthermore, universities act as incubators for firms which manufacturing state of the art technical products. This is because universities have skilled personnel, hardware infrastructure and technical funding. However, at a theoretical level, the transmission of new knowledge into commercially viable products was to overcome barriers which effectively represent a 'knowledge filter' (Acs et al. 2005). This 'knowledge filter' may be represented by a lack of knowledge on the part of academics about how to set up a business, lack of managerial skills, lack of financial resources to commercialise knowledge, lack of realisation of the commercial potential of the new knowledge and even poor marketing of the new knowledge to commercial ventures. However, it has been found that the stronger are the levels of university–industry linkages and the greater the level of firm formation and entrepreneurship, then the more 'permeable' will be the knowledge filter and the greater the probability that new knowledge will be transformed into new products (Mueller 2006). Entrepreneurship may involve an incumbent firm recognising the commercial potential of new knowledge and transforming it into a new product or the setting up of a start-up firm with the specific intention of converting a specific piece of new knowledge into a totally new product. While the survival rate of university–industry spin-offs is high, it will take several years for a spin-off to have any impact on regional and national economic growth (Leydesdorff and Meyer 2006). Furthermore, the funding from venture capital firms is easy to attract if the university has a good track record. The first University Science & Technology Research Park was opened in 1989 at Northeast University in Sheng Yang City. After five years of operation, its gross production value was 150 million Yuan, exports were worth US$ 700,000 and its two main industries were industrial robotics and computer software.[33] The establishment of the first Science & Technology Research Park was followed by the establishment of others all around the country.

The Science and Technology Research Park at Beijing University had an income exceeding two billion Yuan, in 1998. The university parks provide an effective mechanism, whereby knowledge created in the university can be transferred to business enterprises. They also provide funding for enterprises in the form of share issues or loans.[34] The university parks management functionality monitors incubated enterprises and ensures that any problem encountered by the enterprise is resolved as soon as possible. Within a science and technology park, a number of a range of services are offered.[35] These services include human resources, funding advisory services, legal advice, accountancy advice, management consultancy services, marketing services as well as concentrated infrastructure.

Science & Technology Parks

It is the stated aim of the Chinese government that science and technology should generate economic growth and facilitate the economic development of China, while the productive forces that produce economic growth are innovation led by Science & Technology Research. China's Science & Technology research efforts can be broken down into three levels.[36] Firstly, there is a need to develop a high-technology industry and accelerate technological innovation by following a series of programs such as the '863 Program' and the 'Torch Program'.

The purpose of following these programs is to ensure that Chinese Science & Technology enables the industry to function at the frontiers of innovation. Furthermore, these programs are characterised by targeted research on a small number of projects with specific objectives with the results of the research used for commercial purposes. Secondly, it is important to resolve technological problems which hinder China's economic development by following a series of programs such as the 'National Program for Key S&T Projects', 'Industrial Experiment Program', the 'Spark Program', 'National S&T Achievements Dissemination Program' and the 'National Program for Science & Technology for Sustainable Development'. Finally, the importance of specific programs cannot be understated because applied and basic research can be conducted by following the 'Scaling the Heights Program' and establishing the 'National Natural Science Foundation' mechanism. Both program and mechanism will seek to provide a firm footing for scientific and technological innovation in the long term to suit the demands of China's social and economic development. There are also a number of priority areas for science and technology in China.[37] These include increasing the quality and quantity of agricultural products, developing innovation in industry, commercialising the results of research and promoting development through sustainable means. A key component of China's R&D strategy was the '863 Program', which resulted in eight sectors being designated as a priority for R&D. The sectors included information technology, biotechnology, energy technology, space technology, advanced materials, laser technology and ocean technology. Ten years of the '863 Program' yielded over 1000 commercially applicable achievements, and these include biomedicine, state of the art computers, artificial intelligence, fibre optic telecommunications, satellites, high definition lasers and advanced materials. The Medium to Long-Term Plan for Science and Technology Development (2006–2020) [MLTPDST 2006-2020] was launched in 2006. The aim of the MLTPDST (2006–2020) was to ensure that China became an economy dominated by innovation by 2020.[38] Thus, since 2006 the annual growth rate of government-led R&D investment was 20% (Tagscherer 2015). And according to the latter by 2013, government-led R&D expenditure represented 2% of GDP, surpassing the EU average R&D expenditure. One area of focus of the MLTPDST was the development of nanotechnology and the recognition that developing China's nanotechnology sector would contribute towards China's long-term economic growth. The Ministry of Science and Technology implemented the Medium- to Long-Term Plan for Science and Technology Development, and it is also responsible for Nanoscience Research (Dong et al. 2016). According to the latter, to date 28 nanotechnology projects have been financially supported with an investment of 1 billion RMB. The main centres of state-funded nanotechnology research have been in Beijing, Shanghai, Jiangsu and Zhejiang where R&D incubators have been built.[39] Nanotechnology research publications are concentrated in a handful of universities and research institutes. However, while China ranks 2nd in the world, behind the USA, in the number of nanotechnology publications, its ranking in terms of the quality of publications, as measured by the number of publications in journals with an impact factor greater than 20, is much lower (Dong et al. 2016). For example, according to the latter, the USA has 1068 papers in journals with an impact factor greater than 20, Germany 221, UK, 193, France 149 and Japan 121. In comparison, China only has 76 papers in journals with an impact factor greater than 20. Nevertheless, of the top 20 nanotechnology researchers in the world, China hopes to be at 18 of these.[40] These findings suggest that while Chinese research is at the forefront of nano-technology research, it still needs to improve the quality of the research by introducing further market reforms to increase the incentives for researchers, by improving the quality and operations of nanotechnology R&D incubators and perhaps by introducing more diversified sources for funding nanotechnology R&D.

Science & Technology Regional Policy

The purpose of S&T Parks was to foster local economic development assisted by strong government planning.[41] The evolution of the S&T Parks can be traced through three stages reflecting the progression of China's economic reforms (Zhu 2012). The first phase was during the period 1988–1998 during which economic development zones and S&T Parks were established in China's Coastal region allied with government-funded infrastructure and preferential policies to attract foreign multinational firms. The second phase occurred during the period 1998–2006 in which the Parks became technology led, and 1998 represented the pivotal year after which the Parks were no longer focused on manufacturing industry but on technological industry. The third phase began from 2006 when the Parks became 'Knowledge-Based Parks'.[42] The theme of the third phase was to make China an innovation-based economy by 2020. To achieve this aim, by 2010 12 'mega' facilities, 30 national science centres and 300 key labs had been set up.[43] Furthermore, in 2006 the Dushuho Science Higher Education and Innovation Zone was initiated as a knowledge-based project in Suzhou.[44] Technologically led economic growth which was sustainable was also a theme after 2006 with the establishment of eco-parks such as the Hangzhou Xixi Eco Park and the Tianjin Eco-City (Zhu 2012). In the context of environmental sustainability, the need for which increased over the reform years, research institute and government collaboration resulted in scholars gaining experience and expertise in providing solutions to projects in either the Pearl River Delta of Mainland China or to solutions to projects involving both Mainland China and Hong Kong.[45]

Finance for start-up investment was first mentioned in the 'Decision on Science and Technology Reform' in 1985, and it acted as a catalyst for the development finance for Chinese start-ups. The first start-up investment corporation was set up in the latter part of 1985 under the guise of 'China New Technology Start-up Investment Corporation'. In 1986, the 'Spark Program' was established to assist in the formation of SMEs in rural areas to facilitate in the diffusion of Science & Technological achievements to assist in the development of the rural economy through technological innovation and the development of small and medium enterprises. There were a number of criteria used to determine which projects would be supported under the Spark Program.[46] These criteria included the type of resources required, extent of minimal investment required, time period for the flow of returns to investment and the level of technology to be used. In 1988, the 'Torch Foundation' was set up by the central government to ensure that high-tech enterprises set up under the 'Torch Program' would have the financial resources to get established. The major objective of the Torch Program was to ensure that the scientific and technological achievements of China would become[47] commercialised, globalised and industrialised.

In conjunction with the 'Spark' and 'Torch' programs, another program, which had repercussions for science and technology in China, was the 'National Science and Technology Achievements Spreading Program'. This program was designed to utilise all technological resources for the economic benefit of the national economy including those of the rural hinterland and industrial and mining enterprises. The '863 Program' was rolled out in 1988 and was aimed at advancing basic research in the research institutes. It is thought that research is best conducted in an academic environment in the long term as opposed to research being conducted in an industrial/commercial environment (Suresh 2015). The reason for this is that academics would be under less pressure than would researchers in a commercial enterprise to produce results quickly because academics would not be answerable to shareholders like commercial researchers would be. Shareholders would want to see a rate of return on any investment funding. However, in an academic environment researchers would not be answerable to shareholders or a rate of return and so can afford to spend time developing ideas, reinterpretate results until the final solution offers a viable rate of return.[48] According to Jing (2000), this program had little if any benefits for the industrial and manufacturing sector. Also in 1988, the central government sets up a scientific and technological centre in the Zhongguancun area of Beijing and by offering preferential policies lured technologically proficient entrepreneurs to set up firms in the area. Following the establishment of the Zhongguancun centre, in 1991 the central government issued policy guidelines encouraging the establishment of a venture capital fund to finance start-up firms in the centre. In order to strengthen and provide a solid base for venture capital funding, the central government issued one more policy document in 1995. This facilitated the development of venture capital funding. In 1996, a policy document was issued which facilitated the transfer of the results of technological research from research institutes to industrial companies. A guidance document giving advice to research personnel on the transfer of the results of research was issued in 1999.

The reform of the Science & Technology Research Sector, which began in the early 1980s, decentralised decision-making power with regard to the administration of the sector and has increasingly given provincial and regional governments more autonomy in this respect. The effects of technological innovation on economic growth were so great that a provincial slogan became commonly voiced, 'developing vigorously a province or city by the application of science and technology'.[49] In order to facilitate regional development through technological innovation, the central government issued a number of policies and guidelines. In 1991, a document was issued regarding the establishment of high-tech zones in the local economy and stipulating the preferential policies applicable to them. In 1996, a policy document was issued which stipulated the preferential policies applicable to and the qualification required to become a National High-tech Innovation Centre. Furthermore, in 1999 a policy document was issued which would facilitate the establishment and improvement of private science and technology research enterprises. Also in 1999 and as a direct consequence of the National Technological Innovation Conference, a policy document was issued which called for more research devoted to market-oriented projects, deepening of scientific reforms and the enhancement of scientific legislation.[50] The main feature of the document was twofold.

Firstly, it sought to encourage enterprises to upgrade their technological facilities to become more competitive in the marketplace. Secondly, the document sought to encourage more collaboration between enterprises and institutions of research to ensure that the results of the technological and scientific research could be commercialised. The central government was also keen on promoting the development of Non-governmental Science and Technology Incentive Enterprises (NSTIE) because these institutions had the features of firms most likely to succeed in a free market such as self-regulation, self-funding, self-managing and distributing personnel, and bearing the sole responsibility for its own profits and losses. It has been found empirically that direct government support to firm's innovation activities has a negative impact on firm-level innovative performance, while free market-based reforms on research and development have a positive impact on firm-level innovative performance (Guan and Yam 2015).

High-Tech Zones

High-tech enterprises concentrated in high-tech zones and were set up as a backdrop to the 'Open Door' policy. These enterprises were engaged in R&D, sales and industrial management and gathered in high-tech zones due to the preferential policies applied in these zones, lack of state control and the concentration of infrastructure. In 1985, preferential policies were applied in the first high-tech zone set up in Shenzhen; and in 1988, the Zhongguancun high-tech centre was set up in Beijing. The setting up of high-tech zones had been an important feature of the 'Torch Program'. Indeed, it was because of the 'Torch Program' that high-tech zones were set up all over China. However, in order to ensure consistency in the way that each high-tech zone was set up and administered on a daily basis, a policy document was issued in 1991. According to Jing (2000), the high-tech zones were set up in such a fashion that fifty per cent were set up in central provincial cities, twenty-five per cent in Coastal cities and the remaining in the industrial cities. The primary purpose of the high-tech zones was to act as an incentive for academics and researchers to engage in entrepreneurial activity, transform traditional industry through technological innovation, encourage commercially applicable technical innovation, facilitate and increase the growth of high-tech industry, and unleash the productive forces of Chinese R&D.[51] These purposes for the zones were to be served by a number of objectives, which included acting as an area where workers could gain new technical skills, technological-oriented firms could establish themselves and knowledge transfer could be facilitated with the outside world.[52]

Specific fields were selected to which the above objectives could be applied. These fields included biotechnology, new materials, new energy, electronic technology, environmental protection and information and electronics. China's high-tech zones were developed all over the country using the concept of the 'three pillars'—cutting edge technology, government policies regarding high-tech zones and infrastructure. Nevertheless, the central government only macro-manages activities in the high-tech development zones. The total income generated by fifty-two high-tech zones from 1991 to 1998 increased by 5442%. Moreover, the export value of the high-tech zones over the same period jumped by 4638%. Furthermore, Jing (2000) notes that the growth of high-tech enterprises has also created employment within the high-tech zones; by 1998, the number of people employed in the high-tech zones had reached 1.83 million. Therefore, it would seem that high-tech zones and central government's macro-management of them had been a success. Some of the enterprises which became established in the high-tech zones included Sichuan Changhong Co, Shenzhen Huawei Co, Legend Co, Stone Co, Founder Co, Changsha Yuanda Co and Qingdao Haire Co.[53] The Legend Co has gone global and bought the PC business of IBM for $1 billion. The companies, which have become established in the high-tech zones, have also contributed significantly to the local economy. However, even though the high-tech zones have been an overall success story, there are some lingering problems which need to be looked at by the central government. [54]

The vigour with which high-tech zones are promoted across China is very much dependent on the local government. Therefore, regions experience disparities to the extent to which high-tech zones develop.

There are deficiencies in the capital market which services the investment function for high-tech enterprises, especially with regard to central government policy. There are duplications of both product lines and research projects in high-tech zones. The Chinese government has set to resolve these issues by opening up channels of funding available to high-tech enterprises and ensuring that a venture capital system is set up to cater for the funding needs of high-tech enterprises. Furthermore, ensuring that intellectual property laws are respected and ensuring that a transparent legal system is in place will motivate researchers to conduct research with the full knowledge that when their discoveries are commercialised, then they will reap the full economic benefits. The government is also proposing to internationalise high-tech zones and ensure that there is fair competition among the enterprises within the zones.

Incubators

Business incubators in China were set up in high-technology development zones as a government initiative. Therefore, the main feature of business incubators in China is that they are under government control (Ping 2005). Incubators are nurseries in which small and medium-size enterprises are sheltered from the vagaries of free market forces and can grow to such a size that they have sound finances and strong product lines allowing them to compete with other firms once they are de-incubated. The first incubator was opened in 1987, and by the beginning of 2000, there were 110. There are different types of incubators in China: [55]

(a) Specific sector incubators,
(b) Science and technology enterprise incubators providing an all-round service,
(c) The University Science & Technology Research Park,
(d) Returning students innovation park and
(e) International enterprise incubators providing services to enterprises they would expect if they were in a developed country.

These incubators have contributed to the transfer of knowledge, which has been created in a research setting, into commercially viable products able to compete in the domestic and global marketplace. The success of the incubators has been mainly due to the availability of funding, a comprehensive environment for enterprises to operate and knowledge exchange between academia and business.[56] However, a recent analysis of incubators in Xian, Shannxi Province shows that while incubators are necessary to allow SMEs to grow and develop through a path of 'entrepreneurship, innovation and technologies'[57] by giving the SMEs a competitive advantage over their external environment, they are strong enough to stand by themselves. It is on the basis of the commercialisation of new knowledge that new jobs are created and economic development takes place. Nevertheless, in the case of the Xian incubators it was found that government control was reducing the efficiency of the incubators and degrading their performance (Mahmood et al. 2016). Therefore, in order to reinvigorate the incubators and make them more efficient, it is necessary to improve the financial, managerial, legal, organisational and operational areas of incubator control. Furthermore, in order to best support the development of technology firms, the services provided by the incubators should be matched to the needs of the technology firm according to its state in the development cycle (Chan and Lau 2005). However, other empirical work suggests that the performance of technology incubators in China actually increased over the period 2002–2012 (Mahmood et al. 2015).

A Phase 2 development of the incubators occurred after 1997 in a bid for China to attract students who had gone overseas to return to China upon graduation. In this case, more profit-oriented incubators were created in the Coastal region in Shenzhen and Guangzhou in order to encourage technology-based entrepreneurship (Chandra and Chao 2011). For firms in technology business incubators, in Wuhan, it was found that networking and government grants were more important at building the capabilities of the firms to acquire venture capital than was the business support provided by the incubator (Guo et al. 2012). However, according to Chandra and Chao (2011) after 1997 some incubators, mainly those in China's Coastal region, were able to receive funding from a diverse range of sources including government, the private sector and universities and research institutes. While less government control and more free market forces involvement make strengthen incubators, which are similar if not the same as clusters of innovation, an analysis of the strengths of Silicon Valley, in the USA, might perhaps give a recipe for designing and implementing a successful cluster of innovation. In this case, it was found that innovation and entrepreneurship flourish when innovative activities, venture capital, management know how, effective organisation and operations are all located at a single point in space, in a cluster. However, due to the nature of today's telecommunications, a cluster of innovation on one continent can work with a cluster of innovation on another continent. Innovation and entrepreneurship can be geographically independent unlike manufacturing activities. Thus, the best recipe, based on an analysis of Silicon Valley, for a successful cluster of innovation would require a cluster, clusters which are located over different sites, corporate collaborations, business models which are transportable from one geographical location to another and a willingness to build and exploit local skills (Engel 2015).

SMEs

China's central government passed the 'Small Enterprises Promotion Law' in 2003.[58] The main purpose of this law was to stimulate local governments to set up clusters and incubators to attract high-technology start-up firms which were either the results of university spin-offs for the commercialisation of new knowledge or high technology firms set up by Chinese returning from other parts of the world. While the main objective of universities is the 'preservation and the transmission of knowledge'[59], universities have become one of the primary stimulators of regional and national economic growth by transforming the use of knowledge from being purely an internal one to an external use as well (Etzkowitz 2003). In other words, the nature of new knowledge is transformed from being a pure teaching resource to one that is commercially transformed for consumer use. In this process, universities, in China's case adopting the statist Triple Helix regime where the government plays the central role, become entrepreneurial by either moving to university–industry collaborations or moving to university start-ups. In contrast to the statist Triple Helix regime, in the laissez-faire Triple Helix regime, industry takes a leading role in the process of transforming new knowledge, through the process of innovation, into commercially viable products.

In China, SMEs account for 99% of all enterprises and they constitute town and village enterprises, foreign-funded enterprises, joint venture enterprises and non-state research enterprises. The gradual transition of the Chinese economy as one being based on the manufacture of light export goods to an economy which is based on knowledge creation and innovation requires more knowledge-based skilled workers such as professional managers.[60] The reform of SoEs to become more efficient, the increase in the number of private enterprises as well as the increased competition faced by Chinese firms because of China's entry into the WTO in 2001 increased the demand for vocational and executive education. Moreover, SMEs also face a shortage of qualified and experienced professional managers which acts as a constraint on their expansion and growth. As a result of these factors and the UN Millennium Development Goals (UN 2000), the Chinese government has been expanding the provision of vocational and entrepreneurial education.[61] Empirical analysis suggests that a SME owned by one entrepreneur is more efficient at converting raw research and development knowledge into commercially viable products.[62] On the other hand, SMEs with multiple owners will not be focused on endogenous knowledge but with exogenous knowledge. The main feature of SMEs was that there was no legal framework in place to protect either their development or day-to-day existence. Furthermore, the central government had not devised any policies for the development, regulation and growth of the SME sector. This combined with the fact that SMEs, because of their small size, found it difficult to obtain funds for investment from state or non-state sources. The implication of this is that the SMEs will have difficulty in transferring to market the results of S&T research and innovation. In order to resolve issues regarding the investment funds required by SMEs, 'China's Small and Medium Enterprises Innovation Fund' (CSIF) was approved and set up by the central government. The main functions of the CSIF were to allow the commercialisation of research and facilitate the industrialisation of the high-technology sector.[63] However, it is still the case that the slow development of SMEs is most acute in central provinces such as Hubei, where there is an SME financing bottleneck (Fangchun and Lihong 2011). Nevertheless, the CSIF may lay a firm foundation for the development and growth of the SME enterprise sector, although its benefits may not have been felt across all of China's regions, the creation of jobs and the growth of the economy through innovation. The CSIF supports projects which have a high-technology content offering a positive rate of return on investments and projects which result directly from the '863' program and the 'Tackle Key' program with a high export potential.[64] Funding from the CSIF for SMEs includes funding for S&T enterprise start-up capital, low-interest loans for innovative projects and capital investment for innovative industrial projects.[65] Due to the problems associated with SME development and growth, the Bureau of SMEs was established in order to resolve some of the problems associated with SME administration. China's SMEs have numerous advantages associated with their establishment. These advantages include flexible management, low funding requirements, ease of adaptability to market conditions, quick start-up, superior innovation mechanism and low costs associated with management.[66] According to Jing (2000), SMEs are an effective method by which the results of research can be transferred into the market. Therefore, SMEs are an important source of economic growth. However, differences exist between Indian and Chinese SMEs (Singh et al. 2010). Firstly, Indian SMEs are more focused on the development of their suppliers as well as the development of organisational culture. On the other, Chinese SMEs are focused on cost reduction and on the management of relationships. The implication is that Chinese SMEs may be more sustainable in the long run, being more profit oriented and with the ability to ask favours due to the management of relationships than their Indian counterparts.

Returning Students

A direct result of the post-1978 economic reforms in China, Chinese students were sent abroad to study. Deng Xiaoping felt that if Chinese students went abroad to study for foreign degrees, then they would bring back to China new ideas and become change agents for technological and knowledge transfer from the rest of the world to China. Moreover, sending Chinese students abroad to study for advanced degrees would also go some way to correct deficiencies and shortages of trained academic staff in Chinese universities resulting from the effects of the Cultural Revolution. However, not all Chinese students sent to study abroad returned to China. Moreover, this was a considerable source of 'brain drain'. Nevertheless, those students who did return to China not only contributed to academic life but also started up companies themselves, notably in the Zhongguancun district of Beijing. Furthermore, returnees who have gained specific knowledge of public services have been found to reinforce local knowledge and expertise, for example, in the development of health services in China and India.[67] Data[68] suggests that although postgraduate Chinese students began returning home to China in the mid-1970s, the phenomena did not really take off until the early 1990s during the second tranche of the economic reforms. Nevertheless, it would seem that of those postgraduate students who originally left China to study abroad, a smaller number returned in subsequent years. In 1996, the government initiated the 'hundred talents program' to bring back to China those students who had gone abroad for further postgraduate study. Due to this program, in the last 10 years over '20,000 researchers have been attracted back to China via 100 channels'.[69] The power of returning Chinese students to facilitate knowledge creation in China can be illustrated by three examples.[70] In the first case, Jian Wei Pan completed his postgraduate training in Austria before returning to China to set up a research group at the University of Hefei. Pan's research focuses on the development of Quantum computers. In the second case, Andrew Yao and Nobel Laureate Chen Ning Yang, the former contributing to the theory of cryptography and communication, both have labs at Tsinghua University in Beijing. And finally, although

Shi Zhengrong does not head a research group in China, he is an example of a returning academic entrepreneur. In the 1980s, Zhengrong moved to UNSW in Sydney. After completing his fellowship at UNSW, he got a job at a UNSW spin-off company, Pacific Solar, which developed solar cells and where Zhengrong's group was the first in the world to facilitate the growth of silicone at low temperatures. This was the main feature which allowed solar cells to be used for commercial purposes. In the late 1990s, Zhengrong returned to China with the intellectual property of his inventions abroad and subsequently set up Suntech Power in Wuxi, Jiangsu Province. In December 2005, Suntech floated on the NYSE for US\$ 5 billion. However, the company's sales in China represent only 1.5% of its worldwide total.

Innovation Systems in India

Cassiolato and Gonzalo (2016) assert that despite India's macroeconomic performance, the country has been unable to solve the basic technological needs required for its economic development, the provision of infrastructure and public services as well as the needs of India's defence sector. However, India showed its technological prowess when it launched the Mars Orbiter Mission on the 5th November 2013 at a cost of US\$74 million compared to a cost of US\$671 million for NASA's Maven Mars Mission (Amos 2014). According to the latter, why India's successful mission was so cheap was due to the comparatively low cost of Indian engineers and scientists compared to their US counterparts as well as Indian reliance on home-grown technologies and components compared to foreign imports. The successful launch of India's Mars Orbiter Mission but its lower success at being able to solve the needs of its economic development, infrastructure and public policy through the use of technology would seem to suggest that what India lacks is not technology, but central and state government resilience at formulation appropriate policies to fulfil India's economic development, public policy and infrastructure needs coupled with a lack of funding.

The development of innovation systems in India has gone through several distinct phases. The first of these was the pre-1947 colonial period. This was followed by the period 1947–1964 which was characterised as the period in which policies to strengthen Indian sciences were formulated under Prime Minister Nehru. The third period which characterised the development of India's innovation system was the period of self-sufficiency between 1965 and 1989 under Nehru's daughter, Indira Gandhi. The next as yet unfinished period began in 1990 with India's New Economic Policy which can be characterised by the coupling of the Indian economy to the global one at an external level and decentralisation at an internal level. Britain's colonisation of India and subsequently nearly three centuries of British colonial rule did nothing much to establish or to improve India's innovation system. Indeed, in colonial India, there was no technological or innovation policy put in place by the colonial government (Rao 2008). Any innovation policy in place was that which was needed in order to support the extraction and the exploitation of India's resources for the accumulation of wealth by the colonial power. Three universities, Calcutta, Bombay and Madras, were set up in 1857 with the specific purpose of training colonial administrative personnel who were required administer India at the behest of the colonial power, Britain.[71] Furthermore, the original agrarian system of the Indian subcontinent was changed by the introduction of new crops and by the expansion of existing crops for export (Cassiolato and Gonzalo 2016). In order to produce more crops, there was a technology transfer from Britain to India accompanied by a loss of forests for new farmland. Railways were built strategically so that agricultural and commodity produce could be transported to ports and then export markets expediently and at minimal cost. The most important commodity production was that of cotton for the Lancashire mills. Furthermore, railways were built strategically in order to open new markets in India for manufactured goods from Britain. However, railways were also built with a secondary and possibly more important purpose to transport troops to any location on the continent when they were needed. While the focus of colonial administration of India was to maximise agricultural production for export, there was no alignment of agricultural production with the needs of the growing Indian population with the result that there was mass starvation in India in 1877[72]. During the colonial period, Britain only set up two significant institutions in India. In 1867, the Survey of India was established, and in 1875, the Meteorological Department was established (Cassiolato and Gonzalo 2016). However, as India moved towards independence in the late 1930s and early 1940s and as Indian politicians gained more and more autonomy, various other relevant institutions were also established. For example, the Council of Scientific and International Research (CSIR) was established in 1942, and the Industrial Research Planning Committee (IRPC) was established in 1944 (Phalkey and Wang 2016). According to the latter, the CSIR was brought under the control of the IRPC in 1944, but by the mid-1960s control of the CSIR had been given to the Ministry of Education. Technologically, India seems to have been behind China even in the early 1950s, and the continuation of this trend was not because of a lack of qualified researchers, engineers or scientists but infrastructure bottlenecks.[73]

The second stage of the development of India's national innovation system (NIS) occurred between 1947 and 1964. Cassiolato and Gonzalo (2016) call this the planning and confirmation stage. The main feature of this second stage in the evolution of India's NIS was to establish the infrastructure framework from which Indian Science and Technology could develop. Prime Minister Nehru's Science Resolution Policy of 1958 was seen as the key turning point in the evolution of India's NIS (Cassiolato and Gonzalo 2016). According to the latter, Nehru's economic policies during the second evolutionary phase of India's innovation system were:

(a) Technological and industrial self-reliance,
(b) State control of all sectors of the economy, including the financial system,
(c) Low inflows of foreign capital,
(d) Sustaining the Gandhian economic philosophy of the village enterprise,
(e) The state setting prices of goods and factors of production rather than the price mechanism,
(f) A reliance on heavy industrialisation,
(g) And state ownership and control of technology. The third stage of the evolution of India's NIS occurred during the period 1965–1989. Cassiolato and Gonzalo (2016) refer to this period as that of

'institutional consolidation and internal deregulation with Indira and Rajiv Gandhi'. During this third period, the development of Indian innovation and technology was on a selective self-sufficiency basis rather than general self-sufficiency.[74] The pharmaceutical industry was dominant because of 30 years of reverse engineering and a reduction in time for the validity of foreign patents for drugs in India. However, patent violations would stop with India's accession to the WTO. Moreover, it was during this period that India's low economic growth rates since independence from Britain were purely down to Nehru's command economy. The main dateline for technology and innovation during the third stage was as follows:[75]

(a) Improvements in agricultural irrigation and the introduction of high-yielding seeds led to an almost doubling of agricultural output between 1966 and 1978,

(b) The inauguration in 1972 of the National Commission of Science,

(c) The Science and Technology Plan (STP) for 1974–1979. The objective of this plan was for a technical change to be brought about in the Indian economy under the direction of the National Committee on Science and Technology (NCST) (Phalkey and Wang 2016). Furthermore, the NCST was tasked with aligning the priorities of research, development and resources allocation. Moreover, the NCST was required to link the STP 1974–1979 with India's Five-Year Plan as well as to the newly created departments of Electronics, Space and S&T.[76]

(d) The ascendancy of India to the space and nuclear clubs in the early 1980s as envisaged by Nehru,

(e) The Technology Policy of 1983 stipulating the need to develop Indian technology and to adapt the technology of other countries for India's needs. The focus of development was ICT, biotechnology and nanotechnology,

(f) An expansion of India's higher education system so that the country had the skilled labour to help the innovation and technology sector expand in line with government policy. By 1990 the number of universities in the country has almost tripled, the numbers of engineering graduates had increased by 360%, while the numbers of science graduates tripled. Many Indian graduates moved abroad for better pay and conditions but some returned to India in the years following the opening up of its economy in 1991,

(g) A new Science Advisory Council was set up, staffed by scientists and technologists and

(h) The use of computers by the population was promoted.

The fourth and final stage of the evolution and the development of India's innovation system occurred after the year 1990 and it is still in that stage. The period is characterised by what Cassiolato and Gonzalo (2016) refer to as the 'New Economic Policy' which began in 1990 with a focus on the economic liberalisation of the Indian economy, internalisation and decentralisation. As part of the economic liberalisation policies of the 1990s, Prime Minister Singh promoted exports and inward bound FDI; 51% foreign ownership of Indian firms in high-priority sectors began to gain government approval, coupled with this was selective privatisation of state-owned firms. This thus introduced limited market forces into the Indian economy. In 2003, a new technology policy was adopted in India. The crux of the new technology policy was to increase the number of scientists and engineers as a total percentage of the workforce as well as to increase national spending to a level of 2% of GDP (Cassiolato and Gonzalo 2016). According to the latter, a number of challenges exist for India to attain its objective of being an economy that is driven by innovation. Firstly, access to education has to become more open. Currently, only 7% of India's population has access to its educational institutions and university infrastructure remains poor. Secondly, the links between universities, government and firms need to be improved and made stronger so that scientific skills can be transformed into innovation. Thirdly, the level of national and state spending on R&D needs to be improved and the retention rate of staff at universities has to be improved. It seems to be evident from the preceding discussion that India's innovation system remains weak compared to that of China's. Furthermore, the India's innovation system is best modelled as a NIS but China's innovation system is best modelled from the Triple Helix perspective where there are strong linkages between universities, governments and firms.

New Economic Geography Revisited

As previously discussed, Krugman (1991) sought to answer the question 'Why does manufacturing end up being concentrated in one part of a country leaving the other parts to play a peripheral role?' In China's case, the answer to this question arises from the fact that due to government-initiated reforms in 1978 SEZs were established in other Coastal regions of China. The SEZs were followed by NHTIDZs. Both economic structures ensured the realisation of China's comparative advantage in cheap labour and the Coastal regions ease of access to overseas markets, through a concentration in infrastructure. It was the cheap labour and low transport costs which ensured the efficient use of foreign capital.

The economic development of China since 1978 has led to the manufacture of light goods and high-technology goods being concentrated in the Coastal provinces. However, agriculture remains the way of life for a significant majority of China's population in its interior hinterland. Special economic zones (SEZs) have allowed for the export led manufacture of light goods. These SEZs were followed by high-technology development zones (NHTIDZs) which facilitated the export of high technology goods from the Coastal provinces giving these provinces an advantage in terms of economic and social prosperity, as well as contributing to the increase in income disparity between the Coastal provinces and China's interior hinterland. The essence of both SEZs and NHTIDZs is that they represent a concentration of firms and physical infrastructure at a point in space, and where knowledge transfer occurs between Chinese companies and foreign MNCs through joint ventures. It is easy to see that the Chinese economy has moved from the stages of the manufacture of light goods and the production of goods with a high-technology content by knowledge transfer to an economic growth trajectory based on endogenous knowledge creation due to the government's policy of 'endogenous innovation and harmony'. The reform of the educational and R&D sectors in the 1980s and 1990s has placed the Chinese economy in such a position that it can only positively benefit from such a policy. Furthermore, such a policy can only assist in the formation of a homogenous NIS. Nevertheless, the lack of a unified national education system is hindering the formation of a NIS, and in this regard, the Japanese educational model applied to the Chinese system would bring numerous economies of scale. A critical appraisal of the NEG reveals that five restrictions exist in the model devised by Krugman (1991). Firstly, only the agricultural and manufacturing sectors are considered. Secondly, the model does not account for agglomeration economies which arise due to the creation of knowledge in the spatial economy. But centres of innovation tend to lie in urban locations. While the polarisation of innovation is in urban centres for both India and China, the reasons for the polarisation of innovation are different for both countries.[77] In China, the centre of innovation is in the Coastal region due to the forces of agglomeration which are strongest in that region, a region characterised by a rising population, and well-endowed with industry and infrastructure (Crescenzi et al. 2015). Moreover, innovation in the Coastal region, according to the latter, tends to result in backwash effects rather than externalities due to knowledge spillovers. However, in India the polarisation of innovation in urban centres tends to occur because of societal values, such as the importance of education, the family as well as investment in science and technology. Furthermore, in India, innovation results in externalities due to knowledge spillovers.[78] Thirdly, the model assumes that the core-periphery pattern forms due to pecuniary externalities. Fourthly, the model suggests that manufacturing is concentrated in order to minimise transport costs and has therefore excluded the role of infrastructure in economic development. Finally, a key assumption in the model is that the peasant population is immobile between regions. In China's case while, the NEG offers a framework of analysis, deficiencies in the theory can easily be identified. Firstly, China's economic growth has been driven by the manufacturing sector with agriculture playing an insignificant role. Secondly, China's transition to an industrialised economy has necessitated the movement of peasants from the rural hinterland (periphery) to the Coastal regions (core). Thirdly, due to the role of FDI, China's transition to a market economy has been characterised by knowledge transfer. Finally, the Chinese economy is itself transitioning to a knowledge creation economy. In the Chinese context, the NEG is an abstract model and should be remodelled in order to factor in the differences.

Some key points have been established. In Chap. 5, Vol. 1, the link between infrastructure, trade and market size was established. In Chap. 7, Vol. 1, the relevance of infrastructure to the differing stages of China's development was evaluated. In Chap. 2, Vol. 2, and Chap. 3, Vol. 2, the concept of Innovation Systems and the competence block was introduced. Moreover, the relevance of telecommunications and the Internet to knowledge creation and spillovers to a non-fixed location was introduced. In Chap. 3, Vol. 2, the importance of education and centres of knowledge creation to the formation of innovation systems was discussed. This is true specifically with regard to innovation systems which had been modelled on the basis of the Triple Helix Model which emphasises the role of university–government–firm linkages which causes new knowledge to diffuse from academic research to firms due to entrepreneurship, as a direct result of government policy and guidance.

Chapter 4, Vol. 2, will evaluate the nature of entrepreneurship from both theoretical and practical perspectives in China and in India.

Notes

1. Huang, C., and Sharif, N. (2015), Global technology leadership: The case of China, Science and Public Policy, pp. 1–12.
2. Behrens (2004), 'On the location and lock-in of cities: geography vs. transportation technology'. Mimeograph. Centre for Operations Research and Econometrics, Universite Catholique de Louvain.
3. Turpin, T & Liu, X (2002) 'Introduction' in 'Innovation, Technological Policy and Regional Development', Turpin, T (Eds), Edward Elgar, Cheltenham, UK.
4. Etzkowitz, H., and Leydesdorff, L. (2000), The dynamics of innovation: from National Systems and 'Mode 2' to a Triple Helix of University-industry-government relations, Research Policy, 29, pp. 109–123.
5. Ibid.
6. Li, T., Fu, M., and Fu, X. (2013), Regional technology development path in an open developing economy: evidence from China, Applied Economics, 45, pp. 1405–1418.

7. Ibid.
8. Liu, X & Guo, Z. (2002), 'Integrated innovation in Ningxia: natural resources and new knowledge', in 'Innovation, Technological Policy and Regional Development', Turpin, T (Eds), Edward Elgar, Cheltenham, UK.
9. Ibid.
10. Ibid.
11. Chang, P., and Shih, H. (2004), The innovation systems of Taiwan and China: a comparative analysis, Technovation, 24, pp. 529–539.
12. Sigurdson (2004), 'Regional Innovation Systems in China(RIS) in China', EIJS Working Paper No. 195.
13. Ibid.
14. Wang, J. (2013), The economic impact of Special Economic Zones: Evidence from Chinese municipalities, Journal of Development Economics, 101, pp. 133–147.
15. Kang, Q (2004), 'Higher Education Reform in China Today', Policy Futures in Education, Volume 2, Number 1, 2004.
16. Ibid.
17. Letwin, K.M et al. (1994), 'Educational Innovation in China: Tracing the Impact of the 1985 Reforms', Longman.
18. Agelasto. M and Adamson. B (1998), 'Introduction' in 'Higher Education in Post-Mao China', Agelasto.M and Adamson.B (Eds), Hong Kong University Press.
19. Ibid.
20. Ibid.
21. Ibid.
22. Kai-Ming, C. (1998), 'Reforms in the Administration and Financing of Higher Education' in 'Higher Education in Post- Mao China', Agelasto. M and Adamson. B (Eds), Hong Kong University Press.
23. Fan, C. (2006), China's Eleventh Five Year Plan (2006–2010): From 'getting Rich First' to 'Common Prosperity', Eurasian geography and Economics, 47, No. 6, pp. 708–723.
24. China Daily (2000), Major Objectives for Next Five Years', http://www.china.org.cn/e-15/15-3-b/15-3-b-2.htm.
25. BritCham (2011), China's Twelfth Five Year Plan (2011–2015) the English Version—http://www.britishchamber.cn/content/chinas-twelfth-five-year-plan-2011-2015-full-english-version.

26. Wenbin, H. (2012), Looking Back at Thirty Years of Educational Reform and Development in China, Chinese Education & Society, 45:1, 3–6.
27. Kroeber, A. (2013), Xi Jinping's Ambitious Agenda for Economic Reform in China, Brookings, https://www.brookings.edu/opinions/xi-jinpings-ambitious-agenda-for-economic-reform-in-china/.
28. Wong, C. (2016), Budget Reform in China: Progress and Prospects in the Xi Jinping era, OECD Journal on Budgeting, Volume 2015/3.
29. CCP (2014), CCP Central Committee Resolution Concerning Some Major Issues in Comprehensively Deepening Reform, Chin Copyright Media, https://chinacopyrightandmedia.wordpress.com/2013/11/15/ccp-central-committee-resolution-concerning-some-major-issues-in-comprehensively-deepening-reform/.
30. Kang, Q (2004), 'Higher Education Reform in China Today', Policy Futures in Education, Volume 2, Number 1.
31. Kafouros, M., Wang, C., Piperopoulos, P., and Zhang, M. (2015), Academic collaborations and firm innovation performance in China: The role of region-specific institutions, Research Policy, 44, pp. 803–817.
32. Singh, A., Wong, P., and Ho, Y. (2015), The role of universities in the national innovation systems of China and the East Asian NIE's: An explanatory analysis of publications and patenting data,' Asian Journal of Technology Innovation, Vol. 23, No. 2, pp. 140–156.
33. Jing, S (2000), 'The Comparative Study of Regional Innovation Systems of Japan & China', Department of Policy, Regulation and System Reform, Ministry of Science & Technology, China.
34. Ibid.
35. Ibid.
36. Ibid.
37. Ibid.
38. Tagscherer, U. (2015), Science-industry-linkages in China: What drives MNCs to collaborate with Chinese academic partners and what makes them successful, Fraunhofer ISI Discussion Papers Innovation Systems and Policy Analysis, No. 47.
39. Dong, H., Gao, Y., Sinko, P., Wu, Z., Xu, J., and Jia, L. (2016), The nanotechnology race between China and the United States, Nano Today, 11, pp. 7–12.
40. Ibid.
41. Zhu, D. (2012), Chinese S&T parks: the emergence of a new model, Journal of Business Strategy, Vol. 33 Iss 5 pp. 4–13.

42. Ibid.
43. Ibid.
44. Ibid.
45. Zhong, L., Louie, K., Zheng, J., Yuan, Z., Yue, D., Ho, J., and Lau, A. (2013), Science-policy interplay: Air quality management in the Pearl River Delta Region and Hong Kong, Atmospheric Environment, 76, pp. 3–10.
46. Jing, S (2000), 'The Comparative Study of Regional Innovation Systems of Japan & China', Department of Policy, Regulation and System Reform, Ministry of Science & Technology, China.
47. Ibid.
48. Suresh, S. (2015), Research Universities, Innovation and Growth, Research-Technology Management, 58:6, pp. 19–23.
49. Ibid.
50. Ibid.
51. Jing, S (2000), 'The Comparative Study of Regional Innovation Systems of Japan & China', Department of Policy, Regulation and System Reform, Ministry of Science & Technology, China.
52. Ibid.
53. Ibid.
54. Ibid.
55. Jing, S (2000), 'The Comparative Study of Regional Innovation Systems of Japan & China', Department of Policy, Regulation and System Reform, Ministry of Science & Technology, China.
56. Ibid.
57. Mahmood, N., Jianfeng, C., Munir, H., Yanran, M., and Cai, Y. (2016), Incubators, SME's and Economic Development of China, International Journal of Multi-Media and Ubiquitous Engineering, Vol. 11, No. 1, pp. 311–318.
58. Li, C. (2015), Beyond Conventional Perceptions: The Power of Rising SME's in China's Innovative Transformation, Presentation to the DRUID Academy Conference in Rebild, Aalbord, Denmark.
59. Etzkowitz, H. (2003), Innovation in innovation: The Triple Helix of University-industry-government relations, Social Science Information, 42(3), pp. 293–337.
60. Millman, C., Matlay, H., Liu, F. (2008), Entrepreneurship education in China: a case study approach, Journal of Small Business and Enterprise Development, Vol. 15 Iss 4 pp. 802–815.

61. Ibid.
62. Deng, Z., Hofman, P., and Newman, A. (2013), Ownership concentration and product innovation in Chinese private SME's, Asia Pac J Manag, 30, 717–734.
63. Ibid.
64. Ibid.
65. Ibid.
66. Ibid.
67. Huang, C., and Sharif, N. (2015), Global technology leadership: The case of China, Science and Public Policy, pp. 1–12.
68. National Bureau of Statistics, China Statistical Yearbook 2014.
69. New Scientist, 'China: Birth of a Superpower', Tenth November 2007.
70. Ibid.
71. Cassiolato, J., and Gonzalo, M. (2016), Emergence, consolidation and main current challenges of India's National Innovation System: a historical interpretation from Latin America, Discussion Paper 010/2016, Institutio de economica.
72. Ibid.
73. Phalkey, J., and Wang, Z. (2016), Planning for science and technology in China and India, BJHS; Themes 1, pp. 83–113.
74. Ibid.
75. Ibid.
76. Phalkey, J., and Wang, Z. (2016), Planning for science and technology in China and India, BJHS; Themes 1, pp. 83–113.
77. Crescenzi, R., Rodríguez, A., and Storper, M. (2015), The territorial dynamics of innovation in China and India, Journal of Economic Geography, 12, pp. 1055–1085.
78. Ibid.

References

Acs, Z. J., Audretsch, D. B., Braunerhjelm, P., & Carlsson, B. (2005). *The knowledge filter and entrepreneurship in endogenous growth.* Papers on Entrepreneurship, Growth and Public Policy, No. 08. Max Planck Institute of Economics, Jena, Germany.

Agelasto, M., & Adamson, B. (1998). Introduction'. In M. Agelasto & B. Adamson (Eds.), *Higher education in Post-Mao China.* Hong Kong University Press.

Amos, J. (2014). *Why India's Mar's mission is so thrilling—and cheap*, http://www.bbc.co.uk/news/science-environment-29341850.

Behrens, K. (2004). On the location and 'lock-in' of cities: geography vs. transportation technology', Mimeograph. *Centre for Operations Research and Econometrics, Universite Catholique de Louvain.*

BritCham. (2011). China's Twelfth Five Year Plan (2011–2015)—the Full English Version—http://www.britishchamber.cn/content/chinas-twelfth-five-year-plan-2011-2015-full-english-version.

Cassiolato, J., & Gonzalo, M. (2016). Emergence, consolidation and main current challenges of India's National Innovation System: a historical interpretation from Latin America. Discussion Paper 010/2016, Institutio de economica.

CCP. (2014). *CCP Central Committee Resolution concerning some major issues in comprehensively deepening reform, China Copyright Media*, https://chinacopyrightandmedia.wordpress.com/2013/11/15/ccp-central-committee-resolution-concerning-some-major-issues-in-comprehensively-deepening-reform/.

Chakrabarti, S. (2014). China's compulsory education law. ICS Working Paper 2014/03/6.

Chan, K., & Lau, T. (2005). Assessing technology incubator programs in the science park: the good, the bad and the ugly. *Technovation, 25,* 1215–1228.

Chandra, A., & Chao, C. (2011). Growth and evolution of high technology business incubation in China. *Human Systems Management, 30,* 55–69.

Chang, P., & Shih, H. (2004). The innovation systems of Taiwan and China: a comparative analysis. *Technovation, 24,* 529–539.

China Daily. (2000). *Major objectives for next five years*, http://www.china.org.cn/e-15/15-3-b/15-3-b-2.htm.

Clark, S. (2016). China: The new space superpower. *The Guardian*, https://www.theguardian.com/science/2016/aug/28/china-new-space-superpower-lunar-mars-missions.

Crescenzi, R., Rodríguez, A., & Storper, M. (2015). The territorial dynamics of innovation in China and India. *Journal of Economic Geography, 12,* 1055–1085.

Deng, Z., Hofman, P., & Newman, A. (2013). Ownership concentration and product innovation in Chinese private SME's. *Asia Pacific Journal Management, 30,* 717–734.

Dong, H., Gao, Y., Sinko, P., Wu, Z., Xu, J., & Jia, L. (2016). The nanotechnology race between China and the United States. *Nano Today, 11,* 7–12.

Engel, J. (2015). *Global clusters of innovation: Lessons from silicon valley* (Vol. 57, No. 2). University of California Berkeley.

Etzkowitz, H. (2003). Innovation in innovation: The Triple Helix of university-industry-government relations. *Social Science Information, 42*(3), 293–337.

Etzkowitz, H., & Leydesdorff, L. (2000). The dynamics of innovation: From national systems and 'Mode 2' to a triple helix of University-industry-government relations. *Research Policy, 29,* 109–123.

Fan, C. (2006). China's eleventh five-year plan (2006–2010): From 'Getting Rich First' to 'common prosperity'. *Eurasian Geography and Economics, 47*(6), 708–723.

Fangchun, P., & Lihong, C. (2011). SMEs cluster financing: General theory and China's practice, Computer Science and Service System (CSSS), 2011 international conference, Nanjing, 2011, pp. 744–747. doi:10.1109/CSSS.2011.5972077.

Gu, J. (2012). Harmonious expansion of China's higher education: A new growth pattern. *Higher Education, 63,* pp. 513–528.

Guan, J., & Yam, R. (2015). Effects of government financial incentives on firm's innovation performance in China: Evidences from Beijing in the 1990s. *Research Policy, 44,* 273–282.

Guo, T., Hong, J., Zhao, D., Wu, Y., & Fan, J. (2012). The incubators, venture capital and new ventures in China. *International Journal of Innovation Management and Technology, 3*(4).

Huang, C., & Sharif, N. (2015). Global technology leadership: The case of China. *Science and Public Policy*, pp. 1–12.

Jing, S. (2000). The comparative study of regional innovation systems of Japan & China. Department of Policy, Regulation and System Reform, Ministry of Science & Technology, China.

Kafouros, M., Wang, C., Piperopoulos, P., & Zhang, M. (2015). Academic collaborations and firm innovation performance in China: The role of region-specific institutions. *Research Policy, 44,* 803–817.

Kai-Ming, C. (1998). Reforms in the administration and financing of higher education in higher education in Post-Mao China, In M. Agelasto & B. Adamson (Eds.), Hong Kong University Press.

Kang, Q. (2004). Higher education reform in China today. *Policy Futures in Education, 2*(1), 2004.

Kroeber, A. (2013). Xi Jinping's ambitious agenda for economic reform in China. *Brookings*, https://www.brookings.edu/opinions/xi-jinpings-ambitious-agenda-for-economic-reform-in-china/.

Krugman, P. (1991). Increasing returns and economic geography. *The Journal of Political Economy, 99*(3), 483–499.

Letwin, K. M., et al. (1994). *Educational innovation in China: Tracing the impact of the 1985 reforms.* Longman.

Leydesdorff, L., & Etzkowitz, H. (1998). The triple Helix as a model for innovation studies. *Science and Public Policy, 25*(3), 195–203.

Leydesdorff, L., & Meyer, M. (2006). Triple Helix indicators of knowledge based innovation systems, introduction to the special issue. *Research Policy, 35,* 1441–1449.

Li, C. (2015). *Beyond conventional perceptions: The power of rising SME's in China's innovative transformation.* Presentation to the DRUID Academy Conference in Rebild, Aalbord, Denmark.

Li, T., Fu, M., & Fu, X. (2013). Regional technology development path in an open developing economy: Evidence from China. *Applied Economics, 45,* 1405–1418.

Liu, Y., & Dunne, M. (2009). Educational reform in China: Tensions in national policy and local practice. *Comparative Education, 45*(4), 461–476. doi:10.1080/03050060903391594.

Liu, X., & Guo, Z. (2002). Integrated innovation in Ningxia: Natural resources and new knowledge. In T. Turpin, T (Ed.), *Innovation, technological policy and regional development.* Edward Elgar, Cheltenham, UK.

Mahmood, N., Jianfeng, C., Munir, H., Yanran, M., & Cai, Y. (2016). Incubators, SME's and economic development of China. *International Journal of Multimedia and Ubiquitous Engineering, 11*(1), 311–318.

Mahmood, N., Jianfeng, C., Jamil, F., Munir, H., Lu, J., Khan, M., et al. (2015). Snapshot of technology business incubators in China. *International Journal of U- and e- Service, Science and Technology, 8*(7).

Millman, C., Matlay, H., Liu, F. (2008). Entrepreneurship education in China: A case study approach. *Journal of Small Business and Enterprise Development, 15*(4), 802–815.

Mok, K. (2013). *The Quest for entrepreneurial universities in East Asia.* US: Palgrave Macmillan.

Mueller, P. (2006). Exploring the knowledge filter: How entrepreneurship and University-industry relationships drive economic growth. *Research Policy, 35,* 1499–1508.

New Scientist, China: Birth of a Superpower, Tenth November 2007.

Phalkey, J., & Wang, Z. (2016). Planning for science and technology in China and India. *BJHS; Themes, 1,* 83–113.

Ping, H. (2005). *Business incubator industry in China. Tech Monitor, 23.*

Rao, C. (2008). Science and technology policies: The case of India. *Technology in Society, 30*(3), 242–247.

Rhoads, R., Shi, X., & Wang, X. (2014). Reform of China's research universities: A new era of global ambition. *Education and Society, 32*(1), 5–28.

Sigurdson. (2004). *Regional innovation systems in China (RIS) in China.* EIJS Working Paper No. 195.

Singh, A., Wong, P., & Ho, Y. (2015). The role of universities in the national innovation systems of China and the East Asian NIE's: An explanatory analysis of publications and patenting data. *Asian Journal of Technology Innovation, 23*(2), 140–156.

Singh, R., Garf, S., & Deshmukh, S. (2010). The competitiveness of SME's in a globalised economy, observations from China and India. *Management Research Review, 33*(1), 54–65.

Suresh, S. (2015). Research universities, innovation and growth. *Research-Technology Management, 58*(6), 19–23.

Tagscherer, U. (2015). *Science-industry-linkages in China: What drives MNCs to collaborate with Chinese academic partners and what makes them successful.* Fraunhofer ISI Discussion Papers Innovation Systems and Policy Analysis, No. 47.

Turpin, T., & Liu, X. (2002). *Introduction in innovation, technological policy and regional development.* In Turpin, T (Ed.), Edward Elgar, Cheltenham, UK.

UN. (2000). *Youth at the United Nations, United Nations.* Available at: www.un.org/esa/socdev/unyin/qanda.htm.

Wang, J. (2013). The economic impact of special economic zones: Evidence from Chinese municipalities. *Journal of Development Economics, 101*, 133–147.

Wang, Q., & Liu, N. (2014). Higher education research institutes in Chinese universities. *Studies in Higher Education, 39*(8), 1488–1498. doi:10.1080/0 3075079.2014.949544.

Wenbin, H. (2012). Looking back at thirty years of educational reform and development in China. *Chinese Education & Society, 45*(1), 3–6.

Wong, C. (2016). Budget reform in China: Progress and prospects in the Xi Jinping era. *OECD Journal on Budgeting, 2015/3.*

Zhong, L., Louie, K., Zheng, J., Yuan, Z., Yue, D., Ho, J., et al. (2013). Science-policy interplay: Air quality management in the Pearl River delta region and Hong Kong. *Atmospheric Environment, 76*, 3–10.

Zhu, D. (2012). Chinese S&T parks: The emergence of a new model. *Journal of Business Strategy, 33*(5), 4–13.

4

Entrepreneurship in China and India

Entrepreneurship encompasses a creative phenomenon in which an individual or a group of individuals are able to identify a niche in the market for a good or service and exploit this niche by allocating resources such as labour, land and capital in order to make a profit. Entrepreneurs seeking profit are able to allocate resources such as labour and capital in the context of a firm, and by doing so entrepreneurs facilitate the division of labour and economic growth (Smith 1776). Furthermore, an understanding of the role of the entrepreneur will allow for a successful analysis of how labour, capital and technology are able to interact in order to facilitate economic growth (Holcombe 1998). According to Solow (1956, 1957), economic growth occurred because of increases in investment in capital which allowed workers to become more productive over time. However, over time any additional investment was 'swallowed' up by having to replace existing capital so 'new' investment resulted in diminishing increases in worker productivity. Knowledge was assumed to be freely accessible to all firms and in the econometric estimation of the production function, knowledge was assumed to be represented by the residual (Solow 1957). And economic growth occurred in the long run through permeable technological

© The Author(s) 2017
S. Ramesh, *China's Lessons for India: Volume II*,
DOI 10.1007/978-3-319-58115-6_4

change. Therefore, economic growth and economic development, in the long run, are facilitated by entrepreneurship (Carree et al. 2007). However, two distinct types of entrepreneurship have been identified (Koster and Rai 2005). These include the opportunistic entrepreneur and the necessity entrepreneur. The former base their firms on unexplored niche markets and/or innovative products. However, necessity based entrepreneurs who undertake entrepreneurial activities only do so because they do not have any other way to generate sustainable income. The Schumpeterian view on economic growth is that it is facilitated by opportunistic firms establishing new processes and new product lines; and by so doing challenge the products and processes of incumbent firms. The latter have to innovate in order to survive, and if not the market is reorganised by a process of 'creative destruction'. According to Koster and Rai (2005), the process of 'creative destruction' facilitates regional productivity and regional competitiveness leading to regional economic development. 'Creative destruction' is also more likely to occur in developed countries with more mature markets than it is in developing countries in which necessity-based entrepreneurship is more likely to be dominant (Koster and Rai 2005). According to the latter, this is due to the lack of employment opportunities as well as other opportunities to develop a sustainable income.

The work of Lucas (1993) and Romer (1986) ensured that knowledge became associated with externalities and spillovers, and knowledge creation in one form or organisation spilt over into the market due to commercialisation. Once knowledge spillovers were included in economic growth models, the focus of public policy shifted from economic growth on the basis of investment in capital and the subsequent increase in labour productivity to knowledge (Audretsch 2007). The latter suggests that knowledge spillovers were constrained because of 'knowledge spill overs' which prevented the commercialisation of knowledge originating in one firm being commercialised by a third party. Thus, public policy initiatives to invest in knowledge promotion projects did not generate the required level of economic growth, an example being the 'European paradox'. Entrepreneurship bypasses the knowledge filter and thus represents the 'missing link between investments in new knowledge and economic growth' (Audretsch 2007). However, the allocation of entrepreneurial capital amongst different types of economic activity depends on government laws, regulations and public and economic policies (Baumol 1990). For example, housing reform in urban China which allowed state employees to buy the state-owned housing they were renting at subsidised prices facilitated an increase in self-employment (Wang 2012). The latter suggests that the positive relationship between urban housing reform and self-employment resulted from reduced labour mobility costs and a reduction in household capital constraints due to the wealth effect arising from property ownership.

Measuring Entrepreneurship

Determining and understanding the factors which facilitate entrepreneurial activity will allow an insight into why some countries have higher levels of economic growth than do other countries (Hafer and Jones 2015). People with more ability in terms of motivating and managing others, strong time management and organisational skills, tenacity, good interpersonal skills and the ability to take risks seem to have higher incomes as entrepreneurs than the wages they would be able to earn as workers. Thus, general cognitive ability is more important and as a bigger impact on entrepreneurs than on workers (Hartog et al. 2010). This is because people with a high level of cognitive skills will be better able to start and manage a firm in order to innovate than those with a lower level of cognitive skills who would more likely be workers (Van Praag et al. 2013). The education of entrepreneurs rather than that of workers has a bigger impact on a country's economic growth and economic development (Gennaioli et al. 2013). However, according to research, opportunistic entrepreneurs tend to be more educated than are necessity-based entrepreneurs (Bergmann and Sternberg 2007). Furthermore, necessity-based entrepreneurs are less likely to be educated in the sector in which they start the business (Block and Sandner 2009). Perhaps education may better improve the cognitive skills of the entrepreneur class than the cognitive skills of the worker class. A higher level of cognitive skills will reduce income inequality (Meisenberg 2012). Income inequality is measured using the Gini coefficient. The

Gini Coefficient has a value between 0 and 1. If the Gini coefficient is close to 0 then it means that there is perfect income equality, and if it is close to 1 then it means that there is complete income inequality, Arnold (2008). In China, income inequality tends to be lower for urban residents than it is for rural ones (Zhou and Qin 2012). This difference could be explained by the knowledge that urban areas tend to represent an environment which is conducive to innovative entrepreneurship than are rural areas (Baporikar 2015). This could be because urban areas represent a bigger market, economic density as well as a more educated workforce than can be found in rural areas of China.

Entrepreneurship can be measured by using both the Global Entrepreneurship and Development Index (GEDI), developed by Acs and Szerb (2010), and by the Global Entrepreneurship Monitor (GEM). Another measure of entrepreneurship, is an output-based one which is based on the number of private limited liability companies which are entering the market. This is the World Bank's Entrepreneurship Survey 2014. One disadvantage of using this measure is that it may not be a universally comparable measure of entrepreneurship because different countries have different regulations regarding how firms are set up. Furthermore, the nature and the development of entrepreneurship vary from country to country due to cultural, historical, linguistic, religious, institutional, resource access and infrastructural differences, Bruton et al. (2008). The implication is that research into entrepreneurship should not be generalised but should be dependent on country by country. Secondly, the measure does not account for the informal entry of firms into the market. So, it may underestimate the level of entrepreneurial activity in the economy (Hafer and Jones 2015). The level of cognitive skill can be measured using the IQ series published by Lynn and Meisenberg (2010).

Entrepreneurship in Transition Economies

The Chinese economy like the Indian economy is an economy in transition. The economic reforms began in China in 1978. However, in India, the economic reforms progressed in spasms with initial reforms in the 1980s embracing the private sector followed by necessary reforms in the early 1990s due to India's balance of payments crisis. The reforms in both countries have ensured that entrepreneurship has occurred in the background of chaotic, unstable institutional transformation (Yang and Li 2008). The evolution of entrepreneurial activity in India and in China has been different to that in advanced economies (Ahlstrom and Bruton 2002). In China, to a greater extent than in India, entrepreneurship evolved in response to the economic reforms which introduced market forces into the Chinese economy. In a country, whose economy had been based on central planning for twenty-nine years, the removal of the pillars of central planning from the various sectors of the economy left a void for goods and services which could only be filled by the emergence and the activities of the entrepreneur (Tan 2005). Furthermore, government initiatives to introduce new programs (the Spark Program), institutions, such as Science and Technology Research Parks as well as the deregulation of the economy (Yang and Li 2008), has facilitated economic growth through supply-side policies. Thus, these initiatives have facilitated more firms to be set up and to thus enter the market with a resultant increase in aggregate supply and national output. The rise of the middle class in China has also resulted in an increase in consumption which has again given rise to opportunities, to correct market distortions and market deficiencies, which could be grasped by entrepreneurial activity (Tsang 1994). However, the market transition of the Chinese economy is not yet complete because the Chinese economy remains a hybrid market centrally planned economy, and entrepreneurship may still face constraints not present in more advanced economies (Zapalska and Edwards 2001). Furthermore, in the initial stages of economic reform, the economy was dominated by the state and non-state enterprises had a subsidiary role of supporting state enterprises (Fan 1996), putting them at the mercy of local government policies (Wing and Yiu 2000). The evolution of Chinese entrepreneurship is clearly different from entrepreneurship in advanced economies due to the problems it faced in its emergence. These problems included fragmented markets resulting in poorly developed market forces and a lack of clearly defined property rights (Ahlstrom and Bruton 2002). Furthermore, in China, *guanxi* plays a significant role in doing business.

Guanxi refers to the use of contacts and networks in order to further and progress business interests. According to Phan et al. (2010), the 'result of guanxi is a network of social obligation'.

Entrepreneurship in China

The Communist victory in 1949 led to the private sector being eliminated in China by 1956. Under the Communists, China became a centrally planned economy with the government deciding on what was to be produced and how much was to be produced. In effect, the government decided on the allocation of specific factors of production in order to produce specific outputs. As a result, the government would maintain a monopoly on the production and the distribution of goods and services. While the formal private sector had been eliminated, an informal and efficient rent-seeking private sector emerged by filling gaps which the formal economy could not fulfil (Liao and Sohmen 2001). The inability of the Chinese economy to offer a decent standard of living to the people led to the 1978 economic reforms which started with the decollectivisation of agriculture. However, it was the Third Plenum of the Eleventh Central Committee of the Chinese Communist Party which laid the roots for the re-emergence of entrepreneurship in China. This is because it emphasised individual incentives and economic development (Liu 2002). According to the latter until mid-1988, the main component of the private sector was the *getihu* or the individual household unit. However, at that time, the government issued the tentative Stipulations on Private Enterprise (TSPE). The TSPE stipulated that if a unit with private assets hired more than eight workers, then it would be recognised as a private enterprise or *saying qiye*. Furthermore, the TSPE classified private enterprise in three ways (Liu 2002). These included sole ownership, partnership and limited liability corporations. However, in addition to the well-known forms of private enterprise, China's economy gave rise to additional forms of private enterprise. These included the red hat firm, the rented collective, the shareholding firm and the foreign investor joint enterprise (Liu 2002). The red hat firm obtained a licence from local government for production and paid a percentage of its output value or turnover as a fee. Town and village enterprises, urban collective enterprises and state-owned enterprises were red hat firms. Rented collectives were collectives which were rented out to private enterprise. These types of firms were collective only in name as they operated according to the private sector mechanism in terms of generating profits. In a shareholding firm, shares in the collective assets of firms are distributed to employees and a share of the profits is distributed to workers as a bonus. Some state-owned enterprises have been privatised in this way and the evolution of town and village enterprises from collectives as also taken the same route (Liu 2002). The last form of enterprise was the foreign investor joint enterprise. Foreign investors and firms investing in China were required to form joint ventures with a Chinese firm with tax advantage incentives. In order to take advantage of this, Chinese entrepreneurs registered offshore accounts to invest in China as foreign investors. In order to facilitate the transition to a market economy and entrepreneurship, the Chinese government also improved the legal framework by enacting the Company Law in 1993, followed by amendment in 1999, the Partnership Enterprise Law in 1997 a so enacted laws and regulations to improve the rights of parties to contracts, the payment of bills and the availability and the purchase of insurance. The legal system progressively also placed emphasis on ensuring fair competition, improving product quality and consumer protection (Longbao 2009). Nevertheless, the legal protection of personal assets and the legal enforcement of contracts in China are on a weak institutional footing (Lu and Tao 2007). According to the latter, this is in sharp contrast to advanced economies in which a strong and supportive institutional environment with regard to property rights and contract enforcement leads to only the personal attributes of the entrepreneur being the limit to the extent and the nature of entrepreneurship. The lack of a solid institutional footing in China would also suggest that entrepreneurial creativity is also constrained. Although, from a wider perspective, the country's rote learning educational system, reform of which has been attempted, also plays a role in constraining creativity in general.

The decollectivisation of agriculture led to rising unemployment in the rural sector. As a result, this led to the emergence of town and village enterprises or TVE's. The latter were collectively owned by local governments and the workers while not being owned by the state itself. The output of the TVE's contributed to 20% of China's gross output by the 1990s (Liao and Sohmen 2001). In comparison on the state-owned enterprises, the operation of the TVE's reflected the flexibility of its managers to control production and distribution of goods and services in order to maintain low costs and price levels which would best promote the profitability of the enterprise. The focus of the managers of TVE's on profitability, in contrast to the managers of SOE's, would suggest that they represent the roots of modern entrepreneurship in China (Liao and Sohmen 2001). In the 1980s institutional and resource constraints restricted the growth of entrepreneurship in China. The institutional constraint was represented by a law which restricted the number of employees of a private enterprise to just seven. The resource constraint was represented by the lack of availability of funding to entrepreneurs. This was mainly due to the low level of savings in China as well as the discriminatory behaviour of the state banks in restricting lending to just state-owned enterprises. Private enterprises complain of the frustration in dealing with state-owned banks as well as the problems which arise from having to deal with corrupt government officials, Kshetri (2007). However, the government perception of the role of private enterprise changed with the realisation that state-owned enterprises were inefficient with regard to the allocation of the factors of production and with the production of goods and services. The realisation of the inefficiency of state-owned enterprises and the repeal of the law limiting the number of employees of private enterprises to seven signalled the state's shift towards recognising the importance of private enterprise to the Chinese economy.

In the post-economic reform period, the emergence of several types of entrepreneurship can be identified (Liao and Sohmen 2001). According to the latter, the first type of what could be loosely called entrepreneurs were street vendors providing retail and services who emerged prior to the 1978 economic reforms but persisted after the reforms progressed. Street vendors were self-employed and often were associated with illegal emigrants or those who either had a criminal background or low levels of education (Liao and Sohmen 2001). These street vendors, self-employed 'entrepreneurs', were effectively shut out of the state system, and they earned enough to barely survive. The second type of entrepreneur emerged during the reform period, and they can be characterised as being educated and having managerial experience with State Owned Enterprises. They operated in all sectors of the economy on a large scale in businesses known as 'siying qiye' which supplied state-owned enterprises with intermediate goods. The third type of entrepreneurship in China can be associated with foreign educated or trained Chinese returning to China to set up businesses mainly in the Internet sector (Liao and Sohmen 2001).

There are also a number of barriers in China which have a tendency to constrain entrepreneurial emergence and activity. These barriers include political and legal uncertainty, access to resources and cultural perception. Political and legal uncertainty arose due to the infancy of property rights and the rule of law. For example, in the context of gender and entrepreneurship, Deng et al. (2011) find that a law of gender equality will fill an institutional gap which would allow female entrepreneurs in China to 'emerge on a solid footing'. Another strand of political and legal uncertainty may be the conflict of the objectives of central and provincial governments as well as the change of leadership at the top of the Communist Party. Access to resources, mainly finance, is constrained by the Confucian belief in self-sufficiency within the family. However, according to Krug and Hendrischke (2002), because China represents a 'new market' in which entrepreneurs face high transactions costs associated with 'start-up' know and insecurity due to developing institutions, such as property rights and business protocol, entrepreneurship occurs through a process of 'experimentation' and 'selection' on the basis of performance. According to Krug and Hendrischke (2002), 'experimentation' and 'selection' explain why the family is no longer the basis of entrepreneurship in China, why networks are assessed on performance potential, and as to why Chinese firms may not care about developing a core business. The uncertain environment created by the transition of the Chinese economy from a command economy to a socialist market economy has created a number of uncertainties associated with property rights, the image of the entrepreneur and legal institutions themselves. This gap in business confidence created by an uncertain business environment has been filled by the emergence of Guanxi (Kshetri 2007). Furthermore, according to Kshetri (2007), overseas Chinese returning to China are bringing new business knowledge and skills associated with the Western entrepreneurial style. This is an example of a knowledge spillover which differs from learning by doing.

The traditional role of the Chinese family in entrepreneurship is different from the view that entrepreneurs in China prefer to draw on the savings of family members rather than to borrow from willing state-owned banks or venture capital funds. Nevertheless, when entrepreneurs are able to 'tap' venture capital funds, social capital plays an important role (Batjargal and Liu 2004). This social capital can be considered to be similar if not the same as the Chinese social phenomenon of *guanxi*. In this case, networked relationships play a very important role in entrepreneurship in China. Parties to a business transaction which has resulted in a beneficial result for both parties tend to ensure that the positive experience of both parties will allow then to not only transact again but also to act as 'recommenders' to third parties. In such away is the *guanxi* network established. The advantages of doing business by experience can be associated with each party having more information about how the other party behaves. This allows trust to be established between the two party's better information and greater trust allows for better business decisions leading to a more efficient allocation of the factors of production. In the case of venture capital, through better information and greater trust, investors can conduct deeper due diligence tests; and a more accurate valuation of the business they are investing in (Batjargal and Liu 2004). Guanxi thus reduces the uncertainty around the behaviour of investors and entrepreneurs. However, in Italy it has been found that the size of the initial investment in a new venture is not affected by the perceived uncertainty associated with the investment (De Marco 2000). On the other hand, the latter suggests that the size of the initial investment does affect the sales growth rates of the new venture.

According to Huang (2008), the phenomenal growth of the private sector can be explained by access to financial resources through foreign direct investment which permeated all sectors of the Chinese economy as a direct result of the economic reforms. However, a constraint on entrepreneurship is access to resources such as labour. Chinese graduates lack workplace skills; and risk averse peasants prefer to stay with inefficient state-owned enterprises if they can (Liao and Sohmen 2001). According to the latter, the third constraint to entrepreneurship in China is the cultural perception that entrepreneurship is of low status. However, there was also political contempt of private enterprise which as a tendency to restrict their activities, Huang (2008). Nevertheless, Kirby and Ying (1995) analysed the overlap between Chinese cultural values and generalised entrepreneurial values and found overlap with regard to perseverance, resourcefulness and diligence but profit orientation, change and initiative were in conflict with traditional Chinese cultural values. Holt (1997) found that due to the assiduous constraints faced by entrepreneurs in China, they were more risk tolerant than were entrepreneurs in the USA. Culturally, the Chinese place greater emphasis on fate than do their Western counterparts. This implies that Chinese entrepreneurship may benefit from a long-term strategy and opportunism (Liao and Sohmen 2001). On the other hand, another study has found that Chinese and Russian entrepreneurs had childhood friends and family members who were also entrepreneurs (Djankov et al. 2006). Furthermore, Djankov et al. (2006) also find that Russian and Chinese entrepreneurs valued work-related activities more than leisure activities, and they also placed emphasis on the accumulation of wealth. The finding by Holt (1997) that Chinese entrepreneurs are more risk seeking compared to their US counterparts is similar to the findings of Djankov et al. (2006) that Chinese entrepreneurs are also more risk seeking than are their Russian counterparts. Nevertheless, whereas Russian entrepreneurs are better educated than are Chinese entrepreneurs, Chinese entrepreneurs have more family members and childhood friends who are also entrepreneurs (Djankov et al. 2006). Thus, Chinese entrepreneurs may emerge through spillover effects associated with entrepreneurial knowledge. At an intuitive level, it would seem that people in China who become entrepreneurs do so because of a lack of access to good jobs due to their low/no level of education. It could be because of this that Chinese entrepreneurs are also more risk seeking than are entrepreneurs in either Russia or the USA. It is due

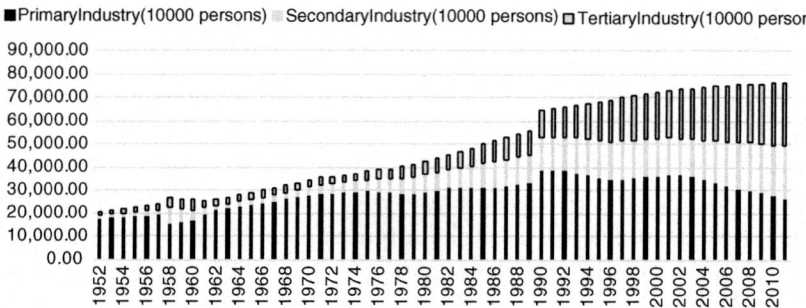

Fig. 4.1 Employment in China's primary, secondary and tertiary industry: 1952–2012. *Source* Compiled by author using data from National Statistical Bureau of China

to the economic reforms in China that have led to the emergence of entrepreneurial opportunities which have been seized by Chinese entrepreneurs who lacked access to secure well-paid jobs due to a poor education and due to a declining and inefficient state sector.

Changes in Firm Ownership in China

Since the late 1970s China's labour market has shifted from a centrally planned one to a market which is increasingly being driven by market forces, Meng (2012). One consequence of this is that, as can be seen from Fig. 4.1, the proportion of workers employed in Primary Industry has been volatile between 1952 and 2012. But the trend in employment in Primary Industry has been downward and the fall in employment in the Primary Industry has been balanced by an increase in the number of workers employed in Secondary and Tertiary Industry. While the number of workers in Secondary and Tertiary Industry in the period 1952–1978 was relatively low compared to the number of workers employed in Primary Industry, after 1978 this changed. Furthermore, after 2002, the number of workers employed in Primary Industry began to fall while the number of workers employed in Secondary and Tertiary Industry began to rise. Employment in the Secondary and Tertiary

Industry began to absorb the workers who had left employment in the Primary Industry more significantly after 2002.

However, the trend in Secondary and Tertiary Industry was upwards after 1978, only after 2002 did employment levels in Primary Industry show a downward trend. Before 1978, up to 80% of workers were employed in the agricultural sector, which comprises Primary Industry, in China, in farms organised as collectives or communes which provided a basic level of health, education and pensions to workers, Meng (2012).

The reason for this that the government wanted to ensure that food was plentiful in supply to the cities. Rural to urban migration was severely constrained by the Hukou System, Meng (2012). In the urban sector, the country's central planners ensured that city dwellers had lifetime employment with centrally planned wages as well as a cradle-to-grave welfare system. China's economic reforms impacted on the country's rural sector first followed by the urban sector. Reforms in the rural sector boosted agricultural productivity but by the mid-1980s underemployment in the agricultural sector had become a serious problem and workers were encouraged to set up township and village enterprises, Meng (2012). By the mid-1990s workers in the state-owned urban sector began to be made redundant due to the governments restructuring of state-owned enterprises and the emergence of the private sector, Meng (2012). Necessity-based entrepreneurship may have increase; and there was convergence between rural and urban employment levels as shown in Fig. 4.2. There are a number of interesting features which characterise the Chinese labour markets transition from a centrally planned one to one based on market forces besides the traditional distinction between rural and urban labour, Fields and Yang (2013). Firstly, the Chinese labour market became increasingly segmented between state, private and agricultural employment.

The change in the Chinese labour market from a centrally planned one to one which is increasingly underpinned by market forces can also be seen from the way in which firm ownership has changed in China over the reform years. Secondly, the increasing effect of the operation of market forces in China may be evidenced by increasing wage levels, Li et al. (2012). However, increasing wages in the Chinese labour market

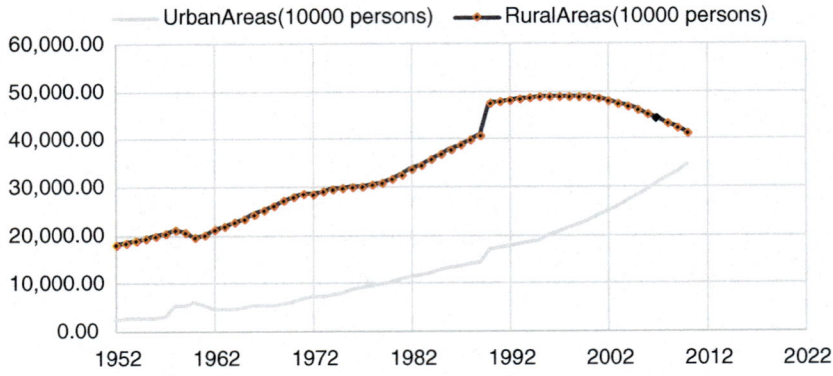

Fig. 4.2 Employment in urban and rural areas of China: 1952–2010. *Source* Compiled by author using data from National Statistical Bureau of China

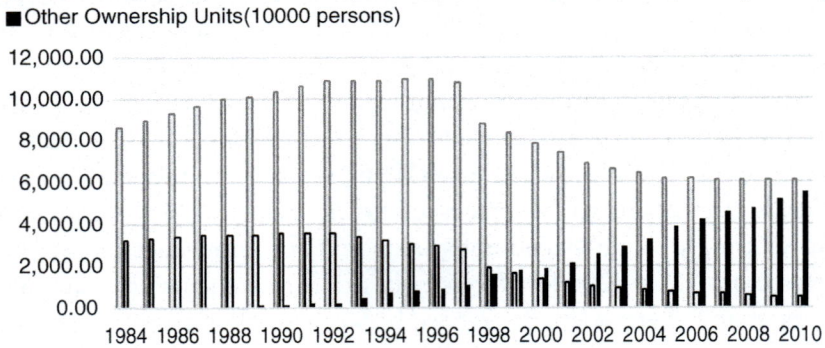

Fig. 4.3 Change in firm ownership: 1984–2010. *Source* Compiled by author using data from National Statistical Bureau of China

may also be evidenced by increasing employer costs due to government labour legislation, Ramesh (2012). Figure 4.3, shows the change in firm ownership in China from 1984 to 2010 between state ownership, urban collective-owned and other ownership types. It can be clearly seen from Fig. 4.3 that between 1984 and 1999 that state ownership of firms and urban collective-owned units was more dominant than other types of firm ownership. However, after 1999, other ownership of firms began to increase while state ownership and urban collective ownership of firms began to decline. By 2000, other ownership of firms had overtaken urban collective ownership with the former becoming comparable to state ownership by 2010. Thirdly, the Hukou worker registration system which maintained the rural–urban divide became increasingly flexible as millions of rural Chinese migrated to the urban regions to find work. Finally, there was a shift from less employment in the rural sector to more employment in the urban sector, as can be seen from Fig. 4.1. Despite the previous discussion on how the Chinese labour market could be segmented, the urban labour market can itself be segmented into three types of workers, Appleton et al. (2004). Firstly, the recently retrenched and reemployed urban workers. Secondly, the non-retrenched urban workers. And finally, rural to urban migrants. Although the Hukou system is more flexible today than it has ever been, it still continues to play a role in the Chinese labour market, Fields and Yang (2013).

China's labour market transition also meant that increasingly workers were able to select the employers they wanted to work for and employers were left to hire and fire workers as they liked. At a demographic level, the young and the old have seen reductions in employment levels with no significant differences due to gender, Meng (2012). The transition of the Chinese labour market from a centrally planned one to one which functioned on market forces drew the attention of the central government in the early part of this century.

By 2003, the newly emerging leadership wanted to formulate the countries policies from three perspectives. These included social justice, social harmony and environmental protection, Cooke (2009). The first two signalled the protection of the rights of workers and employers through increasing regulation of the Chinese labour market. Three new laws which would affect the Chinese labour market came into effect in 2008, Cooke (2009). These were the first since the Labour Law enacted in 1995 and included the Labour Contract Law, the Employment Promotion Law and the Labour Dispute Mediation and Arbitration Law. The Labour Contract Law set out to delineate the rights and responsibilities of workers and employers. The Employment Promotion Law sought to strengthen worker employment and rights. While the Labour Dispute Mediation and Arbitration Law sought to ensure the

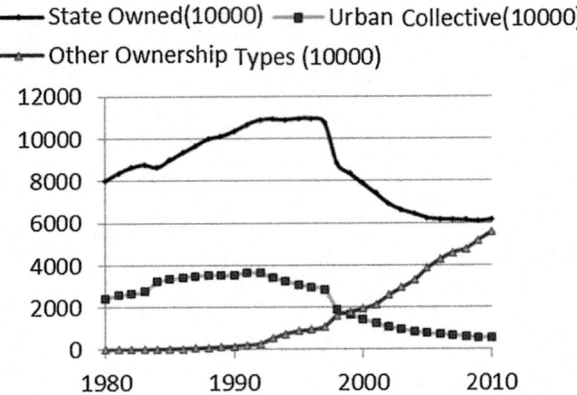

Fig. 4.4 Employees by enterprise type—1980–2010. *Source* Compiled by author using data from National Statistical Bureau of China

fulfilment of the rights of workers and employers enshrined in the Labour Contract Law.

Figure 4.4 shows the changing nature of the number of employees by enterprise type from 1980 to 2010. It can be clearly seen that especially after 1997, the number of employees by other ownership types of enterprise is on the rise while the number of employees by state-owned and urban collective enterprises is decreasing. The other ownership types of enterprises include private enterprises and self-employment, wholly owned foreign enterprises, Hong Kong/Taiwan/Macao-owned enterprises and joint venture and other corporate venture enterprises (Li Gan et al. 2012). According to the latter in 2012, private enterprises and self-employment accounted for nearly two-thirds of employment. While in the context of rural and urban employment, private enterprises and self-employment contributed more to rural employment than to urban employment. The data[1] also shows the number of private industrial enterprises by region for China in 2013. In descending order, the Coastal region has the greatest number of such enterprises followed by the Central and then the Western region. The number of private enterprises in the Coastal region is almost three times the number of such enterprises in the Central region. On the other hand, the Central region has just over twice the number of private enterprises found in the

Western region of China. This would suggest that the economic reforms which started in China's Coastal region helped entrepreneurship to embed and grow more in that region than in either the Central or the Western regions of China. Furthermore, according to the data,[2] the Coastal region has more persons self-employed or employed by enterprise in any sector in any region comparison to the either the Central or the Western regions in 2012. Furthermore, construction and wholesale and retail trade are by far the largest in the Coastal region compared to either the Central or to the Western regions. These findings at a regional level are mirrored at a provincial level. This is because, according to the data,[3] Jiangsu, a Coastal province, has more people who are either self-employed or employed by private enterprises than does either Hubei, a Central province, or Gansu, a Western province. This is specifically true in the context of wholesale and retail trade and construction. Furthermore, at a provincial level, it becomes clear that the number of people self-employed or employed in private enterprises in manufacturing in Jiangsu overshadows the numbers employed in that sector in either Hubei or in Gansu. This finding reiterates previously established evidence that China's economic reforms have embedded secondary and tertiary level activities such as manufacturing, wholesale and retail trade and construction in China's Coastal region. It logically follows that more manufacturing would lead to more imports and exports and increasing wholesale and retail trade. The result would be that Gross Regional Product is on the rise and as a result, increasing provincial affluence and increased economic activity will lead to more construction. In 2007, the government launched the Eleventh Five Year Plan for Western economic development. At the heart of the plan was the establishment of economic zones in Chengdu-Chongqing, Guanzhong-Tianshui and Guangxi Northern Gulf areas. The idea behind the establishment of these economic zones was to make use of these geographical areas natural resources, industrial capacity, urban development and labour supply in order to allow enterprise to increase the productivity in the zones. It is hoped that the establishment of these economic zones will allow the Western region to economically develop as rapidly as did Chinese Coastal region through the establishment of economic zones in the Yangtze River Delta (YRD), the Pearl River Delta (PRD) and the

Beijing-Tianjin-Hebei Metropolitan Area (BTHMA). The YRD focused on technological and manufacturing industries, the PRD focused on various manufacturing industries, the BTHMA on petroleum and natural gas exploitation, and the production of electronic equipment, publishing and printing equipment and communications equipment (Longbao 2009).

Available data[4] can also be used to analyse R&D expenditure by firm ownership type in 2012. In this case, it can be seen that those firms which are independent of the state in terms of funding and more reliant on market forces tend to be the most innovative as measured by the amount spent on R&D. Thus, private enterprises, shareholding corporations and limited liability corporations have spent more money on R&D than has been spent on R&D by state-owned enterprises. Firms which are not dependent on state funding for day-to-day operations and more dependent on market forces compete for revenue and market share. As such any competitive advantage which may arise to these firms is dependent on the innovativeness of the firms. The greater the amount of money which each firm will spend on innovation, through R&D expenditure, the bigger will be the potential to innovate and develop new products and processes. Firms which are innovative develop new products and processes are likely to capture market share and sales from firms which are less innovative. However, state-owned enterprises do not need to compete to survive as they receive state funding in order to ensure their day-to-day operational survival. Such firms will have less incentive to use R&D money provided by the government efficiently because of the problem of moral hazard. In other words, the government will always be at hand in order to supply more R&D funding if the state-owned enterprise runs out of money and needs more money. This type of government expenditure is wasteful and tends to act as a 'drag' on the effectiveness of central government funding. Data[5] can also be used to analyse the number of inventions and patents and inventions by enterprise type for 2012. The number of inventions in force is those inventions for which the firms have a patent. Inventions may be those inventions for which the firm has applied for a patent. An analysis of this data shows that non-state-owned enterprises are more innovative, as measured by the number of inventions in force and the number of inventions compared to state-owned enterprises. Amongst the non-state enterprises, limited liability corporations have the most number of inventions in force as well as the number of inventions in comparison to either private enterprises or shareholding corporations. However, private enterprises had slightly more number of inventions in force as well as slightly more inventions compared to shareholding corporations. On the other hand, state-owned enterprises have a much smaller number of inventions in force as well as a lower number of inventions. This finding gives some credibility to the idea that State Owned Enterprises do not need to be competitively efficient to survive. It's perhaps because of this that State-Owned Enterprises have a far smaller amount allocated to R&D expenditure in comparison to private enterprises, shareholding corporations or limited liability corporations. The low levels of R&D expenditure by state-owned enterprises could also suggest that state-owned enterprises have less financial resources available in comparison to other firm types especially private enterprises, shareholding corporations and limited liability corporations. Yiu and Lau (2008) empirically show that the generation of profits from networked resources is due to the mediating effects of corporate entrepreneurship.

The view that market-oriented, and, therefore, more entrepreneurial firms in China are more likely to be innovative than are state-owned enterprises is supported by the data[6]. In this case, it can be clearly shown that private enterprises, shareholding corporations and limited liability corporations had a greater output in 2012 than did either state sole funded enterprises or State-Owned Enterprises. Furthermore, the new product output of limited liability corporations and private enterprises is over three times the output of state-owned enterprises. But the new product output of shareholding corporations is just over twice the new product output of state-owned enterprises. This indicates that new product development by shareholding corporations maybe hindered by ownership limits on borrowing and/or a smaller proportion of the profits being available for R&D expenditure. On the other hand, the new product output of limited liability corporations is slightly greater than is the new product output of private enterprises. These two firm types may have access to more funds either by being able to borrow more or due to larger profits, allowing them to finance a higher level of R&D expenditure in comparison to either state-owned enterprises or too shareholding corporations. The greater funds accessible for R&D expenditure, the greater will be the level of new product innovation by the firms. However, an interesting finding is that shareholding corporations generate more revenue from the sales of its new products than do private enterprises. This is in contrast to the finding that private enterprises produce more new products than do shareholding corporations. One explanation of this paradox is that shareholding corporations may produce a small number of high-value new products, while private enterprises produce a large number of low-value new products. However, limited liability corporations still generate the most sales revenue from new products in comparison to the sales revenue generated by either private enterprises, shareholding corporations or state-owned enterprises.[7] The findings of the comparison of the sales revenue generated domestically by private enterprise, shareholding corporations, limited liability corporations and state-owned enterprises are mirrored in the data[8] for export value of new products by enterprise type for 2012. The export value of new products is greater in descending order for limited liability corporations, shareholding corporations and private enterprises. In contrast, the export value generated by new products for state-owned enterprises is by far much smaller in comparison to that generated by the three other types of firm ownership, private enterprises, limited liability corporations or shareholding corporations. China's economic growth since 1978 has been based on a manufacturing-led export strategy. Naude and Rossouw (2010) conducted an analysis of the nature and of the determinants of early entrepreneurship in China based on data from the World Bank's Investment Climate Private Enterprise Survey of 3948 Chinese private sector firms in 2002 and in 2003. The findings of the analysis by Naude and Rossouw (2010) suggest that firms in China which export tend to

(a) Directly export without the need for intermediaries,
(b) Be bigger than firms which do not export,
(c) Displayed much faster growth than forms which did not export,
(d) Be younger than firms which did not export,

(e) Develop new products at a faster rate as a result of a higher level of R&D expenditure.

(f) Employ more managers with an international background as well as having more foreign ownership/shareholding.

Since Chinese economic growth has been driven by the export of light manufactured goods, facilitating more entrepreneurial activity in the development of exporting firms is an important policy objective. Furthermore, the importance of this policy objective is underlined by the fact a number of positive spillovers can be associated with the activities of exporting firms and their value creating activities. These positive spillovers include increases in firm size and employment numbers, learning by doing and accumulating experience, the transfer of knowledge and technology due to foreign ownership as well as the indirect benefits of R&D (Naude and Rossouw 2010). In this regard, a single R&D project could lead to multiple sources of innovation. Chinese technological entrepreneurship has been facilitated by government initiatives such as the Torch Program which was initiated in 1988. The motive for the development of the Torch Program was to foster the development of institutions which would generate indigenous innovation and technological innovation (Yu et al. 2009). The latter suggests that the main contribution of the Torch Program to China's innovation system was the science parks and business incubators, also known as high-tech innovation centres. Whereas China's technological entrepreneurship policies were modelled on other Western and other countries innovation programs, they deviated in a number of ways (Yu et al. 2009). Firstly, innovation policy tended to drift with the requirements of central government macroeconomic policies. Secondly, innovation policies at the provincial level were influenced by local officials in association with local stakeholders. Lastly, science parks in China combined manufacturing with technological innovation whereas in Western countries the focus of science park policy was the integration of research and development with education and the needs of industry. In the context of manufacturing given the fact that young firms tend to export more than do older firms, policymakers should focus on facilitating policies which 'enable, motivate, mediate and moderate factors' which allow firms to export sooner rather than later (Naude and Rossouw 2010). Nevertheless, allied to such policies, the policymakers should ensure that the market is competitive in order to allow more forms to enter the market and that these firms are not only efficient and healthy but also innovative. Alon and Lerner (2008) found that that the higher the number of projected employees of the firm, the greater the educational and skill level of Chinese entrepreneurs than the greater the likelihood of international exposure. On the other hand, risk-averse behaviour of Chinese entrepreneurs and lack of competition in the Chinese market would reduce the likelihood of Chinese private enterprises international exposure (Alon and Lerner 2008).

China's transition to an export-led economy was facilitated by foreign enterprises setting up manufacturing operations in China. Three laws provided the legal framework which governed the way in which foreign enterprises interacted with China in the context of creating a favourable investment climate (Longbao 2009). These laws included the Law on Joint Chinese and Foreign Investment Enterprises in 1979, the Law on Foreign Funded Enterprises and the Sino-foreign Cooperative Joint Venture Law. According to Longbao (2009), foreign entrepreneurship and foreign capital have contributed to China's economic development in five ways. These include increased employment, advances in technology through spillover effects due to foreign enterprises R&D centres in China, increased industrial output, increased foreign trade and increased tax revenue for the government. However, the Chinese government was keen to be not to be dependent on foreign enterprises for the evolution of Chinese industry. In this case, the government implemented the Top Ten Industry Promotion Planning initiative in 2009 (Longbao 2009). The initiative ran for two years and it allowed for increased industrial capacity and the upgrading of equipment, increasing technological innovation in order to improve global competitiveness. Longbao (2009) also suggests that the aim of this initiative was to strengthen indigenous Chinese industrial capacity in the production of automobiles, iron and steel, textile equipment, manufacturing, shipbuilding, electronic information, light industry, petrochemicals, nonferrous metal and logistics.

Indian Entrepreneurship and Innovation

In the pre-colonial and in the colonial period the trader merchant and the moneylender represented the entrepreneurial class, embedded and held in place in society by a rigid caste system and by the Hindu religion which hinged on the philosophy of fate (Swetha and Rao 2013). According to the latter, the history of entrepreneurship in India starts with the Indus Valley civilisation which forged trade links with Iran and with Central Asia. The types of entrepreneurial phases in India by historical period can be broken down into five distinct types (Gupta 2008). According to the latter, these include the Panchayati Raj (pre-1700), the British Raj (1700–1950), the License Raj (1950–1985), the Jugaad Raj (1985–1995) and the Invisible Raj (1995–2010). The Panchayati Raj saw the emergence of village craft entrepreneurship and entrepreneurship at the local level. Trade in the village revolved around the barter system with the blacksmith being paid in agricultural produce. The British Raj saw the demise of village craft entrepreneurship and the artisan in India. An example would be India's hand looming village industry. This was due to the introduction of the modern factory system (Medhora 1965). India's textile exports to Britain were heavily taxed whereas Britain's textile exports to India were not. The result was a decline in India's textile industry. The British Raj also represented a hostile environment for Indian entrepreneurship (Swetha and Rao 2013). However, in pre-British India, enterprise was limited to mainly money lending and trade due to low expectations of reward and the occupational rigidity of the caste system (Tripathi 1981).

A managing agency system emerged following the loss of monopoly trading rights by the British East India Company (Brimmer 1955). The managing agency system is unique to India, and it is one in which one firm manages the finance, promotion and the administration of other legally separate firms. The single controlling firm is the 'firm' as known in conventional Industrial Economics. It is the pervading form of economic organisation in industry, trade and in commercial agriculture (Brimmer 1955). Indian agency firms can take the form of private limited companies but are usually partnerships, in the context of family relationships and stratified by caste. According to Brimmer (1955), the managing agency system has legal roots in the Indian Companies Act 1913, as amended in 1936, and it evolved due to two reasons. Firstly, there was a shortage of venture capital in India. And secondly, there was a shortage of entrepreneurial capital in India. However, Indian managing agency firms were formed because the Indian owners had accumulated wealth through trade but lacked technical expertise in contrast to the British owners of managing agency firms in India. Furthermore, in contrast to the Western experience of start-up innovation, risk taking and wealth creation in entrepreneurship remain limited in the Indian experience (Jain 2013).

A License Raj came into being in an independent India. One of the implications of the License Raj was that the public sector took control of major investments and India's economy became centrally planned. Under the License Raj, large private sector investments required licences which were hard to get. However, under the License Raj, two types of entrepreneurship flourished in India due to central government initiatives (Gupta 2008). These included farm and defence entrepreneurship. Farm entrepreneurship was the basis of the Green Revolution in India which allowed the country to escape the famine and starvation of the 1960s (Gupta 2008). Farming entrepreneurship was facilitated by state funding of R&D in farming allied with capacity building due to extension networks which allowed Indian farmers to allow India to achieve self-sufficiency in food. Defence entrepreneurship was facilitated by the state 'borrowing' military technology from other countries and then extending capacity to local private entrepreneurs to develop and build Indian versions of the defence technology (Gupta 2008). The period 1985–1995 is often referred to as the Jugaad Raj. The relaxation of the License Raj led to the emergence of software developers and hardware designers and dealers from the educated professionals who emerged as a result of the License Raj (Gupta 2008). The shift in Indian economic policy from import substitution to market liberalisation, state-sponsored development of the Software Technology Park in Bangalore in 1990, and the outsourcing of the development and design of software systems by MNC's to Indian firms such as Tata, Wipro and Infosys led to the emergence of local technological entrepreneurship (Parthasarathy and Aoyama 2006). According to the latter was the upgrading of the Indian software industry from the provision of low-skill software services to the provision of high-skill R&D services.

Despite the distinct phases of entrepreneurship in India, Medhora (1965) identifies two types of entrepreneurship by nature. Firstly, innovative entrepreneurship facilitates a dynamic economy. Secondly, an imitative entrepreneurship allows for spread effects of new products to a wider market. However, this would depend on the social and on the economic environment (Medhora 1965). In India, the social environment is influenced by the Hindu religion's segregation of Indian society by caste. In this case, there are four main castes: the Brahmin or priest class, the Kshtriya or warrior class, the Vaishya or the trader class and the Shudra or the artisan class. While the caste system may lead to the immobility of labour, it does not necessarily lead to a reduction in entrepreneurs. The vertical integration of the Vaishya caste would lead to entrepreneurship (Medhora 1965). However, the latter argues that for a British style Industrial Revolution to have occurred in India, it would also have required a social revolution which could only have happened with state backing as had happened in Japan. But trading by the Vaishya caste signalled that the three properties of entrepreneurship: risk taking, trading for a profit and speculation all existed (Medhora 1965). Nevertheless, the latter suggests that although entrepreneurial aptitude had existed in India, the lack of opportunity enticed moneylenders and traders to migrate to east Africa and south-east Asia. Furthermore, in the four decades of economic reform, the upper caste has become prosperous while the lower caste (scheduled castes, SCs and scheduled tribes, STs) has not done as well (Varshney 2007). Moreover, in contrast to countries who at similar levels of income, India's level of entrepreneurship lags behind (Ghani et al. 2011a, b). On the other hand, the number of entrepreneurs in the Other Backward Classes (Dalits) category seems to have reflected the increase in India's economic growth especially in the 1980s and the 1990s. Whereas in the fifteen-year period to 2005, the increase in entrepreneurship amongst the SCs and the STs was not significant (Iyer et al. 2013). According to the latter SC and ST entrepreneurs face prominent barriers to entry to become entrepreneurs and to benefit from economies of scale. However,

OBCs seem to be making a lot of progress in the field of entrepreneurship (Iyer et al. 2013). The difference in the ease of access to entrepreneurial opportunities between OBCs, SCs and STs cannot be explained simply on the basis of differences in literacy rates, years of schooling or by choice of industry (Iyer et al. 2013). Furthermore, according to the latter, the under-representation of the SCs and the STs in entrepreneurship and firm ownership is also common within India's states. This implies that this phenomenon cannot be due to specific regions of underdevelopment (Iyer et al. 2013). Firms owned by SCs and STs tend to be smaller than the firms owned by non-SCs. According to Iyer et al. (2013) SCs and STs may not be able to expand the size of their firms because the caste system constrains networking which facilitates finding the right employees as well as the building of relationships with customers and with suppliers. Another factor which may be constraining the expansion of firms by SCs and STs is the lack of infrastructure, especially that associated with the reliable supply of electricity, water, the provision of transport, indisputable title to land as well as the ability to associate a particular rate with a future pay-off (Bhide 2004). The latter also suggests that small-scale entrepreneurs place more emphasis on the reform of indirect taxes rather than direct taxes and on the prevention of the theft of physical goods rather than on contract enforcement.

There were also other local private enterprise initiatives in states such as Gujarat which would have national ramifications. The Entrepreneurship Development Program (EDP) was set up in Gujarat, India in 1970 in order to promote small business enterprise (Bhatt 1986). This was around the same time that town and village enterprises began to emerge in China. The EDP was established under the supervision of the Gujarat Industrial and Investment Corporation, and its main purpose was to select, train and guide potential entrepreneurs to identify suitable projects. However, in 1978, the Centre for Entrepreneurship Development (CDE) was established in order to oversee and administer the EDP. According to Bhatt (1986) in the fourteen years from 1970, in Gujarat, 312 entrepreneurial programs with 7710 participants were conducted in 130 locations. The results suggest that 60% of the potential entrepreneurs selected and trained through the program successfully set up a business, 75% of which were profitable.

The success of the CDE in promoting the EDP and small business enterprises brought Gujarat's program to national attention, and the Entrepreneurship Development Institute of India (EDI-I) was established in 1983. The aim of the EDI-I was to 'conduct research, offer consultancy and training, and assist state-level agencies in carrying out their programs' (Bhatt 1986). In the period 1995–2010, the Invisible Raj, private enterprise was free to enter and set up in most parts of the economy and did not require licences to do so. However, foreign MNCs entering the Indian market lured experienced professionals from Indian enterprises which then resulted in the formation of small local microenterprises. Koster and Rai (2005) suggest that small-scale enterprises remain a very important measure of entrepreneurship in India, while the share of small-scale enterprises in the Indian economy is increasing. On the other hand, the share of registered firms seems to be static and not prone to any big changes, Koster and Rai (2005). According to the latter the predominance of small-scale enterprises in the Indian economy, and a weak relationship between the level of GDP and the market share of registered firms suggests that entrepreneurship in the Indian economy has not yet shifted to a more formal orientation. The implication is that the level of Indian economic growth has not been sufficient enough to generate the required number of jobs to reduce necessity-based entrepreneurship (Koster and Rai 2005). For the Indian government, the low number of registered firms in contrast to the number of small-scale enterprises suggests that policy needs to be formulated at the state level which facilitates the development of entrepreneurial quality (Koster and Rai 2005). Increasing the level of entrepreneurial quality equates to increasing the number of registered firms in the economy in comparison to the number of small-scale enterprises. Moreover, increasing the quality of entrepreneurship will have a positive impact on the level of economic development (Wong et al. 2005). However, according to Gurtoo and Williams (2009) found that not only did a large proportion of informal workers work on their own account but that not all work was due to economic necessity. Furthermore, that workers in the informal sector work because of need is an assumption rather than being based on evidence (Gurtoo and Williams 2009). This is in contrast to the structural approach which distinguishes between 'necessity' entrepreneurs and 'opportunity' entrepreneurs (Aidis et al. 2006). The dichotomy between necessity-based entrepreneurs and opportunity-based entrepreneurs has been incorporated into the Global Entrepreneurship Monitor (GEM) survey (Minniti et al. 2006). GEM survey data can provide a better insight into how entrepreneurship may either be need or opportunity based. In this case the need-based drivers of entrepreneurship have been under scrutiny more than ever, especially in Western nations (Gerxhani 2004). Interest in the nature of the informal sector in India has been spurred by the revelations that it is both large and expanding (Chaudhari and Banerjee 2007). Some estimates suggest that the informal sector in India is composed of 93% of the country's total workforce (Kapoor 2007). In contrary to conventional wisdom, it would seem that the formal sector exists on the margin while the informal sector is mainstream (Gurtoo and Williams 2009). Furthermore, according to the latter, the conventional held view was that workers worked in the informal sector simply because they could not find any work or were excluded from working in the formal sector (Gurtoo and Williams 2009). In order to investigate this phenomenon, the latter conducted a nationwide survey-based investigation between 2006 and 2007. The findings were in contrast to the conventional structuralist view that workers in the informal sector were largely waged workers. Moreover, the findings suggested that 49% of the workers in the informal sector worked as entrepreneurs or on their own account (Gurtoo and Williams 2009). The 2004 GEM survey also supported this view on the basis that 107 million people were keen to set up their own firms. For policy makers, the finding that informal entrepreneurs may represent the mainstream workforce in developing economies and that informal entrepreneurs are in the mainstream suggests that policies supporting informal entrepreneurs need to be developed (Gurtoo and Williams 2009).

A number of explanations can be found in the literature for the nature of entrepreneurship in India. Some empirical studies suggest that Indian entrepreneurs are risk averse and so favour the service sector rather than the manufacturing or industrial sector as the service sector would require less investment and less sunk cost (Gupta 2008). However, other studies suggest the lack of availability of capital as well as a poor institutional support environment for entrepreneurs (Veen 1976). Nevertheless, other studies showed how local microenterprises evolved into industrial enterprises, thus refuting the risk-averse Indian entrepreneur empirical findings (Gupta 2008). Another constraint on entrepreneurship in India is a lack of achievement motivation which is truer in the context of female entrepreneurs (Shivani et al. 2006). However, according to Ghani et al. (2013), the better the local infrastructure (in rural counties as opposed to cities), the faster the relative rate of entry of females into entrepreneurship in either manufacturing or services. As females in India have a tendency to do all household and other manual chores, better infrastructure would mean that less time would be required to complete these tasks which would mean that they would have more time to engage in entrepreneurial endeavours. At a general level, Monsen et al. (2012) find that living in urban areas increases the probability of an individual transitioning into self-employment.

The greater the access to local education for women, the higher the literacy rate, and the tougher the labour laws and regulations than the higher will be the level of female participation in entrepreneurship in the services sector (Ghani et al. 2013). At a general level, the quality of infrastructure and the quality of education are strong predictors of entrepreneurship into manufacturing (Ghani et al. 2014) and manufacturing and services in India (Ghani et al. 2012). The latter suggests that these relationships are much stronger in India than in the USA. This could be because India is still at an earlier stage of development in the context of structural transformation, urbanisation and the development of the manufacturing sector (Ghani et al. 2012). The implication is that because structural transformation, urbanisation and the development of the manufacturing sector are still at the early stages of development, central and local government economic policies will have a strong impact on the change and direction of these factors. High levels of local entrepreneurship also result in higher levels of local job creation, with entrepreneurship helping to allocate resources efficiently, enhancing competition and innovation while promoting trade (Ghani et al. 2012). According to Ghani et al. (2014), strong labour laws and access to financial institutions by households also play a positive role in the nature of entrepreneurial activity in the manufacturing sector. Poor gender legislation protecting and ensuring women's rights equal treatment in the jobs market and the workplace means that the number of women employed in the formal sector of the economy is smaller to the numbers of women employed in the informal sector (Torri and Martinez 2014). The informal sector of the economy is that which falls under the 'radar' of the government, and it is that sector of the economy which does not comply with tax collection and labour laws and regulations (Amin et al. 2003). According to Torri and Martinez (2014), the lack of access to jobs in the labour market opens up other job creation opportunities in the informal sector such as community enterprises. While community enterprises such as Gram Mooligai Company Limited (GMCL), a community enterprise in the herbal sector employing untouchable females, enhances women's learning and leadership skills it does nothing to reduce the prejudices of India's caste system or improve legislation better empowering women to successfully find jobs in the formal sector of the economy (Torri and Martinez 2014). Thus, according to the latter, while enterprise opens new sources of income for women excluded from jobs in the formal sector, it does nothing to improve the empowerment of women. This can only be accomplished by improving India's labour laws and regulations to end gender and caste discrimination. However, Ghani et al. (2013) found that female business ownership rates were higher in southern Indian states such as Karnataka, Kerala and Tamil Nadu compared to northern Indian states such as Delhi, Bihar, Haryana and Gujarat. This may indicate that women in leadership positions are valued more in southern India than it is in northern India. However, it has been found that an increase in political reservations, positions in government bodies, resulted in an increase in female participation in entrepreneurship in manufacturing in the informal sector in which 99% of manufacturing businesses lie and which accounts for 80% of employment in India in the 1990s (Ghani et al. 2014). Furthermore, as 70% of India's population still live in villages, with half of this being women, enabling capacity building amongst rural women in India's villages by providing training in finance, management, marketing, production and literacy represents a powerful tool to further India's economic development (Mehta and Mehta 2011). There is also a dichotomy between rich women and poor women in the context of wealth and entrepreneurial ability (Kumbhar 2013). Wealthy women may have access to financial resources but no entrepreneurial ability whereas poor women may have entrepreneurial ability but no access to financial resources. An easy way to resolve this dichotomy is for the government to initiate microfinance initiatives at the rural village level targeted specifically at women entrepreneurs. Nevertheless, a rights-based approach was adopted in order to ensure the development, survival and protection of women and children through the National Policy for Empowerment of Women (2001) which was adopted for implementation by the Tenth Five Year Plan (2002–2007) (Goyal and Parkash 2011). Despite institutional factors, human factors are important for sustainable entrepreneurship (Sinha 1996). According to the latter, these 'human factors' represent the entrepreneur's style of leadership, beliefs, values, orientation, manipulative skills as well as the entrepreneur's demographics and background.

Another factor which constrains the emergence and the development of entrepreneurship is the lack of human capital. In India, human capital is on the rise, especially amongst male entrepreneurs but this is true of only a small part of the population. Despite, the constraints to entrepreneurship in India, self-reliance upon poverty is buoyant in India. For example, over 50% of the identifiable workforce in India is self-employed (Debroy and Bhandari 2007). Furthermore, between 1993 and 2004, there was an increase of 10% in the average income of the 20% of the lowest of the population (Gupta 2008). A similar increase occurred in the average incomes of the top 20% of the population. This suggests that self-enterprise is a feature of the behaviour of both the top 20% and the lowest 20% of India's population. According to some, the entrepreneurial dynamism of the Indian economy is temporary because it is due to exogenous factors such as the return of native business leaders from abroad as well as high-tech start-ups by the returned foreign-born children of Indian parents (Turner 2007).

Some of the factors which have been constraining India's economic growth have been identified as a lack of hard and soft infrastructure which has not only constrained the development of the market in India but has also constrained the increase in the entrepreneurial participation in the economy. However, the scarcity of resources in India maybe facilitating the development of a new type of entrepreneurship which is based on a 'frugal, flexible and inclusive approach to innovation and entrepreneurship in India' (Prabhu and Jain 2015). The latter suggests that the traditional mode of innovative entrepreneurship was one which was based on big corporations spending large sums of money in developing new types of goods for a relatively small number of people. However, with a reduction in costs the goods and services would become available to a bigger proportion of the population through further innovation. Nevertheless, the nature of innovation itself is changing in the context of 'where, how and by whom' innovation is conducted (Prabhu and Jain 2015). The nature of innovation is becoming more emerging markets based, especially in the context of Brazil, China and India. Some of the features of an emerging economy include widening disparities of income between the rich and the poor and as well as a rising middle class. According to Prabhu and Jain (2015) a substantial amount of the innovation in these emerging economies is on a small budget, accommodates circumstances and is based on the needs of the local community. Innovators are adapting to scarcity by making best use of existing technology and resources in order to develop novel solutions to local community-level problems which have not been previously addressed because of high costs, lack of knowledge and lack of commitment (Ahlstrom 2010). Another development in the innovation process is that the innovating agents are increasingly being characterised as social ventures, individuals, local firms and multinational firms (Prahalad 2012). Social ventures and individuals have the advantage of local knowledge and the tenacity and resourcefulness of the practitioners. However, they lack the ability to scale up local solutions up to a state/national level. This is due to a lack of financial resources. On the other hand, large multinational corporations have substantial financial resources in order to fulfil their corporate social responsibility obligations, although they may also be motivated by increased growth and market share, but lack local knowledge in order to provide fully comprehensive solutions. Local firms act as a conduit between social ventures and multinational corporations. According to Prabhu and Jain (2015), local firms have comprehensive local knowledge in order to provide the best solutions to local problems. Furthermore, local firms may have a long-term view regarding its involvement in the social venture project. The implication of this is that the project will become established and so more likely to succeed than if the term takes a short-term view. However, even local firms may be inept in social venture projects, Prabhu and Jain (2015). The latter suggests that the Tata Group was short-sighted in its business strategy with regard to the Tata Nano. While the Tata Nano was marketed as the world's cheapest car, Tata Group failed to realise that a large proportion of the Indian population neither had a bank account or access to loans in order to buy the Tata Nano. Government institutions and agencies have also adopted the frugal, flexible and innovative approach to social entrepreneurship. For example, the Reserve Bank of India sees financial inclusion as one of its objectives. The Aadhaar Service of the Unique ID Authority of India also seeks financial inclusion as one of its financial objectives with the additional objectives of efficiency and transparency in the context of public welfare and distribution programs (Prabhu and Jain 2015). The latter suggests that in some states, this can be also facilitated by GPS and Smart card technology. Furthermore, ICICI Bank in association with EKO, a financial service provider, and local shops has set up a financial system which allows workers from rural villages working in cities to repatriate their earnings back to their home villages. The integrated approach to social entrepreneurship taken by ICICI Bank saves costs by making use of existing technology supplied by EKO in order to deliver financial accessibility in local shops in rural villages. Prabhu and Jain (2015) suggest that the cultural, societal and economical background of India presents an innovation system which is different from the traditional model which is enshrined in the innovation systems of the developed, industrial countries. These differences suggest the frugality of Indian innovators, the ad hoc approach taken to innovation in India and the community-based innovative solutions which are produced. The contemporary Indian approach to innovative social entrepreneurship whether by individuals, governments, not for-profit organisations, local firms and/or multinational organisations can be associated with the existing knowledge of bricolage, output driven processes in a resource constrained environment, and ad hoc organisational processes and structures.

Jain and Sharma (2013) suggest that the frugal, flexible and innovative approach of Indian innovators is due to the volatility and instability of the business environment in India. This may be associated with structural shortcomings, associated with poor hard and soft infrastructure as well as with institutions which are hampered by costly and time-consuming bureaucracy. Another structural deficiency of the Indian economy is that up to 40% of the population do not have bank accounts (Prabhu and Jain 2015). This lack of development of India's financial system means that Indian households are unable to borrow and to save in the conventional sense. Thus, India lacks a transparent and a necessary medium which can channel savings into loans and so, increase investment expenditure. It is also true to say that a large part of India's population does not have access to good housing, access to the electricity grid or to education and health services. The limited income of the majority of India's population, allied with no or limited access to a financial system, means that a substantial proportion of Indian households are illiterateand eat unhealthy foods which are cooked using environmentally unfriendly methods (Dreze and Sen 2013). One of the problems associated with government and agency efforts to reduce the informal sector and to expand the formal sector by improving the living conditions of households is the cost of doing so. In other words, the cost of expanding social programs, for example, to connect all households in a state to the electricity grid would be formidable. A program to expand access to healthcare to all villages in a state would also face similar problems. The cost constraint on providing social services to the urban and the rural poor of India can also be associated with the development of affordable goods and services for this demographic group. While the size of India's middle class is rising, its numbers are still dwarfed by its urban and rural poor. Nevertheless, the incomes of both demographic groups are growing although the middle-class consumption is becoming static. This means that the potential aggregate sales of goods and services to the urban and to the rural poor are huge which is why there is increased interest in the development of innovative goods and services for this demographic group. Prabhu and Jain (2015) suggest that entrepreneurial Indian innovators have facilitated the fulfilment of this need 'through the use of local and cheap technologies combined with clever organisational and logistical arrangements'. The typical characteristics of this approach include the use of available technology and resources, flexible thinking and a realistic approach, and the inclusion of the community with regard to product/service development and delivery.

Two examples of this innovative entrepreneurial approach towards addressing the needs of India's urban and rural poor include the Solar Electric Lighting Company (SELCO) and the Mobile Diabetic Clinic (Prabhu and Jain 2015). According to the latter SELCO, a private for-profit company was set up in 1995 to provide solar powered lighting to the rural poor who would normally use kerosene lamps for lighting purposes. However, the problem was that solar panels and associated batteries were expensive and difficult to sell even to middle-class Indian households, so how could they be sold to poor rural households. The owner of SELCO, Harish Hande found that the rural poor could not afford to large sums of money each day but incurring a smaller cost each day was too much a burden on household income. Hande gained the insight that the rural poor earned small amounts of money each day and spent that money the same day in order to pay for food and fuel for heating, cooking and paying off debts (Prabhu and Jain 2015). According to the latter, Hande found that the rural poor would buy kerosene on a daily basis and spend around 25 cents on doing so. The implication of this revelation was that Hande realised that he had to be in a position to supply solar panel energy to the rural poor on a daily basis at a similar price to the kerosene that they would normally buy. In order to achieve this, Hande made use of local logistics by hiring local entrepreneurs to start up solar energy shops from which local villagers could hire solar panel charged lamps for 20 cents a day. This was a cheaper price at which Kerosene was sold. This would make solar panel charged lamps more economical to use than kerosene as well as being a healthier option as the lamps do not emit unhealthy fumes (Prabhu and Jain 2015). However, the problem is that the local entrepreneurs will not have enough capital to buy solar panels and/or lamps to start renting out solar panel charged lamps. Nevertheless, this problem was solved when Hande guaranteed loans for the local entrepreneurs. These loans allowed the local entrepreneurs to buy the solar panels, lamps and any other equipment which they would need to start operating and renting out solar panel charged lamps to the local rural poor. It is easy to see that the solar panel solution incorporated the main features of the new emerging markets innovative entrepreneurial model. These features included the use of existing technology and innovative thinking to include the local community in the delivery of the solution to the rural poor. Another innovative social entrepreneurship initiative is the mobile diabetic clinic. In this case, local unpaid volunteers were trained in order to assess whether patients had diabetes in a mobile clinic. The local volunteers may not benefit financially but they gain transferable training in the medical sector which can then be used to find other jobs in the sector. SELCO and the mobile diabetic clinic are but a small drop in improving living standards and eliminating poverty. But all such initiatives added together do contribute towards achieving these goals at least at a local level. The problem is that these local social entrepreneurship initiatives are difficult to replicate in other Indian states due to cultural, structural, economic and demographic differences between the states in India.

This chapter has evaluated the nature of entrepreneurship in China and India. Effective entrepreneurship is able to bypass any constraints on the diffusion of knowledge from centres of innovation, such as research institutes and universities to production. The level of economic growth in a country is therefore limited by the quality, quantity and the extent of entrepreneurship in that country. In China, cheap subsidised housing and the impact of ongoing economic reforms provided opportunities for entrepreneurship. There were a number of characteristics associated with the impact of the ongoing economic reforms on entrepreneurship in China. Firstly, there was an increase in the ownership types of firms other than by the state. Secondly, the Coastal region of China experienced the largest increase in the number private enterprises compared to either the Western region or the Central region. And, lastly in terms of innovation, non-state-owned enterprises and limited liability firms produced the most number of inventions compared to other ownership types. Clearly, the government's strategy of facilitating knowledge spillovers from research institutes and universities to the commercial sector through the mechanism of entrepreneurship has been successful. Nevertheless, in China, entrepreneurship and the family business also have deep cultural roots. At the microeconomic level, entrepreneurship permeates throughout Chinese society.

On the other hand, entrepreneurship in India has had a different experience. During the colonial period, Britain maintained an atmosphere which was hostile to Indian entrepreneurship which remained limited to money lending and trade. The traditional Hindu caste system also acted to constrain entrepreneurship in India. Yet another reason why entrepreneurship did not take off in India was that after the British East India Company lost its monopoly on trading privileges, the managing firm emerged. Entrepreneurship failed to take off in India even after independence because the Congress Party, the party of government, governed under a socialist, centrally planned 'license raj'. Under the 'license raj' the government controlled the economy and firms by issuing licences for any type of activity. Even after the economic reforms of the 1980s and the 1990s, while the share of small-scale enterprises is rising in the economy, the share of registered firms has remained unchanged. The fact that the number of registered firms has not increased would suggest that that the Indian economy has not shifted towards a more formal orientation. The Indian government must, therefore, formulate and implement policies designed to increase the quality and the quantity of entrepreneurship in India. These reformist policies could be orientated towards increasing entrepreneurs access to financial resources, reforming the labour market to make the hiring of workers less expensive for firms, strengthening the capability of research institutes and universities to be more innovative, and strengthening the entrepreneurial links between research institutes, universities and industry.

Notes

1. National Bureau of Statistics, China Statistical Survey 2014.
2. National Bureau of Statistics, China Statistical Survey 2013.
Notes: *10000 persons.
3. Ibid.
4. Source: National Bureau of Statistics, China Statistical Survey 2013.

5. National Bureau of Statistics, China Statistical Survey 2013.
6. Ibid.
7. National Bureau of Statistics, China Statistical Survey 2013.
8. Ibid.

References

Acs, A. J., & Szerb, L. (2010). *The global entrepreneurship and development index (GEDI)*. Paper presented at "Opening up innovation: Strategy, organisation and technology". London: Imperial College.

Ahlstrom, D., & Bruton, G. D. (2002). An institutional perspective on the role of culture in shaping strategic actions by technology-focused entrepreneurial firms in China. *Entrepreneurship Theory and Practice, 26*(4).

Ahlstrom, D. (2010). Innovation and growth; how business contributes to society. *Academy of Management Perspectives, 24*(3), 1–23.

Aidis, R., Welter, F., Smallbone, D., & Isakova, N. (2006). Female entrepreneurship in transition economies: The case of Lithuania and Ukraine. *Feminist Economics, 13*(2), 157–183. 142

Alon, I., & Lerner, M. (2008). *International entrepreneurship in China: Lessons from global entrepreneurship monitor*. Paper presented at the Next Globalisation Conference on Transnational Entrepreneurship, April 30, 2008. http://citeseerx.ist.psu.edu/viewdoc/download?doi=10.1.1.475.8637&rep=rep1&type=pdf.

Amin, S., Rai, A., & Topa, G. (2003). Does microcredit reach the poor and vulnerable? Evidence from Northern Bangladesh. *Journal of Development Economics, 70*, 59–82.

Appleton, S., Knight, J., Song, L., & Xia, Q. (2004). Contrasting paradigms: Segmentation and competitiveness in the formation of the Chinese labour market. *Journal of Chinese Economic and Business Studies, 2*(3).

Arnold, R. (2008). *Economics*. Thomson Learning Inc.

Audretsch, D. (2007). Entrepreneurship capital and economic growth. *Oxford Review of Economic Policy, 23*(1), 63–78.

Baporikar, N. (2015). Role of entrepreneurship in the networked Indian economy. In P. Pablos (Ed.), *Technological solutions for sustainable business practice in Asia*. USA: IGT Global.

Batjargal, B., & Liu, M. (2004). Entrepreneurs access to private equity in China: The role of social capital. *Organisation Science, 15*(2).

Baumol, W. (1990), Entrepreneurship: Productive, unproductive and destructive. *The Journal of Political Economy, 98*(5).

Bergmann, H., & Sternberg, R. (2007). The changing face of entrepreneurship in Germany. *Small Business Economics, 28*(2–3), 205–221.

Bhatt, V. (1986). Entrepreneurship and development: India's experience. *Finance and Development, 23,* 1.

Bhide, A. (2004). *What role for entrepreneurship in India,* Memo. Graduate School of Business, Columbia University. https://www0.gsb.columbia.edu/mygsb/faculty/research/pubfiles/2187/Bhideentre.pdf.

Block, J., & Sandner, P. (2009). Necessity and opportunity entrepreneurs and their duration in self-employment: Evidence from German micro data. *Journal of Industry, Competition and Trade, 9*(2), 117–137.

Brimmer, A. (1955). The setting of entrepreneurship in India. *The Quarterly Journal of Economics, 69*(4).

Bruton, G., Ahlstrom, D., & Obloj, K. (2008). Entrepreneurship in emerging economies: Where are we today and where should the research go in the future. *Entrepreneurship Theory and Practice, 32,* 1.

Carree, M., van Stel, A., Thurik, A. R., & Wennekers, A. R. M. (2007). *The relationship between economic development and business ownership revisited.* Rotterdam: Tinbergen Institute.

Chaudhari, S., & Banerjee, D. (2007). Economic liberalization, capital mobility and informal wage in a small open economy: A theoretical analysis. *Economic Modelling, 24,* 924–940.

Cooke, F. (2009). The enactment of three new labour laws in China: Unintended consequences and the emergence of 'new' actors in employment relations. In *Keynote Speech, Conference of the Regulating for Decent Work Network.* Geneva, Switzerland: ILO, July 8–10, 2009.

Debroy, B., & Bhandari, L. (2007). *Exclusive growth—Inclusive inequality.* Working Paper, Centre for Policy Research, New Delhi.

De Marco, A. (2000). Uncertainty and new venture investments: Some empirical evidence from young Italian firms. *International Journal of Entrepreneurship, 4,* 143.

Deng, S., Wang, X., & Alon, I. (2011). Framework for female entrepreneurship in China. *International Journal of Business and Emerging Markets, 2*(1), 3–20.

Djankov, S., Qian, Y., Roland, G., & Zhuravskaya, E. (2006). Entrepreneurship in China and Russia compared. *Journal of the European Economic Association, 4*(2/3).

Dreze, J., & Sen, A. (2013). *An uncertain glory: India and its contradictions.* Princeton: Princeton University Press.

Fan, Y. 1996. Global perspectives: Chinese peasant entrepreneurs: An examination of township and village enterprises in rural China. *Journal of Small Business Management, 34*(4).

Fields, G., & Yang, S. (2013). *A theoretical model of the Chinese labour market.* Discussion Paper Series, Forschungsinstut Zur Zukunft de Arbeit, No. 7278.

Gan, L et al (2012). *Data you need to know about China.* Research Report of China Household Finance Survey. London: Springer.

Gennaioli, N., La Porta, R., Lopez-de-Silanes, F., & Shleifer, A. (2013). Human capital and regional development. *Quarterly Journal of Economics, 128*, 105–164.

Gerxhani, K. (2004). The informal sector in developed and less developed countries: A literature survey. *Public Choice, 120*(2), 267–300.

Ghani, E., Kerr, W., & O'Connell, S. (2011a). Promoting entrepreneurship growth and job creation. In E. Ghani (Ed.), *Reshaping tomorrow: Is South Asia ready for the big leap.* New Delhi: Oxford University Press.

Ghani, E., Kerr, W., & O'Connell, S. (2011b). Local industrial structures and female entrepreneurship in India. *Journal of Economic Geography*, 1–36.

Ghani, E., Kerr, W., & O'Connell, S. (2012). *What makes cities more competitive? Spatial determinants of entrepreneurship in India.* Policy Research Working Paper 6198. The World Bank.

Ghani, E., Kerr, W. & O'Connell, S. (2013). Local industrial structures and female entrepreneurship in India.*Journal of Economic Geography, 13*(6), 929–964.

Ghani, E., Kerr, W., & O'Connell, S. (2014). Spatial determinants of entrepreneurship in India. *Regional Studies, 48*(6).

Goyal, M., & Parkash, J. (2011). Women entrepreneurship in India—Problems and prospects. *International Journal of Multidisciplinary Research, 1*(5).

Gupta, V. (2008). An inquiry into the characteristics of entrepreneurship in India. *Journal of International Business Research, 7*(1).

Gurtoo, A., & Williams, C. (2009). Entrepreneurship and the informal sector: Some lessons from India. *Entrepreneurship in India, 10*(1).

Hafer, R., & Jones, G. (2015). Are entrepreneurship and cognitive skills related? Some international evidence. *Small Business Economics, 44*, 283–298.

Hartog, J., Van Praag, M., & Van Der Sluis, J. (2010). If you are so smart, why aren't you an entrepreneur? Returns to cognitive and social ability; Entrepreneurs versus employees. *Journal of Economics and Management Strategy, 19*, 947–989.

Holcombe, R. G. (1998). Entrepreneurship and economic growth. *The Quarterly Journal of Austrian Economics, 1,* 45–62.

Holt, D. (1997). A comparative study of values among Chinese and US entrepreneurs: Pragmatic convergence between contrasting cultures. *Journal of Business Venturing, 12*(6).

Huang, Y. (2008). *Capitalism with Chinese characteristics: Entrepreneurship and the State.* New York: Cambridge University Press.

Iyer, L., Khanna, T, T., & Varshney, A. (2013). Caste and entrepreneurship in India. *Economic and Political Weekly, XLVIII*(6).

Jain, M. (2013). Role of entrepreneurship in Indian economy. *Journal of Social Welfare and Management, 5*(3), 144.

Jain, S., & Sharma, D. (2013). Institutional logic migration and industry evolution in emerging economies: The case of technology in India. *Strategic Entrepreneurship Journal, 7*(3), 252–271.

Kapoor, A. (2007). The SEWA way: Shaping another future for informal labour. *Futures, 39,* 554–568.

Kirby, D., & Ying, F. (1995). Chinese cultural values and entrepreneurship: A preliminary consideration. *Journal of Enterprising Culture, 3*(3).

Koster, S., & Rai, S. (2005). Entrepreneurship and economic development in a developing country: A case study of India. *The Journal of Entrepreneurship, 17*(2), 117–137.

Krug, B., & Hendrischke, H. (2002). Entrepreneurship in China: Institutions, organisational identity and survival: Empirical results from two provinces. ERIM Report Series *Research in Management,* ERS-2002-14-ORG.

Kshetri, N. (2007). Institutional changes affecting entrepreneurship in China. *Journal of Developmental Entrepreneurship, 12*(4), 415–432.

Kumbhar, V. (2013). Some critical issues of women entrepreneurship in rural India. *European Academic Research, 1*(2).

Longbao, W. (2009). *Regional economic development and entrepreneurship in China.* Paper Prepared for the Conference, "US-China Business Cooperation in the 21st century: Opportunities and Challenges for Enterprises". Indiana University, Indianapolis and Bloomington, Indiana, April 15–17, 2009. http://www.indiana.edu/~rccpb/uschinacooperation/papers/P7%20Wei%20Longbao.pdf

Li, H., Li, L., Wu, B., & Xiong, Y. (2012). The end of cheap Chinese labour. *The Journal of Economic Perspectives, 26*(4).

Liao, D., & Sohmen, P. (2001). The development of modern entrepreneurship in China. *Stanford Journal of East Asian Affairs, 1.*

Liu, Y. (2002). *Development of private entrepreneurship in China: Process, problems and countermeasures.* Chinese Academy of Social Sciences.

Lu, J., & Tao, Z. (2007). *Determinants of entrepreneurial activities in China.* MPRA Paper No. 5675.

Lucas, R. (1993). Making a miracle. *Econometrica, 61,* 251–272.

Lynn, R., & Meisenberg, G. (2010). National IQs calculated and validated for 108 nations. *Intelligence, 38,* 353–360.

Medhora, P. (1965). Entrepreneurship in India. *Political Science Quarterly, 80*(4).

Meisenberg, G. (2012). National IQ and economic outcomes. *Personality and Individual Differences, 53,* 103–107.

Meng, X. (2012). Labor market outcomes and reforms in China. *The Journal of Economic Perspectives, 26*(4).

Mehta, A., & Mehta, M. (2011). Rural women entrepreneurship in India:— Opportunities and challenges. In *International Conference on Humanities, Geography and Economics.* Pattaya, Dec 2011.

Millman, C., Matlay, H.,& Liu, F. (2008). Entrepreneurship education in China: A case study approach. *Journal of Small Business and Enterprise Development, 15*(4), 802–815

Minniti, M., Bygrave, W., & Autio, E. (2006). *Global entrepreneurship monitor: 2005 executive report* (p. 145). London: London Business School.

Monsen, E., Mahagaonhar, P., & Dienes, C. (2012). Entrepreneurship in India: The question of occupational transition. *Small Business Economics, 39*(2).

Naude, W., & Rossouw, S. (2010). Early international entrepreneurship in China: Extent and determinants. *Journal of International Entrepreneurship, 88.*

Parthasarathy, B., & Aoyama, Y. (2006). From Software services to R&D services: Local entrepreneurship in the Software industry in Bangalore. *India, Environment and Planning A, 38,* 1269–1285.

Phan, P., Zhou, J., & Abrahamson, E. (2010). Creativity, innovation and entrepreneurship in China. *Management and Organisation Review, 6*(2), 175–194.

Prabhu, J., & Jain, S. (2015). Innovation and entrepreneurship in India: Understanding Jugaad. *Asia Pac J Manag, 32,* 843–868.

Prahalad, C. K. (2012). Bottom of the pyramid as a source of breakthrough innovations. *Journal of Product Innovation Management, 29*(1), 6–12.

Ramesh, S. (2012). Continental shift: China and the global economic crisis. In L. Wang (Ed.), *Rising China in the changing world economy*. Routledge/ Taylor and Francis Group (April 2012).

Romer, P. (1986). Increasing returns and long-run growth. *Journal of Political Economy, 94*, 1002–1037.

Shivani, S., Mukherjee, S. K., & Saran, P. (2006). Socio-cultural influences on Indian entrepreneurs: The needs for appropriate structural intervention. *Journal of Asian Economics, 17*(1).

Sinha, T. (1996). Human factors in entrepreneurship effectiveness. *The Journal of Entrepreneurship, 5*, 1.

Smith, A. (1776). An inquiry into the nature and causes of the wealth of nations: Representative selections. In B. Mazlish (Eds.), 1961. New York: Bobbs-Merrill Company Inc.

Solow, R. (1956). A contribution to the theory of economic growth. *Quarterly Journal of Economics, 70*(1), 65–94.

Solow, R. (1957). Technical change and the aggregate production function. *Review of Economics and Statistics, 39*, 312–320.

Swetha, T., & Rao, K. (2013). Entrepreneurship in India. *International Journal of Social Science and Interdisciplinary Research, 2*(7).

Tan, J. (2005). Venturing in turbulent water: A historical perspective of economic reform and entrepreneurial transformation. *Journal of Business Venturing, 20*(5).

Torri, M., & Martinez, A. (2014). Women's empowerment and micro-entrepreneurship in India: Constructing a new development paradigm? *Progress in Development Studies, 14*(1), 31–48.

Tripathi, D. (1981). Occupational mobility and industrial entrepreneurship: A historical analysis. *The Developing Economies, 19*, 52–68.

Tsang, E. W. K. (1994). Threats and opportunities faced by private businesses in China. *Journal of Business Venturing, 9*(6).

Turner, P. (2007). Entrepreneurship: Riding growth in India and China. http://knowledge.insead.edu/economics-politics/entrepreneurship-riding-growth-in-india-and-china-2084.

Van Praag, M., van Witteloostuijn, A., & van der Sluis, J. (2013). The higher returns to formal education for entrepreneurs versus employees. *Small Business Economics, 40*, 375–396.

Varshney, A. (2007). India's democratic challenge. *Foreign Affairs* (March–April).

Veen, J. H. (1976). Commercial orientation of industrial entrepreneurs in India. *Economic and Political Weekly, 11,* 35.

Wang, S. (2012). Credit constraints, job mobility, and entrepreneurship: Evidence from property reform in China. *The Review of Economics and Statistics, 94*(2), 532–551.

Wing, C. C. K., & Yiu, M. F. K. (2000). Small business and liquidity constraints in financing business investment Evidence from Shanghai's manufacturing sector. *Journal of Business Venturing, 15.*

Wong, P. K., Ho, Y. P., & Autio, E. (2005). Entrepreneurship, innovation and economic growth: Evidence from GEM data. *Small Business Economics, 24*(3), 335–350.

Yang, J., & Li, J. (2008). The development of entrepreneurship in China. *Asia Pacific Journal of Management, 25.*

Yiu, D., & Lau, C. M. (2008). Corporate entrepreneurship as resource capital configuration in emerging market firms. *Entrepreneurship Theory and Practice, 32,* 37–58.

Yu, J., Stough, R., & Nijkamp, P. (2009). Governing technological entrepreneurship in China and the West. *Public Administration Review, 69,* S95–S100 (Comparative Chinese/American Public Administration, December 2009).

Zapalska, A. M., & Edwards, W. (2001). Chinese entrepreneurship in a cultural and economic perspective. *Journal of Small Business Management, 39,* 3.

Zhou, Y., & Qin, Y. (2012). *Empirical analysis on income inequality of Chinese residents.* Springer.

5

Comparative Study: Jiangsu, Hubei and Gansu: 1949–2014

In previous chapters, infrastructure, knowledge spillovers and knowledge creation have been discussed in broad terms in terms of theory and with relevance to modern China since 1949. However, this chapter will conduct a cross-provincial analysis of a Coastal province (Jiangsu), a Central province (Hubei) and a Western province (Gansu). The analysis is taken further by evaluating infrastructural, knowledge creation and spillover factors which influence Chinese economic growth specifically at the provincial level. These factors are infrastructure, manufacturing industry, S&T research parks, high-technology zones and education. The manufacturing industry has been included because associated with it is a concentration of infrastructure. The analysis will be assessed qualitatively using the case study methodology outlined in Chap. 4, Volume 1. The conclusions to be drawn from the comparative case study of the three provinces will assist in answering the research questions specified in Chap. 3 and in addressing the research propositions outlined in that chapter.

© The Author(s) 2017
S. Ramesh, *China's Lessons for India: Volume II*,
DOI 10.1007/978-3-319-58115-6_5

Cross-Provincial Analysis

The provincial data for each economic feature in Table 5.1 is represented as a percentage of the national one. In this case, the national figure for each economic feature is treated as 100%; and the provincial figure is treated as a percentage of this. This will make a provincial comparison more informative and robust. Table 5.1 clearly shows that Jiangsu has more of each economic feature compared to Hubei and Gansu except land area. Similarly, Hubei has more of each economic feature than Gansu except land area. Nevertheless, although each feature decreases moving from Jiangsu, Hubei and Gansu, it is obvious in terms of manufacturing and knowledge creation that Jiangsu is far better endowed than either Hubei or Gansu in terms of FDI in fixed capital, personnel in experimental development, enterprise R&D funding and foreign funding. Clearly, in terms of the economic reforms, Jiangsu has reaped more benefits in the context of the knowledge economy than either Hubei or Gansu. In terms of population density, Jiangsu is twice as densely populated as Hubei and nearly 6 times more densely

Table 5.1 Comparative Statistics 2009–2010

Statistics[a]	Jiangsu (%)	Hubei (%)	Gansu (%)
Area	1.1	1.9	4.73
Population	5.87	4.27	1.91
Population density	5.34	2.25	0.4
GDP	10.33	4.03	1.03
GDP per capita	13.12	7.04	4.01
FDI in fixed capital	19.42	2.75	0.20
Exports	2.53	0.13	0.02
Imports	2.06	0.12	0.06
Personnel in basic research	5.37	3.91	1.35
Personnel in applied research	5.27	4.50	1.75
Personnel in experimental development	13.68	3.89	0.74
Government R&D funding	6.66	4.11	1.04
Enterprise R&D funding	13.81	3.61	0.50
Foreign R&D funding	20.86	0.92	0.10
Other R&D funding	10.06	3.35	1.12

Source Compiled by author using data from National Statistical Bureau of China, China Statistical Yearbook 2011
Note [a]Percentage of national value

Table 5.2 Percentage of Sources of Funds in Research by Province 2003 and 2007

Region	Total (%)		Government grants (source of funds) (%)		Enterprise funds (source of funds) (%)		Bank Loans (source of funds) (%)	
	2003	2007	2003	2007	2003	2007	2003	2007
National	100	100	100	100	100	100	100	100
Jiangsu	7.48	12.16	6.38	7.04	9.60	13.61	26.28	21.18
Hubei	3.97	3.00	4.10	4.22	5.56	2.54	1.39	1.95
Gansu	1.4	0.94	1.34	1.11	0.93	0.94	2.05	0.26

Source Compiled by author using data from China's National Bureau of Statistics, China S&T Yearbook 2003 and China S&T Yearbook 2007
Note The percentages have been derived by treating the Yuan National Total as a base of 100 and converting the provincial Yuan total figures into percentages as appropriate

populated than Gansu. With regard to the indicators of manufacturing such as exports and imports, the figures suggest even more disparity between Jiangsu, Hubei and Gansu. Clearly, the post-1978 economic reforms have had a self-sustaining effect on the economic growth and prosperity of the Coastal provinces.

Moreover, Jiangsu is favoured by government in comparison with Hubei or Gansu because, as Table 5.2 shows, government grants to research institutions in Jiangsu Province are higher than those to local research institutions in Hubei or Gansu. Due to the opening up of the Coastal regions to international commerce, Jiangsu Province is also favoured by foreign investors who receive a greater return from investments in the province than from investment in either Hubei or Gansu. In Table 5.2, the provincial figures for the source of funds have been represented as a percentage of the national figure which has been used a base of 100. While Jiangsu receives more government grants, enterprise funds and bank loans for research than either Hubei or Gansu, the most significant figure is that for bank loans. This suggests a certain degree of risk taking, an indication of entrepreneurship. Compared to the national average, Jiangsu receives more of its funds as bank loans, while it is only in this category that Gansu receives more funds for research than Hubei. Therefore, entrepreneurship is more active in Coastal provinces such as Jiangsu. This view is also supported by the percentage change in funding from enterprise funds and bank loans over the period 2003–2007. In the case of Jiangsu, the former increases and the latter decreases.

From Table 5.1, it seems that population density has an impact on the economic prosperity of a province. The greater the population density of a province, the greater will be its economic prosperity. It is intuitive that the smaller the provincial population and the greater the provincial land area, the smaller will be the provincial population density (λ) where

$$\lambda = \frac{\text{Provincial Population(persons)}}{\text{Provincial Land Area}\left(\text{km}^2\right)} \qquad (1)$$

The smaller is λ for a province, then the lower will be the person-to-person interactions and the fewer the possibilities for the transfer and creation of knowledge. This effect is further magnified the fewer the quantity and lower the quality of provincial transport infrastructure and telecommunications. The lack of infrastructure also signifies a lower level of entrepreneurial activity in comparison with provinces where there is a relative abundance of such infrastructures. The implication is that as economic prosperity travels from the east of China to its west, it will have fewer and fewer opportunities to take root and grow because the factors of urbanisation such as transport and telecommunications infrastructure are reduced in capacity. The role of transport and telecommunications infrastructure is to reduce the density of space and increase its population density. At the same time, infrastructure simulates the effects of urbanisation in two ways. Firstly, the availability of infrastructure increases the flow of people, facilitating knowledge interactions and the division of labour. Secondly, infrastructure reduces the costs of transporting manufactured goods from and resources to sites of production.

In this way, infrastructure increases the economic density of space, while facilitating in the formation of knowledge linkages. The combination of a sufficient stock of physical [teachers and transport and telecommunication infrastructures] and soft infrastructures [i.e. numbers of universities, numbers of science & technology parks] increases the population and economic density of space, facilitating the transfer and creation of knowledge, as well as its commercialisation through entrepreneurial activity.

The data in Table 5.3 is used to populate Table 5.4. The latter defines a spatial category, the associated spatial features and the respective provincial content. The spatial features can be further defined as being infrastructure, administrative, economic or geographical in nature.

The features in the above table which are highlighted in red are those for which Hubei Province has greater capacity than either Jiangsu or Gansu. The features in black are those for which Jiangsu has greater capacity than either Hubei or Gansu. It can be clearly determined from this table that Hubei Province has greater infrastructural capacity in terms of railway or highway capacity. However, the only economic features which Hubei has greater capacity than Jiangsu are waterway passenger traffic, railway passenger traffic and highway freight traffic. The fact that Jiangsu has greater highway passenger traffic may be explained by the fact that Jiangsu has a greater preponderance for car ownership. With regard to Gansu, the only feature it has which is larger than any of either Jiangsu's or Hubei's features is with regard to railway freight traffic. This is highlighted in grey in the 'economic features' column. The reason why Gansu has the largest amount of railway freight traffic may be because historically there were more railways in the interior of China which also has the largest deposits of natural resources. These and manufactured goods could be transported by rail to either China's coastal regions or countries in central Asia. Nevertheless, in terms of administrative features, Hubei has more regions and cities at county level than either Jiangsu or Gansu. The propositions outlined in Chap. 4, Volume 1, will now be evaluated in the following sections.

Proposition 1

Knowledge creation has sustained income disparities between the Coastal regions of China and the interior hinterland since the post-1978 economic reforms.

Data: [Education] [Patent Registration] **Criteria:** [University Graduates, R&D Spend, Patents registered].

In terms of the creation of knowledge, it would seem that annual average increases in teachers employed at secondary schools, university

Table 5.3 Provincial geographical and infrastructural statistics 2013

Spatial category	Spatial features	Jiangsu	Hubei	Gansu
Prefecture	Regions at Prefecture Level (Regions)	13	13	14
Prefecture	Cities at Prefecture Level (City's)	13	12	12
County	Regions at County Level (Regions)	100	**103**	86
County	Cities at County Level (City's)	23	**24**	4
City	Districts at City Level (District)	**55**	38	17
Cultivated Land	Cultivated Land (10,000 ha)	**480**	309.1	340
Population	Urban Population (10,000 Persons)	**5090**	3161	1036
Population	Rural Population (10,000 Persons)	**2849**	2638	1546
Transport	Railway length (Km)	2599	**3929**	2595
Transport	Highway Length (Km)	156,094	**226,912**	133,597
Transport	Length of navigable inland waterways (Km)	**24,333**	8271	914
Transport	Length of coastline (Km)	**1000**	0	0
Transport	Private Vehicles Owned (10,000 units)	**729**	236	88
Transport	Civil Vehicles Owned (10,000 units)	**840**	282	114
Passenger Traffic	Railway (100 Million per Km)	514	**634**	383
Passenger Traffic	Highway (100 Million per Km)	**847**	415	212
Passenger Traffic	Waterway (100 Million per Km)	**3.97**	3.24	0.16
Freight Traffic	Railway (100 Million Ton per Km)	381	914	**1551**
Freight Traffic	Highway (100 Million Ton per Km)	1790	**2046**	811
Freight Traffic	Waterway (100 Million Ton per Km)	**7753**	1791	0.01
Entrepreneurship	Private industrial Enterprises (Units)	**28,676**	6872	579

(continued)

Table 5.3   (continued)

Spatial category	Spatial features	Jiangsu	Hubei	Gansu
Entrepreneurship	Private industrial Enterprises Total Assets (100 million yuan)	**25,669**	4921	592
Entrepreneurship	State industrial Enterprises Total Assets (100 million yuan)	**16,549**	15,016	7889
Entrepreneurship	State and State Holding Industrial Enterprises (units)	**904**	689	381
Telecommunications	Internet Usage (%)	**51.7**	43.1	34.7
Telecommunications	Utilisation of fixed line and mobile phones (sets/100 persons)	**128.87**	93.13	90.64
Telecommunications	Business Volume of Postal Services (100 million yuan)	**269.59**	74.15	11.38
Telecommunications	Business Volume of Telecoms Services (100 million yuan)	**1133.21**	536.01	227.33

Source Compiled by author using data from China's National Bureau of Statistics, China Statistical Datasheet 2014
Note Economic features of each spatial category for Jiangsu, Hubei and Gansu

enrolments and telephone subscribers would play a significant role. Telephone subscribers have been included in the knowledge creation category because the use of the telephone facilitates the diffusion of knowledge and knowledge creation among the general population.

Figure 5.1 shows the average percentage change for telephone subscribers, university enrolments and teachers in secondary schools for the pre-reform period 1953–1976. In this period, only Jiangsu registered a bigger percentage increase in terms of university enrolments than Hubei or Gansu. However, with regard to teachers in secondary schools both Hubei and Gansu registered bigger increases than Jiangsu. In terms of telephone subscribers, Hubei registered a bigger percentage increase followed by Jiangsu. This increase can be explained by the fact that more land line telephones would have been used by the military and party officials.

Table 5.4 Provincial Spatial Features 2013

Infrastructure	Administrative	Economic	Geographical
Railway length	**Regions**	**Highway freight**	Length of coastline
Highway length	Districts	Waterway freight	Cultivated land
Navigable inland waterway length	**Cities**	Urban population	
		Rural population	
		Post & telecommunications business volume	
		Vehicles owned	
		Railway passenger traffic	
		Highway passenger traffic	
		Waterway passenger traffic	
		Railway freight traffic	

Source Compiled by Author from Table 5.2 using data from the Chinese National Bureau of Statistics

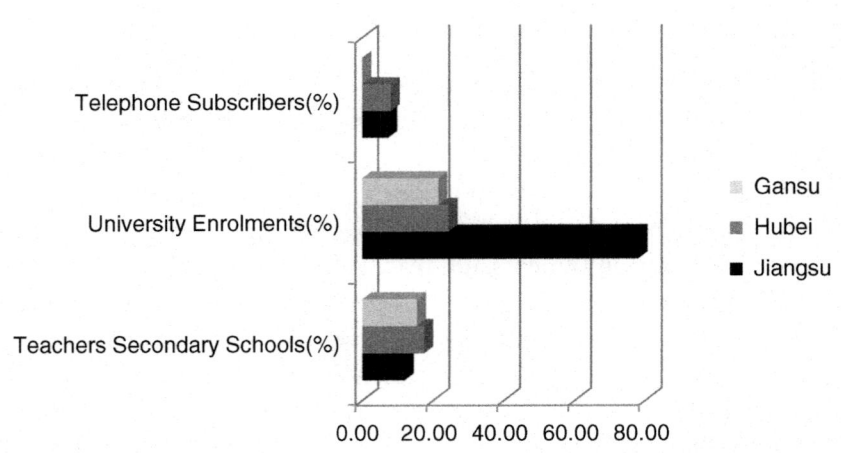

Fig. 5.1 1953–1976: Average percentage annual growth of knowledge factors. *Source* Compiled using data from China's National Bureau of Statistics, China Compendium of Statistics 1949–2004

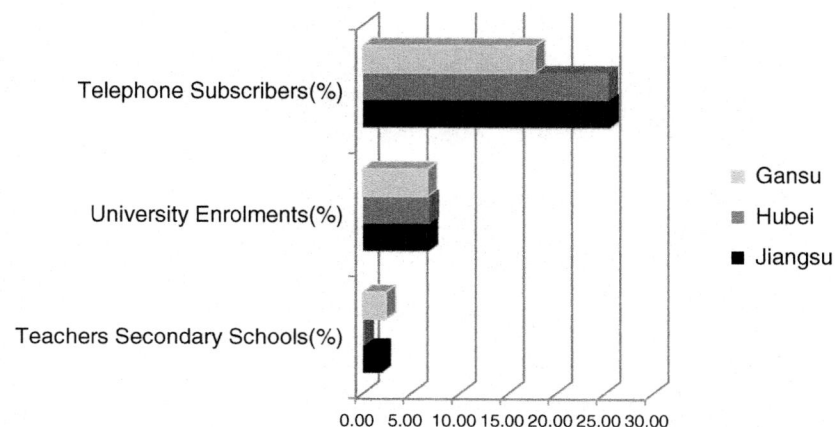

Fig. 5.2 1979–1995: Average percentage annual growth of knowledge factors. *Source* Compiled using data from China's National Bureau of Statistics, China Compendium of Statistics 1949–2004

Figure 5.2 shows the same data in the first reform period 1979–1995. Although the telephone subscribers in Gansu increased in percentage terms, both Jiangsu and Hubei registered bigger increases with Jiangsu showing a slightly bigger increase than Hubei. In terms of university enrolments, all three provinces showed roughly the same increase. Nevertheless, with regard to teachers in secondary schools Jiangsu and Hubei registered larger increases than Hubei with Gansu's increase being larger than that of Jiangsu.

Figure 5.3 shows that in the second reform period, 1997–2004, Gansu registered the largest annual average percentage increase in the numbers of telephone subscribers followed by Jiangsu and then Hubei. In terms of university enrolments, the order of annual average percentage increase is Hubei, Jiangsu and Gansu. The annual average growth of the numbers of teachers in secondary schools was the largest in Gansu, followed by Hubei and Jiangsu. It would seem, from this simple analysis that the inland provinces of Hubei and Gansu should be doing just as well as Jiangsu with respect to the formation of innovation systems. However, the economic prosperity of the Coastal regions due to an influx of FDI; and the decentralisation of education funding

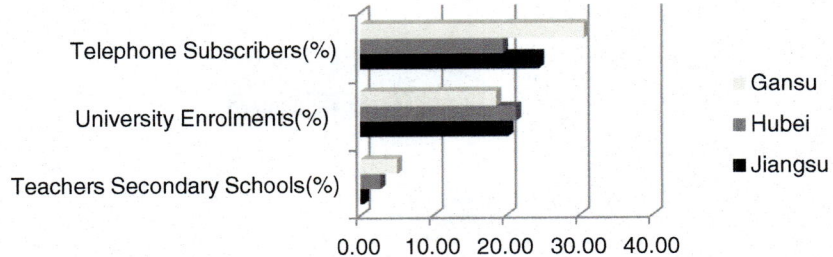

Fig. 5.3 1997–2004: Average percentage growth of knowledge factors. *Source* Compiled using data from China's National Bureau of Statistics, China Compendium of Statistics 1949–2004

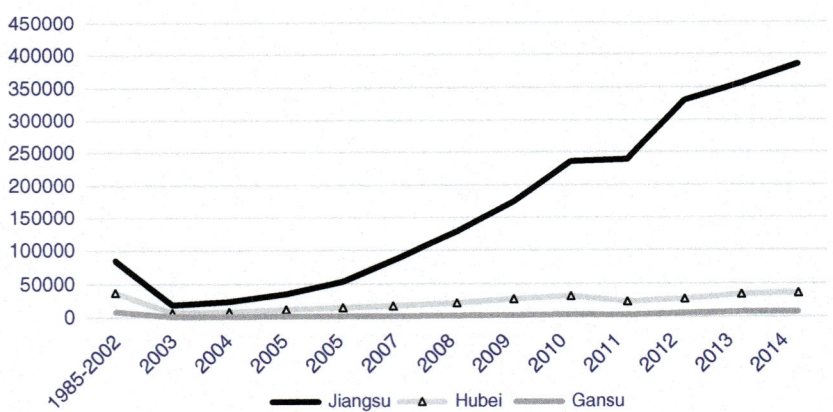

Fig. 5.4 Domestic applications for patents received from 1985 to 2014. *Source* Compiled using data from Intellectual Property Office of PRC. *Note* Patents are in units of numbers received

has resulted in the development of Coastal innovation systems at the expense of a national one. This point is emphasised by the data in Fig. 5.4 which shows the domestic patent applications made is greatest in Jiangsu compared to either Hubei or Gansu in the period 1985–2014. However, the comparison of the growth of telephone subscribers, university enrolments and teachers in secondary schools between the three periods does indicate that Gansu has been engaged in a 'catch-up' with other provinces with regard to the creation of knowledge.

Figure 5.4 indicates that it is the case that Coastal provinces such as Jiangsu are doing better than inland provinces such as Hubei and Gansu with regard to knowledge creation, if the latter can be measured in terms of patents filed and granted. In each of the years from 1985 to 2014, Jiangsu is ahead of both Hubei and Gansu with regard to the number of patents filed with the Chinese Intellectually Property Office. Similarly, Hubei is ahead of Gansu in each of the years from 1985 to 2014 in terms of patents filed. It has already been established in Fig. 4.9, Chap. 4, Volume 1, that the Coastal region [Jiangsu] is ahead of both the Central [Hubei] and Western regions [Gansu] of China with regard to granted patents. However, the data has not been differentiated to distinguish between MNC patents and indigenous Chinese patents. This is because research in China by MNCs is carried out by indigenously educated researchers, perhaps being managed by foreigners because this is cheaper than hiring foreign educated researchers. Thus, the educational reforms have played a critical role in generating the unbalanced development of regional innovation systems in China. Moreover, this has resulted in sustaining disparities in income between the Coastal regions of China and its interior hinterland.

Due to the open Coastal cities, SEZs, NHTIDZs and science and technology research parks and the associated influx of FDI into the Coastal/Coastal Region of China, entrepreneurial and MNC activity has been greater in this region. It would seem that the government reforms, which facilitated horizontal linkages between research institutes and universities R&D with entrepreneurial activity, ensured that the greatest knowledge creation activity occurred in the Coastal regions of China where the majority of entrepreneurial activity took place in the post-reform years. Figure 5.5 illustrates the point that the trend of invention by type of institution has favoured industrial and mineral enterprises. Enterprises tend to be more innovative and favour risk-taking in their activities. The latter may be exhibited by the borrowing of funds at commercial rates of return to finance innovative activities, as well as having access to enterprise funds. It was shown in Fig. 5.21, Chap. 5, Volume 2, that enterprise funds accounted for more S&T funding in Coastal (Jiangsu) than in Central (Hubei) China.

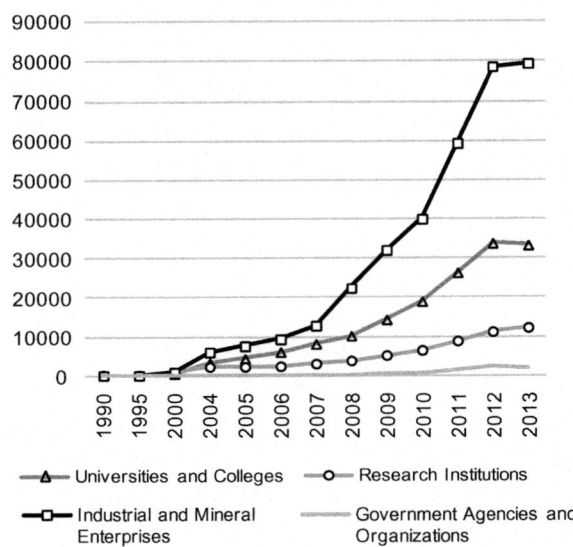

Fig. 5.5 Trend of invention by type of institution 1990 to 2013. *Source* Compiled using data from China's National Bureau of Statistics, Chinese Statistical Yearbook, Various Years

The post-reform trend in the annual average percentage increases in university enrolments, telephone subscribers and teachers employed in secondary schools in inland provinces, such as Hubei and Gansu compared to Jiangsu, suggests two things. Firstly, it can be inferred that educated individuals migrated to the Coastal provinces from inland provinces because of the increased work opportunities. Migration was much easier in the reform years, as previously discussed because educational reform facilitated individual choice as students were not educated to plan and were free to choose courses which offered better employment prospects. The inland provinces, therefore, experienced a 'brain drain' to the Coastal provinces. Secondly, the educational reforms resulted in the decentralisation of educational funding, allowing the Coastal provinces to better fund education compared to China's interior provinces. These two features ensured that knowledge creation activities mainly agglomerated in the Coastal region of China, thus sustaining income disparities between China's Coastal regions and its interior.

Proposition 2 and Proposition 5

In this section, the relevancy of Proposition 2 and Proposition 5 is assessed using annual average yearly growth rates in waterway passengers, highway passengers, railway passengers, length of railways, length of highways, rail freight, waterway freight and highway freight.

Proposition 2 Infrastructure simulates the effects of urbanisation by increasing the geographical and population densities of space by facilitating the mobility of people and resources.

Data: [Physical Infrastructure]

Criteria: [Freight Traffic, Passenger Traffic, highway and railroad length]

Proposition 5: The speed with which knowledge is transmitted varies with the type of infrastructure.

Data: [Infrastructure] Criteria: [Road transport—face-to-face contact] [Telecommunications—Instant]

In the period 1953–1976, the annual average percentage increase in railway freight is largest in Gansu Province. This can be seen from Fig. 5.6. This may have been due to the requirements of the centrally planned economy which was based on the mistaken notion that railways lead to prosperity. In the same period, as Fig. 5.7 shows, Gansu showed the largest annual average percentage increase in the length of highways, length of railways and railway passengers. Similarly, Hubei showed the largest annual average percentage increases with respect to waterway passengers and highway passengers. This may be accounted for the fact that it was in this period that the 'Third Front' program was being actively implemented by the Chinese government. The Third Front program called for the balanced economic development of all of China's provinces as well as the industrialisation of China's interior regions due to military necessity.

In this period, Hubei shows the largest increase in the annual average increase in highway passengers. During this period, knowledge creation activities were associated with process design and military needs. Most of China's knowledge creation activity was military related. Nevertheless, there was a profound lack of facilitation of knowledge creation in the educational sector and a lack of knowledge spillover from institutional research into entrepreneurial activity due to the vertical structure linking research with the end user.

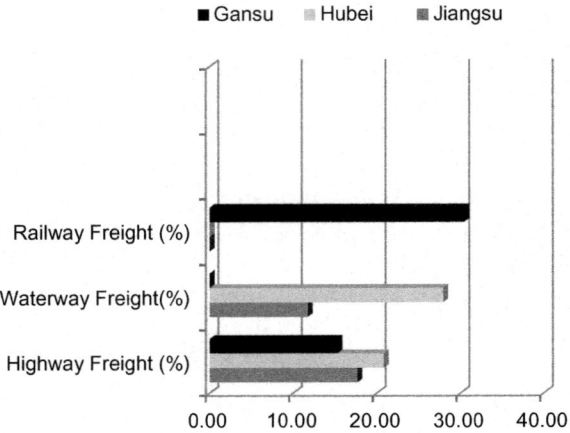

Fig. 5.6 1953–1976: Average percentage growth of provincial Freight Traffic. *Source* Compiled using data from China's National Bureau of Statistics, China Compendium of Statistics 1949–2004

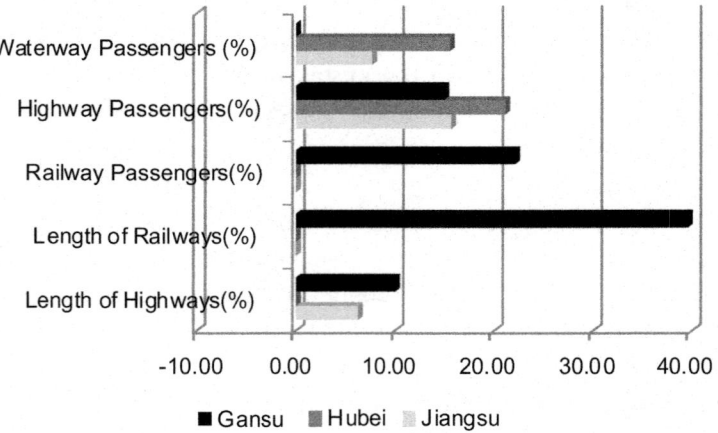

Fig. 5.7 1953–1976: Average percentage growth of Passenger Traffic and transport length. *Source* Compiled using data from China's National Bureau of Statistics, China Compendium of Statistics 1949–2004

Figures 5.8 and 5.9 show the data annual average percentage changes for freight traffic, passenger traffic and infrastructure length for the period 1979–1995.

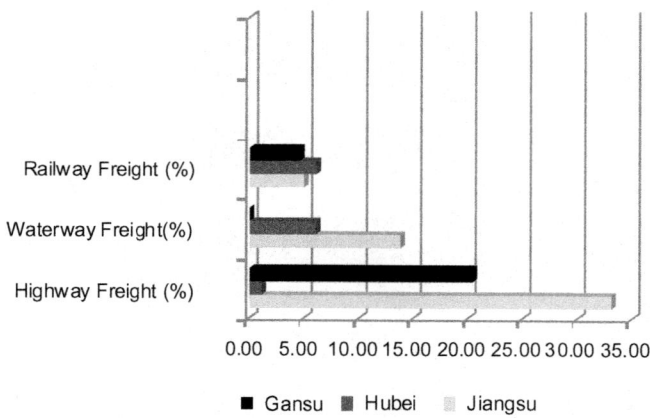

0.00 5.00 10.00 15.00 20.00 25.00 30.00 35.00

■ Gansu ■ Hubei Jiangsu

Fig. 5.8 1979–1995: Average Percentage growth of provincial Freight Traffic. *Source*: Compiled using data from China's National Bureau of Statistics, China Compendium of Statistics 1949–2004

It can be clearly determined from these figures that Jiangsu shows the largest annual average percentage increase in the length of highways, highway passengers, waterway freight and highway freight during the period compared to either Gansu or Hubei. During this period, there was also an increase in vehicle ownership in the more affluent Coastal provinces such as Jiangsu. These observations must clearly be associated with the post 1978 economic reforms. Gansu registers a bigger increase in highway passengers and highway freight than Hubei in the same period. Nevertheless, Hubei shows a slightly bigger increase in railway freight than either Jiangsu or Gansu. This may be indicative of Hubei's role as the transit province through which raw resources may transit from the Western provinces such as Gansu to the Coastal provinces such as Jiangsu.

Figure 5.10 below shows the average percentage growth of provincial freight traffic during the period 1997–2004. As can be seen, the data is dominated by Hubei which shows a 600% annual average increase in highway traffic for the period. This can be accounted for by the fact that the highway freight in ton per km jumps from 500 in 2002 to 22,400 in 2003.

If this outlier is removed, the data can be represented by Fig. 5.11. In this case, it can be seen that Hubei and then Jiangsu register the biggest

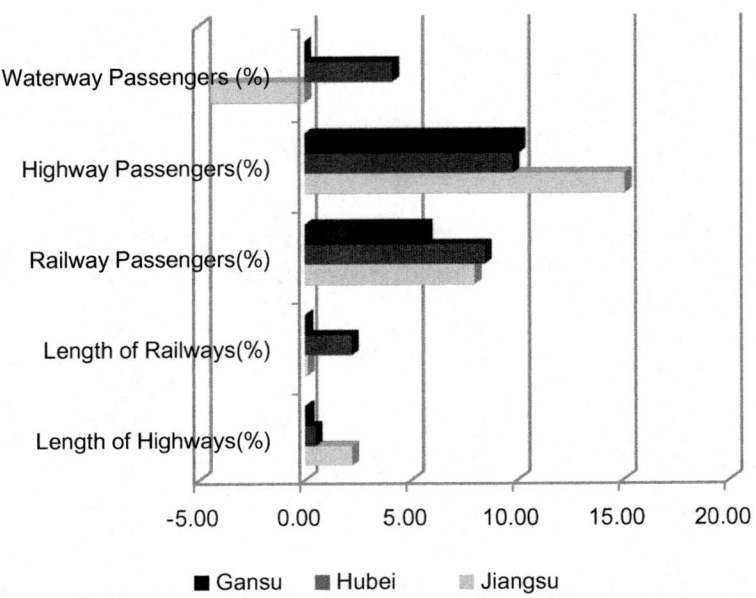

Fig. 5.9 1979–1995: Average Percentage Growth of Passenger Traffic and Transport Length. *Source* Compiled using data from China's National Bureau of Statistics, China Compendium of Statistics 1949–2004

increases in waterway freight. Similarly, Gansu and Hubei register comparatively similar increases in railway freight.

During this period Hubei also registers the largest average annual percentage increases with regard to the length of railways, waterway passengers, highway passengers and railway passengers. This can be seen from Fig. 5.12. These changes maybe associated with the Western Development Program when personnel and capital goods would have been transported from the Coastal regions to the Western regions.

While it can be taken for granted that Proposition 5 is justifiable, it is impossible to assess Proposition 2 on the data available and justify or repudiate it. However, if SEZ's are considered it is easier to do the former than the latter. This is due to the fact that SEZ's are areas of land where infrastructure investment has been concentrated. Within SEZs, undisrupted electricity generation and water supply, education, roads, ports and railways, combined with preferential policies relating to tax

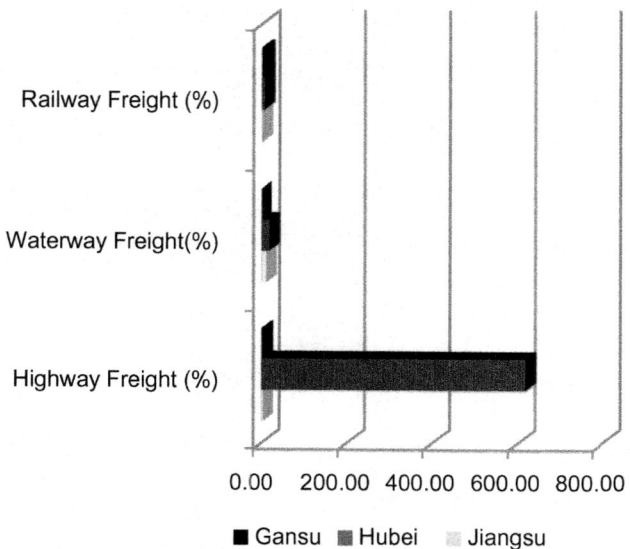

Fig. 5.10 1997–2004: Average percentage growth of provincial freight traffic. *Source* Compiled using data from China's National Bureau of Statistics, China Compendium of Statistics 1949–2004

and foreign exchange earnings have contributed to these zones nurturing and sustaining much of China's post reform economic growth. The importance of zones can be associated with a shift in the significance of highways as opposed to railways in moving from the interior of China to the Coastal regions over the years.

Proposition 3

Infrastructure leads to the specialisation of labour, leading to the integration of fragmented local markets and market integration. In the post reform, period the essence of this proposition can be found in the SEZs and NHTIDZs. This is due to the fact that a variety of physical and non-physical infrastructures has seen concentrated investment in these predefined spatial areas. Thus, it can be expected that the effects of increased infrastructure can be seen with regard to changes in imports, exports, gross regional product (GRP), GRP per capita and total investments in fixed assets over time.

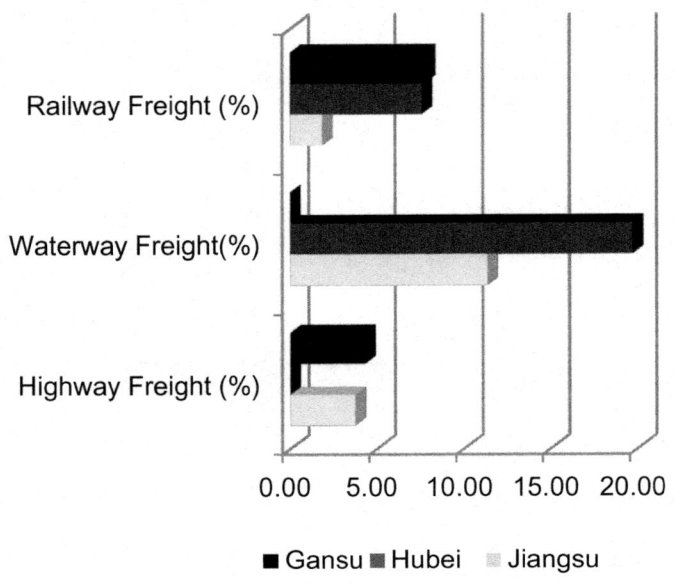

Fig. 5.11 Average percentage growth of provincial freight traffic. Hubei highway freight outlier removed. *Source* Compiled using data from China's National Bureau of Statistics, China Compendium of Statistics 1949–2004

Data: [Manufacturing Output]. **Criteria:** [GIOV] [Imports] [Exports]

As can be seen from Fig. 5.13, in the period 1953–1976, Hubei shows the largest average annual increases in total investments in fixed assets, gross regional product (GRP) and gross regional product per capita. These effects may be due to the 'Third Front' program and agriculture which was the predominant sector in this period compared to manufacturing. During this period, Jiangsu, which had a lively agriculture sector, also showed the larger annual average increase in GRP than Gansu.

In the period 1979–1995, Fig. 5.14, Gansu shows a larger average annual increase in exports than either Jiangsu or Hubei. Nevertheless, Hubei shows bigger average annual increases than Gansu with regard to GRP, GRP per capita and total investments in fixed assets [TIFA]. However, in the same period Jiangsu shows the largest average annual

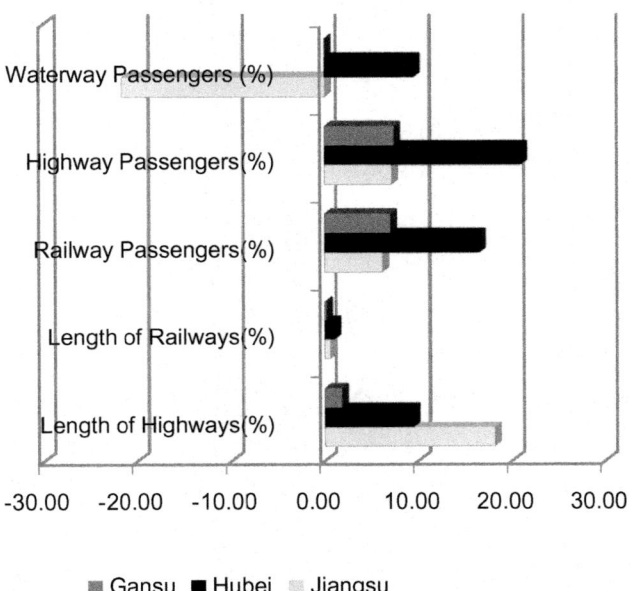

Gansu ■ Hubei Jiangsu

Fig. 5.12 1997–2004: Average percentage growth of passenger traffic and transport length. *Source* Compiled using data from China's National Bureau of Statistics, China Compendium of Statistics 1949–2004

increase with regard to Imports and TIFA than either Hubei or Gansu. The former maybe due to the fact that it was cheaper for Coastal provinces to import resources than have it transported from other inland provinces due to poor transportation and bottlenecks in the transport system. It must also be remembered that the period 1979–1995 was a period in which the economic growth rates of China's Coastal provinces converged with those of its interior provinces which relied heavily on the agricultural sector. The high prices of agricultural produce meant that the interior provinces were more prosperous than the Coastal provinces. However, this changed when the prices of agricultural produce fell towards the late 1980s and early 1990s, and the growth rates of the Coastal provinces began to diverge from the growth rates of the interior provinces following a period of convergence. It is interesting to note that worldwide increase in the cost of food may help China's interior

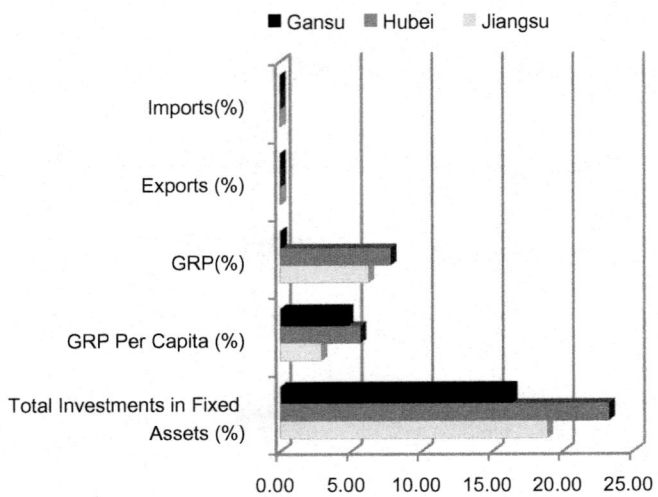

Fig. 5.13 1953–1976: Average percentage growth of economic factors. *Source* Compiled using data from China's National Bureau of Statistics, China Compendium of Statistics 1949–2004

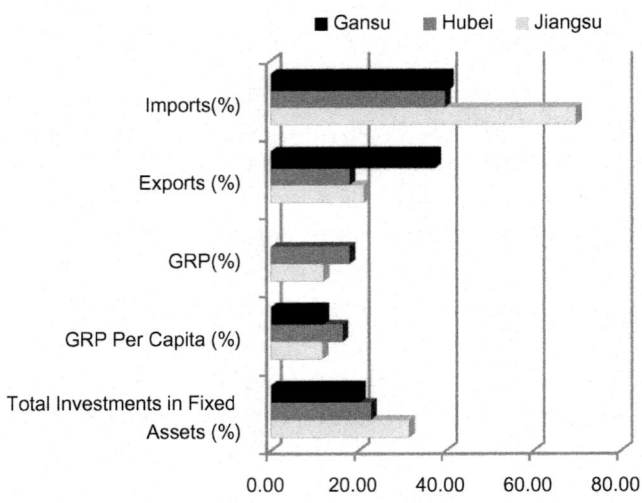

Fig. 5.14 1979–1995: Average percentage growth of economic factors. *Source* Compiled using data from China's National Bureau of Statistics, China Compendium of Statistics 1949–2004

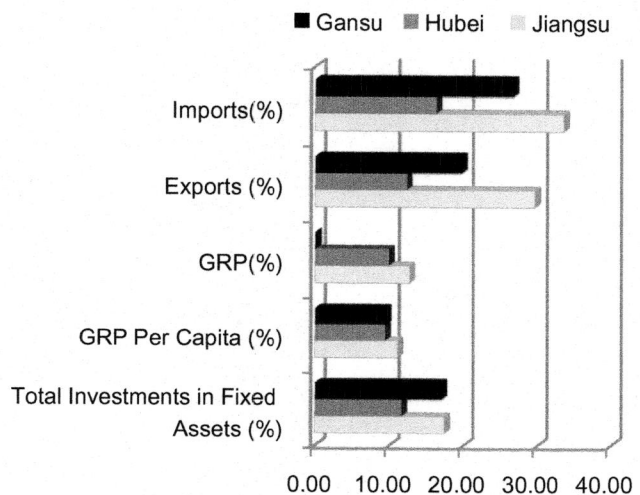

Fig. 5.15 1997–2004: Average percentage growth of economic factors. *Source* Compiled using data from China's National Bureau of Statistics, China Compendium of Statistics 1949–2004

provinces prosper again leading to a reduction in income disparities between China's interior and Coastal provinces.

During the period 1997–2004 there is a perceptible change in the annual average percentage changes of economic factors. As can be seen from Fig. 5.15, Gansu shows the largest average annual percentage increases with regard to imports, exports and total investment in fixed assets compared to Hubei. Nevertheless, with regard to average annual increases in GRP per capita, Gansu is approximately on par with Hubei. These effects may be associated with the Western Development Program which was instituted in 1999.

It is interesting to note that in the period 1979–1995, the increase in total investment in fixed assets [TIFA] was greatest in Jiangsu compared to either Hubei or Gansu. This can be accounted for by the fact that SEZs were evolving in the Coastal provinces at this time. However, in the period 1997–2004, the increase in TIFA was approximately at the same level in Gansu and Jiangsu. This may be accounted for by the effects of the Western Development Program in China's interior

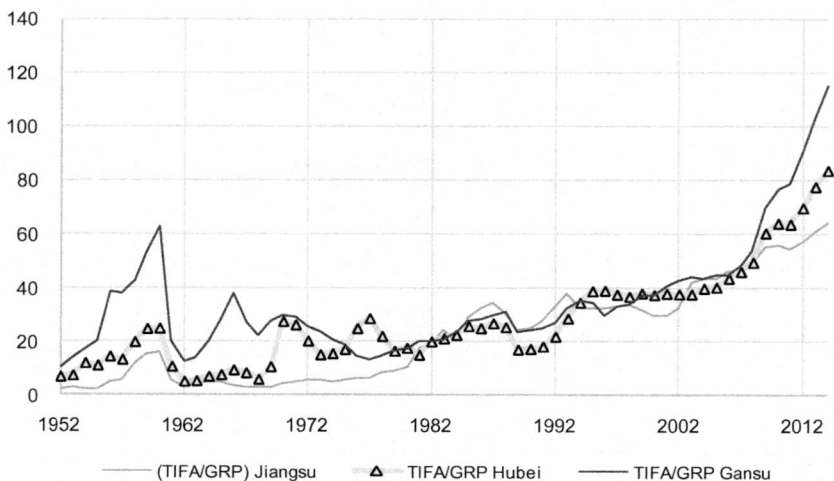

Fig. 5.16 Adjusted Total investments in fixed assets (TIFA) 1952–2014. *Source* Complied using data from China's National Bureau of Statistics. China Yearly Macro-Economic Statistics (Provincial). *Note* Total Investment in Fixed Assets (TIFA) adjusted for inflation by dividing by the respective provincial Gross Regional Products (GRP)

provinces, and the emergence of NHTIDZs in the Coastal provinces. It can also be seen that in the period 1997–2004, the growth rates of GRP per capita, imports, exports and GRP was greatest in Jiangsu Province. This demonstrates the economic dominance of the SEZs and NHTIDZs in China's Coastal provinces over other regions of the country. An adjusted TIFA is analysed below, followed by an analysis of adjusted gross industrial output value [GIOV].

Figure 5.16 shows the change in total investments in Fixed Assets over time after it is adjusted for inflation by dividing by the corresponding provincial gross regional product. The inflation-adjusted figures suggest that total fixed investment in fixed assets was predominant in Gansu and Hubei from 1952 to 1980. After 1980, total fixed investment in fixed assets in Jiangsu began to rise perhaps due to the development of the special economic zones overtook that of Hubei and Gansu. Nevertheless, after 1995, inflation-adjusted total investment in fixed assets of Gansu Province overtook that in Jiangsu and Hubei. These

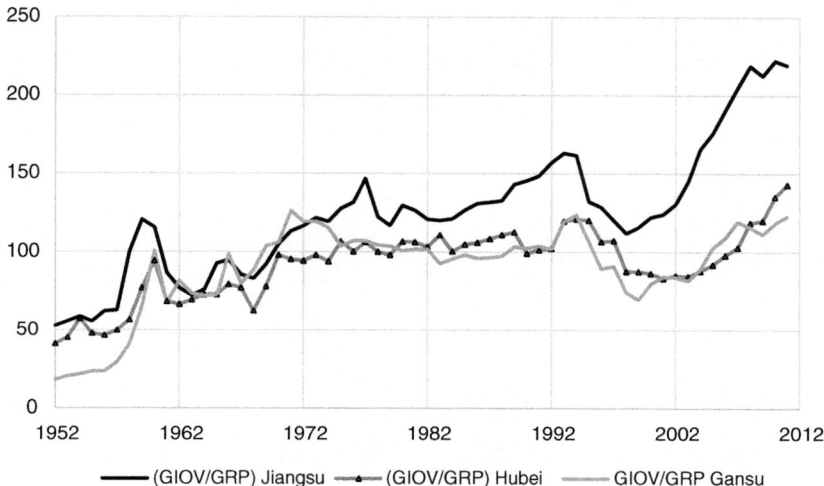

Fig. 5.17 Adjusted Gross Input Output Value (GIOV) 1952–2012. *Source* Compiled using data from China's National Bureau of Statistics. China Yearly Macro-Economic Statistics (Provincial). *Note* Gross Input Output Value (GIOV) adjusted for inflation by dividing by regional GRP

may be attributable to an emerging Western Development Program, which was not officially instituted until 1999.

Figure 5.17 shows that the inflation-adjusted GIOV between Jiangsu and Gansu begins to diverge after 1972, with Jiangsu's GIOV on an upward trajectory, compared to that of Gansu. This may have resulted from the fact that TVEs began to start emerging in Jiangsu around this time, well before the start of the 1978 economic reforms. Furthermore, TVEs were also predominant in other Coastal provinces such as Fujian where the government was reluctant to invest in state-owned enterprises for fear of military attack. The inflation-adjusted GIOV of Hubei and Gansu begins to diverge after the early 1960s. After the mid-1990s, adjusted GIOV showed a much bigger rise than did the adjusted GIOV of either Hubei or Gansu. Although after 2007/2008, the adjusted GIOV began to overtake that of Gansu although the increase was much smaller than the increase shown by the change in adjusted GIOV for Jiangsu. This could be due to the government's fiscal stimulus in November 2008 in response to the global credit crunch of 2008.

Proposition 4: The 'New Economic Geography' is inadequate in accounting for how agglomeration economies form due to knowledge creation because it is missing the micro-foundations of agglomeration economies arising from knowledge linkages caused by knowledge externalities.

Data: [Scientific Personnel] [R&D Expenditure] [S&T Parks]

Criteria: [How research carried out by one firm benefits the economy?]

As outlined in Chap. 5, Volume 1, according to Krugman (1991), there is no role for the creation of knowledge in the framework of the new economic geography [NEG] because it considers only the agricultural and manufacturing sectors and operates within the confines of neoclassical economics and its oversimplifying assumption of perfect knowledge. The NEG does not therefore account for the knowledge externalities which arise from the knowledge linkages due to knowledge creation activities. In the Chinese context, knowledge externalities can be measured by the number of patents granted and the knowledge linkages resulting from knowledge creation activities which have been facilitated between research activities and commercial entrepreneurial activity due to the specific reform of the educational and R&D sectors as discussed in Chaps. 2 and 3, Volume 2. It is apparent that the NEG cannot account for scientific personnel, R&D expenditure and science and technology research parks and university incubators which act as a vehicle for the commercialisation of knowledge in the China. Furthermore, the NRG cannot account for the formation of technological enterprises. Differences in these factors between provinces are therefore important when considering how the NEG is lacking with regard to knowledge creation.

The FDI literature suggests a number of stages in the economic development of China since the start of economic reforms in 1978. The first stage would have been permitting investment under a tightly controlled environment. This would have necessitated a fair degree of political selection bias in favour of the Coastal provinces. However, despite this literature, it is simpler to break down the economic development of China since the start of the economic reforms into three stages. Firstly, infrastructure has played a key role in the success of the SEZs and the subsequent manufacture and export of low-cost light good. Secondly, infrastructure and knowledge transfer played a key role in the success of the NHTIDZs. Finally, China is metamorphosing into a third stage of economic development, that of economic development through indigenous knowledge creation due to specific knowledge-related reforms such as the '863', 'Spark' and 'Torch' programmes as well as other institutional reforms. In retrospect, China has moved from the manufacture of low-technology goods to the manufacture of high-technology goods through imported technology. According to Jakobson (2007), in 2005, 88% of China's high-tech exports were produced by foreign MNCs. Thus, in order for China to become a creator of endogenous knowledge, there is a need for a national innovation system, which can transfer indigenous creativity into economic growth. At present China, there are a number of regional innovation systems, mainly in the Coastal provinces. Nevertheless, the success of China's third stage of economic development will depend on the successful emergence of a national innovation system. The requirements for a unique national innovation system to emerge in China number four.[1] Firstly, it is necessary to make academia more credible by reducing fraud and in general reducing the occurrences of academic misconduct. Secondly, it is necessary to raise the profile and implementation of IPR protection. Thirdly, it is necessary to make Chinese education more conducive to creativity, competition and increasing national standards. And finally, it is necessary to make S&T policy less bureaucratic, promoting an atmosphere which facilitates creativity. It would therefore be useful to examine the key indicators of knowledge creation in China at the provincial level of Jiangsu, Hubei and Gansu.

S&T Personnel by Region

A key feature of Fig. 5.18 is that although Jiangsu has the most number of scientists and engineers compared to Hubei, which has more than Gansu Province, the scientists and engineers are in the main employed by large and medium-sized enterprises in all three provinces with Jiangsu, followed by Hubei leading the way. This suggests two things. Firstly, Jiangsu has the largest pool of human capital compared to the

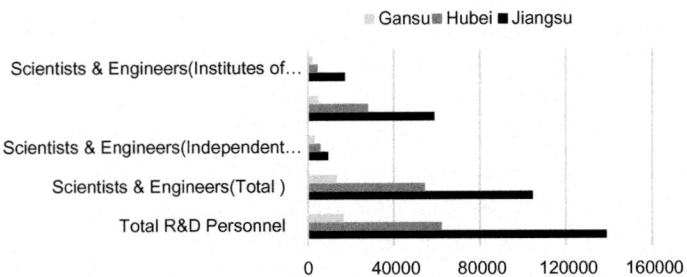

Fig. 5.18 Full-time equivalent of R&D personnel by region (2006). *Source* Compiled using data from China's National Bureau of Statistics. China S&T Statistical Yearbook 2007: Table 1.17: S&T Personnel by Region (2001)

other two provinces. And secondly, the business units which employ the largest number of scientists and engineers are entrepreneurial units which tend to be more prevalent in the Coastal provinces.

Institutions by Region

Figure 5.19 shows that in 2013, Jiangsu Province was predominant in terms of student enrolments. It also had the highest number of secondary school graduates, university and college graduates and

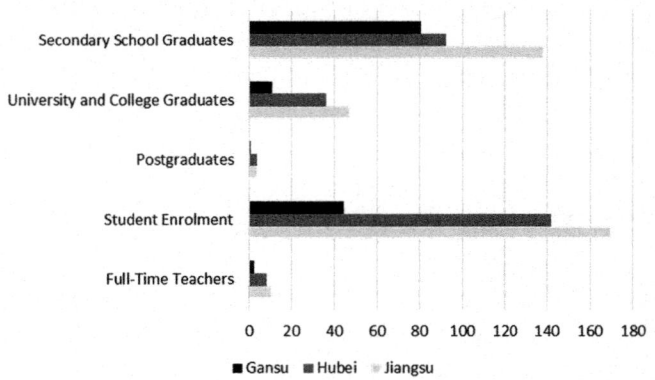

Fig. 5.19 Basic Statistics on Regular Institutions of Higher Education by Region (2013). *Source* Compiled by author using data from China's National Bureau of Statistics. Various statistical yearbooks. *Note* Figures are in 10,000 persons

postgraduates, with Hubei and Gansu following in descending order. However, interestingly, the discrepancy between the number of post-graduates for Jiangsu and Hubei was small. The implication is that both Jiangsu and Hubei may have the same levels of research potential. Nevertheless, the figure for postgraduates for Hubei was taken from those graduating from various institutions of higher education.

Technical Research Topic—Natural Sciences

Figure 5.20 shows that with regard to the natural sciences research, Jiangsu Province experienced the greatest input of funds as well as the largest number of topics under research. The composition of the source of funds for Jiangsu, Hubei and Gansu Province is shown in Fig. 5.21. It can be seen that government is the biggest contributor of funds for S&T research.

Major Indicators of LME by Region

An evaluation of the major indicators of LME by region follows, below.

Figure 5.22 clearly shows that of all the three provinces, Jiangsu has the highest gross output value and the total of new products. The reasons for this are clear.

Firstly, the largest number of scientists and engineers are employed by entrepreneurial-type firms based in the Coastal regions. Secondly, the majority of the research is in the natural sciences where innovation tends to have maximum commercial impact. Thirdly, in a Coastal region such as Jiangsu, government grants and enterprise funds account for the majority of the funding in innovation compared to the other inland provinces of Gansu and Hubei. It is apparent that the post-1978 economic reforms have concentrated economic activity in the Coastal regions. This in turn has created a self-sustaining linkage with knowledge creation activity. Table 5.5 shows the number and value of imported contracts for technology and equipment by province and by region. At a provincial level, Jiangsu substantially leads Hubei and

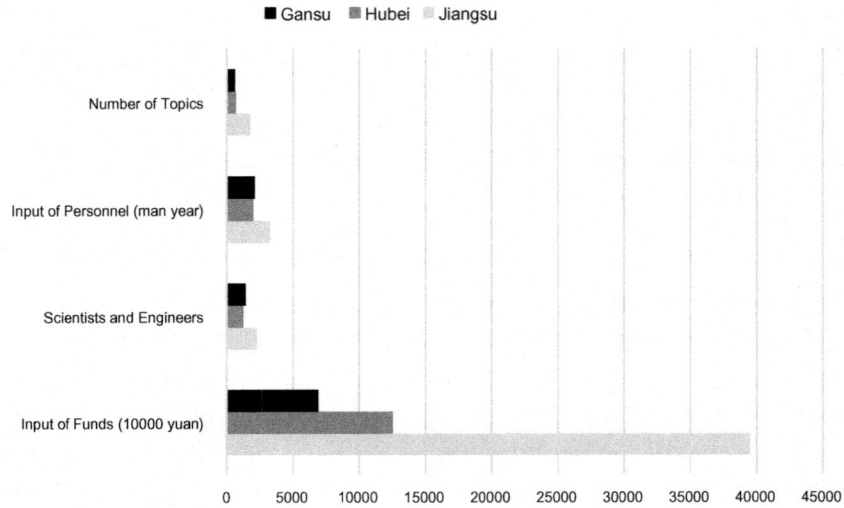

Fig. 5.20 Technical research topic—Natural sciences—2007. *Source* Compiled by the author using data from China's National Bureau of Statistics, China Statistical Yearbook on Science and Technology 2008

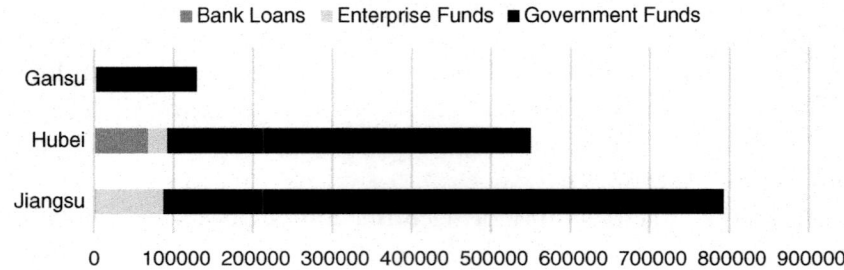

Fig. 5.21 Source of funds for innovation. *Source* Compiled by author using data from China's National Bureau of Statistics. China S&T Statistical Yearbook 2008: S&T Source of Funds by Region (2007*). *Notes* *2006 figure, *Units* 10,000 yuan

Gansu in terms of the number of imported technology and equipment contracts. This feature is repeated at a regional-level analysis encompassing Coastal, Central and Western regions of China. Nevertheless, in the context of academic papers by level of significance, Hubei is not far

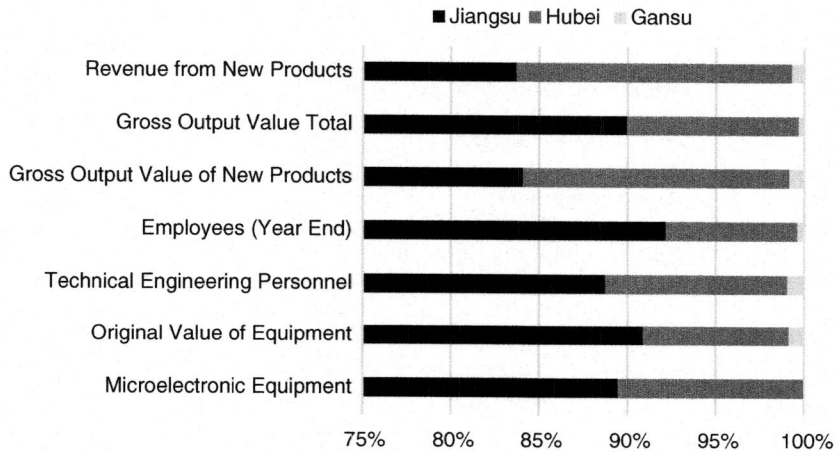

Fig. 5.22 Major Indicators of LME by Region 2007. *Source*: Compiled by author using data from China's National Bureau of Statistics. China S&T Statistical Yearbook 2008: Indicators of LME by Region (2007)

behind Jiangsu although the difference in the significance of academic papers between these two provinces and Gansu is big. This would lead to the view that Coastal and Central provinces have the same level of knowledge creation capacity, but the value in that knowledge creation capacity is greatest in the Coastal provinces.

Private enterprises also seem to play a more significant role in the knowledge and manufacturing sectors in the Coastal provinces than do so in either the Central or the Western provinces. For example, as shown in Table 5.6, the amount of private enterprise funding for R&D was by far the largest in Jiangsu than in either Hubei or Gansu. The R&D funding in Gansu represents that from all sources as no breakdown by firm ownership type is given by China's National Bureau of Statistics. Similarly, the number of enterprises with R&D activities as well as the number of private industrial enterprises is much bigger than in either Hubei or Gansu. This supports the view that the private sector is the key driving force in the knowledge and manufacturing economies of the Coastal provinces of China in comparison with the private sectors in either the Central or the Western provinces. The last row

Table 5.5 Nature of imported technological contracts by Province

	Jiangsu	Hubei	Gansu
Number of imported technology contracts (units)	613	142	11
Value of contracts for technology (US$10,000)	225,945	34,642	970
Value of contracts for equipment (US$10,000)	5614	8	1376
Chinese papers taken by foreign referencing systems by significance	3	5	17
	Coastal	Central	Western
Number of imported technology contracts (units)	8042	832	820
Value of contracts for technology (US$10,000)	1,473,066	107,506	89,928
Value of contracts for equipment (US$10,000)	314,153	44,753	21,508

Source Compiled by author using data from China's National Bureau of Statistics, China Statistical Yearbook on Science and Technology 2008

Table 5.6 Characteristics of Regional Enterprises by Province

	Jiangsu	Hubei	Gansu
Funding for R&D expenditure by enterprises (100 million yuan)	222.41 (private)	36.4711 (private)	66.9194 (all)
Number of enterprises with R&D activities	2091 (all)	575 (private)	579 (all)
Number of private industrial enterprises	28,676	6872	579
Ratio of profits to total industrial costs of private industrial enterprises (%)	6.57	5.89	3.1

Source Compiled by author using data from China's National Bureau of Statistics, China Statistical Datasheet 2014

in Table 5.6 also reveals that costs of production are much higher in Coastal provinces such as Jiangsu. This could be due to tougher environmental and labour laws driving up the costs of production in China's Coastal regions compared to the Central and Western regions.

Case Study Structure

In order to view the effects of the post-1978 reforms with a wider perspective, the case study will be focused on three Chinese provinces [Jiangsu, Hubei and Gansu] on three political periods as follows:

(a) The Maoist period, 1952–1977
(b) Deng Xiaoping's 'Four Modernizations' (agriculture, industry, science/technology, defence) 1978–1995.
(c) The projection of China's Economic Future, 1996–2010. This period includes the Western Development Strategy started in 1999.

Moreover, the impacts of economic development policy on the following components of a competence block will be evaluated:

(a) Physical Infrastructure (roads, railways, telephone and Internet),
(b) Manufacturing,
(c) S&T research parks, high-tech zones and universities, and
(d) Education.

Economic growth in China since the reforms of 1978 has in the main been achieved through growth in exports. Consumption by Chinese consumers has played a contrastingly insignificant part in China's economic growth. However, this has been changing in recent times with government-initiated programmes such as the Western Development Program, and increasing investments in infrastructure by the Chinese government. Figure 5.23 shows how the factors listed in (a)–(d) facilitate the formation of linkages in the Chinese economy and how these linkages interact to influence economic growth in China. Education facilitates knowledge creation, the agglomeration economies of which materialise in universities, research institutes and foreign multinational R&D centres in science and technology parks, high technology development zones and university incubators. Universities and other research institutes established links with industry due to the implementation of government policies in the 1980s and 1990s. These policies tended to

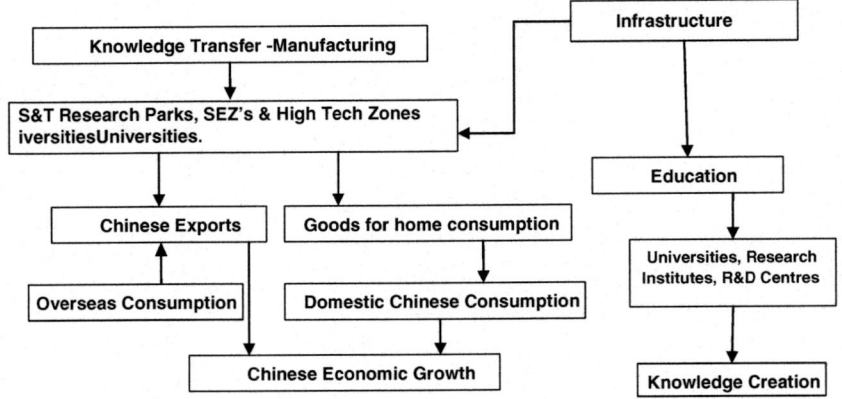

Fig. 5.23 Infrastructure, knowledge transfer & creation, economic growth. *Source* Author

encourage the horizontal integration of knowledge transfer and spillover activities of research institutes with manufacturing industry.

Knowledge transfer and spillover effects occurred because of joint ventures between Chinese companies and foreign multinationals within the SEZs, NHTIDZs and science and technology parks. Physical infrastructure has a role both in knowledge creation and in manufacturing. In the latter case, it facilitates the movement of resources to sites of manufacturing and the movement of final goods to markets. The economic implication of transport infrastructure is that it lowers the costs of production. Physical infrastructure also facilitates the creation of knowledge by facilitating the movement of people. The economic effects of the latter are that knowledge can be disseminated through seminars and workshops. Moreover, the process of innovation and transmission of knowledge is facilitated through the use of technological infrastructure such as the Internet and computers.

Knowledge transfer, spillovers and the manufacture of high-technology goods take place in the high-tech development zones which were set up around the country in the early 1990s. The light manufacturing industry played a role in economic growth through the manufacture of products which are imitations of existing products, and not innovative products. The manufacture of light goods takes place in special economic zones which were created in the first round of economic reforms in the 1980s. It is only recently that the Chinese economy has begun to move on a trajectory of economic growth caused by knowledge creation. This is entirely due to the reform of the educational and R&D sectors which the government focused on in the 1980s and 1990s. The knowledge trajectory of the Chinese economy coincides with the government's 2006–2011 plan objective of economic growth through endogenous harmony and innovation. The case study analysis will begin with Jiangsu which will be followed by case studies of Hubei and Gansu.

Jiangsu

Jiangsu is one of the Coastal provinces of China. Other Coastal provinces and Coastal municipalities include Guangdong, Fujian, Zhejiang, Shandong, Hebei, Liaoning and the municipalities of Shanghai, Beijing and Tianjin. Jiangsu together with the municipality of Shanghai and the province of Zhejiang forms the Chanjiang River system, part of the Yangtze River Delta which is one of the three Coastal innovation systems in China. The other two such innovation systems are the Pearl River Delta and the Bo Hai Sea Rim. The province covers an area of 102,600 km². This area represents approximately 1.1% of China's total land area; its total population is 74 million persons, which is approximately 5.7% of China's total, giving it a population density of 724 persons per km². This province is composed of three regions:

(a) Sunan (Suzhou, Wuxi, Changzhou municipalities),
(b) Subei (Xuzhou, Huaigin, Yancheng and Lianyungang) and,
(c) Suzhong (Nanjing, Zhenjiang, Yangzhou and Nantong).

Of the three regions, Sunan is the more prosperous and Subei the least. In the former, there is a concentration of manufacturing and S&T parks. In Subei, there is a concentration of agriculture. The location of these regions within Jiangsu can be easily visualised from the map in Fig. 5.24.

Fig. 5.24 Map of Jiangsu Province. *Source* http://digital-vector-maps.com

Jiangsu Province has an abundance of features as discussed previously with regard to Tables 5.3 and 5.4. These features included infrastructural, administrative, economic, geographical and entrepreneurial. Industry and agriculture in Jiangsu are very well developed. In 2004, the total agricultural output of Jiangsu (24.2 million tons), almost surpassed the combined total agricultural output of Hubei (21 million tons) and Gansu (4.8 million tons). The common misconception is that a Coastal province such as Jiangsu has no agricultural sector and that all of China's agriculture is based in the Central and Western regions. This is not the case, and neither is this misconception borne out by the data. However, the presence of agriculture and industry in a Coastal province does not necessarily mean that there has been a net transfer of surplus from one sector to the other, and this is true of Jiangsu.

Infrastructure

In addition to having a coastline, Jiangsu has intra-provincial accesses to the sea via the Yangtze River which flows through the province from west to east, as well as the Grand Canal which flows from the north of the province to its south. Ports such as Nantong have easy access to the sea. Moreover, Jiangsu Province benefits from its proximity to Zhejiang and Shanghai which together form the Yangtze River Delta. For example, Suzhou is a city in southern Jiangsu, yet it is only a forty-minute train ride from the centre of Shanghai. Thus, many people who work in Shanghai also live in the towns of Jiangsu. The daily commute is a common feature in any developed region in the world. Therefore, in terms of development, Jiangsu Province is relatively well developed compared to other parts of China. In 2007, the province of Jiangsu invested[2] around forty-six billion RMB for the provision of transport infrastructure. The forty-six billion of investment can be broken down in five ways. Eight billion RMB was used for the construction of railways including the Hu-Tong Railway, Su-Huai Railway, Lian-Yan Railway, Ning-Hang Intercity Railway, Hu-Ning Intercity Railway and the Ning-An Intercity Railway. A proportion of this investment was also used for the expansion of Huai-Yang-Zhen Railway, Zhen-Nan Railway, Xin-Chang Railway and the Ning-Qi Railway. A further eight billion RMB was allocated for port construction, five-hundred million RMB for the construction of passenger and goods stations and two and a half billion RMB for channel construction. A final allocation of twenty-seven billion RMB was made available for highroad construction.

An aggregate assessment of which infrastructural features have been prominent in the various economic phases of provincial and national development can be useful although not as informative as the changes in annual average percentage changes analysis conducted earlier on. It can be seen from Table 5.7 that the periods 1978–1995 and 1996–2004 are clearly the most significant when it comes to physical infrastructure in Jiangsu.

In the period 1978–1995 the railway freight carried, length of highways, number of railway passengers carried feature quite prominently.

Table 5.7 Aggregate Jiangsu infrastructural features

Year	Railway freight	Highway freight	Waterway freight	Business volume of P&T
1949–1977	46,502[a]	7269	82,384	220,993[a]
1978–1995	**488,903**	195,718	482,344	2,499,145
1996–2004	338,575	**301,405**	**755,258**	**25,042,952**
	Export	Imports	Telephone subscribers	Length of railways
1949–1977	47,400[a]		112[a]	**18,036[a]**
1978–1995	4,933,566	2,669,621[a]	1057	13,807
1996–2004	**29,947,570**	**25,339,791**	**11,525**	6817
	Length of highways	Railway passengers	Highway passengers	Waterway passengers
1949–1977	255,453[a]	14,645[a]	36,267	**20,680**
1978–1995	**427,313**	**204,675**	34,297	14,734
1996–2004	399,873	152,001	**570,674**	1065

Source Compiled by author using data from China's National Bureau of Statistics. China Compendium of Statistics 1949–2004
Note Figures denoted by [a]indicates incomplete data for the period under study

However, in the period 1996–2004, highway freight, waterway freight, business volume of post and telecommunications, number of telephone subscribers and the number of highway passengers show the greater aggregate change than in any other period. Indeed, the aggregate number of telephone subscribers in the period 1996–2004 shows a 990% increase compared to that in the period 1978–1995. This is due to the fact that up to the early 1990s, the use of landline phones was restricted to military and party use. In the period 1949–1977, the only features of physical infrastructure of any prominence were the length of railways and the number of waterway passengers transported. Both of these features make sense because at that time, under central planning, the infrastructure of economic development was seen as the railway. The ordinary peasant did not use the highway because he/she did not have access to a car which was only available to members of the party or to the military. It is due to this reason and the river/canal network of the province which may explain why the number of passengers transported by water was greater in the 1949–1977 period than in any other economic period. It can also be noticed that the aggregate length of railways decreases from the first period to the third period. This may be explained by two reasons. Firstly, the implication of the move from central planning to a market-based economy meant that only profitable railways were built and maintained. Secondly, in Jiangsu and other Coastal provinces, a key feature of the post-1978 period was the concentration of infrastructure in the specially designated areas such as the SEZs, S&T parks and technology development zones.

It can be clearly seen from Table 5.7 that the aggregate length of railways in the period 1996–2004 was significantly less than in previous economic periods. This suggests that less railway capacity was added to the provinces stock of railway during this economic period. In fact, during this period, there was only a 0.59% increase in the annual average length of railway lines. Nevertheless, Jiangsu does have a rail network, and it has seven major lines.[3] These include the Jinghu Railway, Longhai Railway, Ninghang Railway, Ninghe Railway, Ningwu Railway, Ningqi Railway and the Xin-Chang Railway. In addition to road and rail infrastructure, Jiangsu Province also has a number of river systems.[4] These include the Grand Canal, the Guanhe River, the Huaihe River, the Qinhuai River, the Shuhe River, the Yangtze River and the Xinyi River. The province also has eight major airports.[5] These include Changzhou Benniu Airport, Lianyungang Baitabi Airport, Nanjing Lukou Airport, Nantong Xingdong Airport, Suzhou Guangfu Airport, Wuxi Shuofang Airport, Xuzhou Guanyin Airport and Yancheng Airport. The close proximity of the province and especially the Sunan part of it to Shanghai gives its resident's access to Shanghai Pudong International Airport and Shanghai Hongqiao Airport. This allows Jiangsu residents easy access to other Chinese and foreign cities, facilitating the formation of communication networks. The majority of the financing of infrastructural projects in recent years resulted from the provincial sharing of costs and bank loans.[6] For example, the Sutong Bridge which is due for completion in 2009 has shared costs. The Sutong Bridge will link Nantong City and Changshu across the Changjiang River at an estimated total cost of US$725.77 million, of which US$ 266.12 million will be collected by Jiangsu Province, Suzhou City and Nantong City in a proportion of 3:1:1.

In Jiangsu Province, the road network is distinguished between highways and expressways. There are ten major highways in, and which pass through, Jiangsu Province.[7] These include Highway G020: Beijing–Fuzhou, Highway G045: Lianyungang–Huerguosi, Highway G055: Shanghai–Chengdu, Highway G065A: Ningbo–Nanjing, Highway G204: Yantai–Shanghai, Highway G205: Shanhaiguan–Guangzhou, Highway G310: Lianyungang–Tianshui, Highway G311: Xuzhou–Xixia, Highway G328: Nanjing–Huai'an, Nanjing Highway Network. In addition to its sprawling highway network, Jiangsu also has ten major expressways.[8] These expressways include the following Beijing–Shanghai, Lianyungang–Suzhou, Nanjing–Changzhou, Nanjing–Hangzhou, Nanjing–Lianyungang, Nanjing–Nantong, Shanghai–Nanjing, Suzhou–Yancheng, Wuxi–Yixing and Xuzhou–Lianyungang.

Manufacturing Industry

By the time the PRC was founded in 1949, Jiangsu Province had established industries. In 1950, the province produced 9.9% of the total industrial output of China.[9] The handicraft, textile and food processing sectors formed the backbone of traditional industry in the province, being located in the urban centres of Sunan such as Wuxi, Nantong and Suzhou. It would be these sectors which would lay the foundations for the development of light industry in Jiangsu in the Mao period from 1952 to 1977. The development of the Sunan region was facilitated by both the development of Shanghai and transportation facilities. In the period immediately preceding the Great Leap Forward, less emphasis was placed on the development of the Coastal provinces, including Jiangsu, due to their vulnerability to enemy attack. Nevertheless, during the Great Leap Forward, decentralisation of central authority took place. Moreover, following Mao's calls for the industrialisation of the countryside, small-scale rural industries took root in Sunan. These small-scale industries revolved around the agricultural sector, mainly in food processing or the production of agricultural machinery. The development of industry in Sunan therefore played a supporting role to agricultural Subei. However, the economic development of Sunan did not continue because of the Cultural Revolution. The region suffered more than the agricultural north due to its embracement of 'capitalistic construction' of enterprises. In the Mao period, the focus of government economic policy was on the development of heavy (chemicals, machinery) and light (textiles) industries through the state-owned enterprise system. Northern Jiangsu (Subei) was less developed than southern Jiangsu (Sunan), but the process of convergence of industrialisation in both parts of the province was driven by the formation of state-owned enterprises.[10] However, at the outset of economic reforms in 1978, it was the municipalities of Sunan which emerged with a stronger industrial base than the municipalities of Subei for two reasons. Firstly, despite the apparent convergence of industrial capacity in both regions of Jiangsu, enterprises in Sunan grew faster. Secondly, the town and village enterprises were significantly and firmly established in Sunan than they were in agricultural Subei. This was due to the fact that in the early 1970s, central government policy shifted towards the development of the Coastal regions through the formation of small-scale rural enterprises.[11] It was at this time that Sunan seized on its historical experience of industrialisation and established town and village enterprises (TVEs) on a large scale. It would be these TVEs which would act as the engines of economic growth following the post-1978 reforms. Bramall (2007) suggests that the success of establishing enterprises in Sunan may be attributable to five factors, of which Sunan has more compared to Subei. These factors included high levels of literacy, enhanced human capital stock, entrepreneurial activity, close proximity to Shanghai and lastly better infrastructure. Subei, on the other hand, has always been dominated by agriculture, and therefore, it has less of a need for more educated and skilled labour. Moreover, it has always been prone to flooding with the subsequent loss of agricultural production.

The post-1978 economic reforms brought with them considerable decentralisation and more empowerment over economic issues for local authorities. It has also been suggested in the literature that a number of factors were in favour of Sunan's economic development.[12] Firstly, local authorities in Sunan have been shown more favour and flexibility with regard to the specifics of central government economic reform policies to be implemented. Secondly, local authorities in Sunan have been more tenacious in the application of economic reforms. Finally, Sunan had non-state TVEs, which were ready to take advantage of the economic reforms as well as the appropriate conditions for taking advantage of the influx of FDI. In contrast, most, if not all, of the interior provinces' economic landscape was dominated by state-owned enterprises. Thus, it can be seen that Jiangsu Province had a predisposed inevitability about its chances of prospering from China's economic reforms due to the evolved industrial base which already existed in the province at the start of the reforms. If the rudiments of entrepreneurship and a substantial industrial base had not already existed in the Coastal provinces at the time of the reforms, then it would have taken longer for the reforms to effect economic growth in China. It is quite interesting to note that at the start of the economic reforms, Jiangsu not only had a prominent manufacturing sector but also a peripheral agricultural base as well.

S&T Research Parks, High-Tech Zones

The geographical distribution and density of science and technology research parks in China falls moving from the Coastal region to the Central region and then to the Western region. In Jiangsu Province there are four of the fifty-three designated science and technology research parks. These include Changzhou Hi-Tech Industry Development Zone, Nanjing New & High Technology Industry Development Zone, Wuxi National Hi-Tech Industrial Development Zone; and the Suzhou Hi-Tech Industry Development Zone. The data in Table 11.5 suggests that the S&T parks in Wuxi and Suzhou contribute significantly to the Jiangsu and Chinese economy in terms of export value, with exports contributing the most value in USD terms. In terms of export value, the most successful high-technology development zones have been Nanjing and Changzhou.

As can be seen from Table 5.8, the increase in export value for these two zones between 2004 and 2013 was 3570 and 833%, respectively. The Suzhou zone was set up in 1992, and most of the initial investment was of Japanese MNC origin. However, this initial investment was followed by investment from MNCs from Hong Kong, Taiwan, Europe

Table 5.8 Jiangsu science and technology research parks statistics 2004 and 2013

S&T Park	Number of enter-prises (2013)	Total business income 2004 (10,000 USD)	Taxes Income (10,000 USD)	Total value of import and export (10,000 USD)	Export value 2004 (10,000 USD)	Export value 2013 (10,000 USD)	Increase in export value (%)	Foreign invested projects	Value of FDI invest-ment (10,000 USD)
Nanjing High-Technology DZ	365	67,847	5367	95,969	21,887	803,245.974	3570	44	5207
Changzhou High-Technology DZ	976	68,965	16,380	115,265	63,676	594,232.7	833	**104**	16,593
Suzhou High-Technology DZ	1234	172,951	21,519	1,934,793	1,090,479	2,389,238.5	119	172	39,689
Wuxi High-Technology DZ	1100	160,646	23,265	1,036,614	511,952	1,863,965.1	264	252	62,321

Source Compiled by author using data from China's National Bureau of Statistics. China Statistical Datasheet 2014 and China Statistical Yearbook 2005

and the USA. There are over three hundred foreign-funded ventures in the zone with a number of high-profile MNCs locating and investing in the Suzhou Park as follows:

(a) **USA**—Motorola, Du Pont, Upjohn,
(b) **Japan**—Fujitsu, Matsushita, Sony, Seiko and Epson,
(c) **Taiwan**—Asus and Acer,
(d) the **Netherlands**—Philips

The majority of research and production in the zone are in the areas of electronic communications, new materials, chemicals and precision machinery. Typical products manufactured within the zone focus on electronics, computing devices and accessories including electronic sensors, computer cameras and LCDs. In addition to placing production facilities within the zone, a number of MNCs have established R&D facilities which employ indigenous Chinese skilled labour. For example, Motorola's 1993 investment of US$120 million had grown to US$3 billion by 1999, and of this US$150 million was focused on R&D. One of the best features of the Suzhou Park is its geographical location, embedded in the Yangtze River Delta, with close proximity to the coast, access to advanced infrastructure, freshwater availability from lake Taihu and enhanced human resources. The effect of the agglomeration of resources (physical, capital and human) within the Suzhou High Technology Development Zone is the lower costs of manufacturing and R&D associated with the nature and availability of infrastructure within the zones and surrounding areas.

Research by Sutherland (2005) suggests that the role of science and technology parks in China is as the conduits of technology transfer and locations of production of high-technology goods rather than centres of innovation. However, it is clear from the discussion in Chap. 3, Volume 2, that this may be a misconception, especially if China's S&T parks are viewed from the perspective of the Triple Helix Model of innovation. In the Western context, S&T parks are conduits through which innovation and knowledge creation are transferred from in-house R&D institutions and universities to commercial enterprises for industrial production. As Sutherland (2005) points out, it is therefore misleading to suggest that

Table 5.9   Number and specialisation of enterprises by region 2006

Number of enterprises	Jiangsu	Hubei	Gansu
Number of enterprises	2501	**489**	**86**
Number of electronic and telecoms equipment manufacturing enterprises	1330	119	13
Number of Aircraft and spacecraft manufacturing enterprises	11	6	3
Number of office equipment manufacturing enterprises	184	14	0
Number of medical treatment instrument and meter manufacturing enterprises	520	87	17
Number of medical and pharmaceutical manufacturing enterprises	456	263	53

Source Compiled by author using data from China's Statistics Yearbook on High Technology Industry 2007

the S&T parks have created a mechanism for the commercialisation and mass production of domestic Chinese knowledge creation. Nevertheless, due to the government's reforms of the education and R&D sectors, this conception of indigenous knowledge creation is changing.

Moreover, in China, the commercialisation of knowledge creation in China is occurring in S&T parks such as Zhongguancun in Beijing as previously discussed in Chap. 2, Volume 2. It is also the case that universities have created incubators to create a company to commercialise an in-house innovation. With regard to the need for the transfer of knowledge and the nature of that knowledge, Li-Hua (2004) has found that in well-developed provinces like Jiangsu, there is a need for tacit knowledge such as management skills, whereas in the least developed provinces, e.g. Gansu, there is a need for explicit knowledge such has technological 'know how'. This may be explained by the fact that Jiangsu is a technically advanced province requiring management 'know how', but Gansu is not as technologically advanced. The technological superiority of the enterprises specialising in the manufacture of technological intensive equipment is also evidenced by the greater number of these enterprises in Jiangsu compared to either Hubei or Gansu, with Hubei coming in second position. However, the disparity in the number of technological-focused enterprises is greatest between Jiangsu and Hubei and Gansu. These features can be clearly seen from Table 5.9.

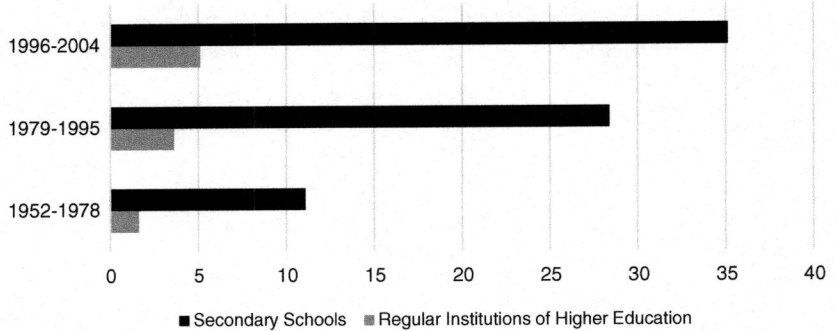

Fig. 5.25 Jiangsu full-time teachers—Three periods. *Source* Compiled by author using data from China's National Bureau of Statistics. China Compendium of Statistics 1949–2004. *Note* The figures in the graph represent an aggregate for each period. Enrolments are per 10,000 persons

Education

The central government's dual-track nine-year compulsory education policy has been implemented very well in Jiangsu Province. The province has a layered education system with preschool, primary, secondary, university, vocational and adult education, with approximately 15% of the population in some form of education.[13] Furthermore, within the province, there are ninety-four universities and colleges with over two hundred thousand students, 2800 scientific research and technology institutes, two hundred secondary vocational schools and six thousand secondary and technical schools.

Moreover, there are over seven hundred thousand adults studying or training at universities and schools in the province.[14] The province is, therefore, well endowed with educational infrastructure, and it has the financial resources to provide such educational resources due to the fact that the province accounts for 10% of China's GDP. A qualitative analysis of the provincial provision of full-time teachers and student enrolments in the three economic and political periods follows. Figure 5.25 shows that the growth in the aggregate number of full-time teachers in secondary schools and higher institutes has been increasing over the three periods with significant growth occurring in the reform period in the number of full-time teachers at secondary schools. This qualitative analysis clearly shows that, in the reform era, government policy has focused on the increase in supply of teachers to all the major sectors of higher education, but more significantly to secondary schools. The significant increase in the number of full-time teachers to secondary schools is in line with the governments' guarantee of giving each child nine years of compulsory education. Nevertheless, although central government has a clearly stated goal with regard to secondary education at the provincial level, the story is different. Typically, a child in a Western province such as Gansu is unlikely to get as much education as a child in a Coastal province such as Jiangsu. This may be due to specific reasons such as providing a livelihood for an extended family, the costs associated with a longer period of learning, likelihood of gaining employment on graduation and the remoteness of the region from the hub of economic activity. Moreover, the funding for education in Jiangsu is more likely more generous than in poorer provinces.

Furthermore, the quality of learning in the remote provinces is also affected by the availability of qualified teachers, the sparsely populated and mountainous landscape. Clearly, the best and brightest teachers will be more attracted to working in a more developed province where the salaries will be higher. Due to its prosperous status, the demand for

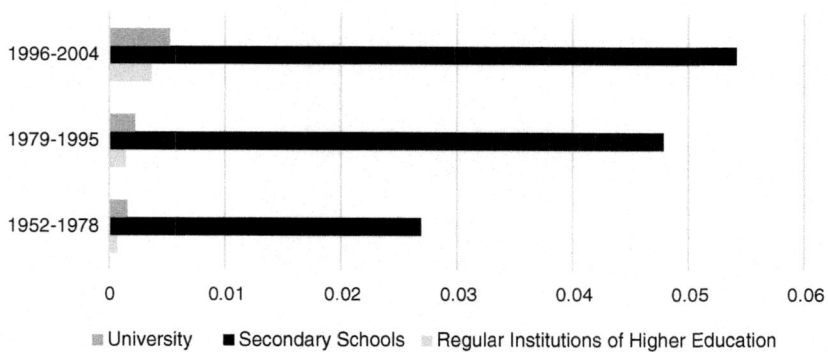

Fig. 5.26 Jiangsu student enrolments—Three periods. *Source* Compiled by author using data from China's National Bureau of Statistics. China Compendium of Statistics 1949–2004. *Note* The figures in the graph represent an aggregate for each period. Enrolments are per 10,000 persons

educated workers is likely to be higher in Jiangsu. Figure 5.26 shows that the biggest increases in student enrolments have been at secondary schools followed by student enrolments at universities. The increase in the former has been more pronounced after the start of economic reforms in 1978 whereas the increase in the latter is more pronounced in the period 1996–2004. In 2004, Jiangsu had the highest number of institutions of higher learning with 105 universities with an annual intake of over 700,000 students. Furthermore, the universities in Jiangsu accept exchange students from over 100 countries from over 300 universities. This is facilitated by the ease of access to airports with domestic and international destinations. A great deal of interaction, therefore, takes place between Chinese students and foreign students. These interactions facilitate the exchange and transfer of knowledge and lead to enhanced knowledge creation in Chinese universities.

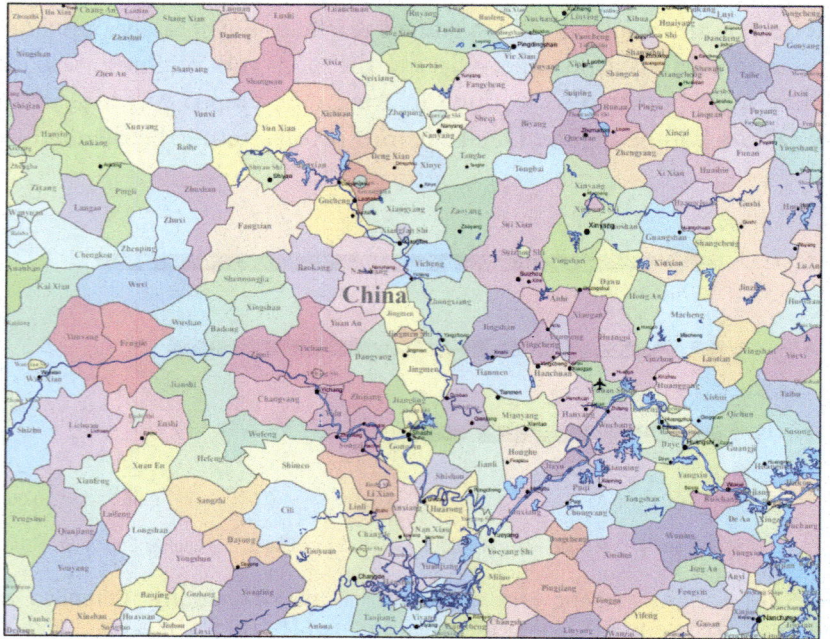

Fig. 5.27   Map of Hubei Province. *Source* http://digital-vector-maps.com

Hubei

Hubei is one of China's central provinces in conjunction with Henan, Hunan, Jiangxi, Anhui, Guangxi and Shaanxi. Like other Western and Central provinces, Hubei is landlocked without a coast. However, it has access to the sea via a river system unlike the Western provinces. Nevertheless, Hubei does not form any kind of innovation and entrepreneurial system like its Coastal neighbours. However, Hubei has an area of 186,000 km² or 1.9% of the total landmass of China; and its provincial population is 60.16 million, giving it a population density of 323 persons per km². A map of the province is shown in Fig. 5.27. The map shows the distribution of urban centres in the province.

Infrastructure

Tables 5.3 and 5.4 showed that, compared to Jiangsu or Gansu, Hubei is superior in terms of infrastructural capacity to the other provinces because it has:

(a) A greater length of railway track and highways,
(b) A greater railway passenger traffic and
(c) A Greater use of the highways for freight traffic.

Nevertheless, the implication of Hubei's large infrastructural capacity is that it is a 'transit' province through which the physical factors of production (resources and labour) are moved from the Western provinces to the centres of manufacturing in the Coastal provinces, rather than the province being a centre of manufacturing itself.

Hubei has a number of infrastructural features.[15] Firstly, Hubei is traversed by the Yangtze River, and the province has two major ports which are Wuhan and Huangshi. Both ports have a capacity to berth vessels with a capacity of up to 5000 tons. Secondly, the province has five major railway lines. These include the Jiaozuo–Zhicheng line, the Shanghai–Wuhan line, the Wuhan–Chengdu line, the Beijing–Kowloon

Table 5.10 Aggregate Hubei infrastructural features

Hubei	Railway freight	Highway freight	Waterway freight	Business volume of P&T
1949–1977		8783	89,223	80,533
1978–1995	**687,159**	26,046	**375,416**	1,393,455
1996–2004	494,338	**51,016**	225,312	**9,556,015**
	Export	Imports	Telephone subscribers	Length of railways
1949–1977	180,972	5911	62	
1978–1995	2,360,936	756,606	620	**31,464**
1996–2004	**3,134,451**	**1,433,562**	**4574**	16,953
	Length of highways	Railway passengers	Highway passengers	Waterway passengers
1949–1977			18,845	21,901
1978–1995	**885,241**	159,977	**168,169**	**49,098**
1996–2004	566,348	**174,584**	140,436	7823

Source Compiled by author using data from China's National Bureau of Statistics. China Compendium of Statistics 1949–2004
Note Figures denoted by ᵃ indicates incomplete data for the period under study
Units of Measurement: Freight (10,000 tons), Length (10,000 km), Passengers (10,000 persons) Imports/Exports(USD10,000), Telephone Subscribers (10,000 subscribers), Business Volume of P&T (10000 yuan)

line, and the Beijing–Guangzhou line. As part of the tenth five-year plan, the Shashi–Yueyang and the Chongqing–Huaihua lines are under construction. The central government is also planning a third line which will traverse the banks of the Yangtze River connecting the provinces of Sichuan, Hubei, Jiangxi, Anhui, Jiangsu, Chongqing and Shanghai. Thirdly, there are 118 highways within Hubei and 8 highways which traverse it. The central government is also planning in the tenth five-year plan to build two highway projects connecting the cities of Nanning and Shanghai and Zhuhai and Beijing, both of which will traverse Hubei. Fourthly, with regard to Civil Aviation, Hubei has over six major airports which include Wuhan, Shashi and Sanxia. The airport at Wuhan is the largest in Hubei, and each week over two hundred flights on average are cleared to land there. The airport has capacity for over four million passengers. There is also an air link between Wuhan and Hong Kong, but this has not given Hubei the same kind of prosperity that Jiangsu has. Finally, the province derives electricity from three major power stations—Gezhouba, Danjiangkou and the Three Gorges Hydroelectric Stations. There is also a gas pipeline, which runs from Chongqing to Wuhan.

In Table 5.10, it can be clearly seen that with regard to the physical infrastructural features of Hubei, the periods 1978–1995 and 1996–2004 are the most significant. Despite the Mao periods comparably long time span, the 27-year period from 1949 to 1977, there was little effect on the physical infrastructural features of Hubei in aggregate terms. Within this context, the period 1978–1995 showed the biggest aggregate increases in railway freight, waterway freight, length of railways, length of highways and in the number of waterway and highway passengers transported.

Nevertheless, it was the period 1996–2004 which showed the biggest aggregate change in the statistics of variables of real economic significance such as the business volume of post and telecommunications, provincial imports and exports, highway freight and passengers transported by the railways. Furthermore, it was in the 8-year period 1996–2004 that the number of telephone subscribers in Hubei increased in aggregate terms by over 600% from the previous economic period of 1978–1995. As previously discussed, Hubei showed the largest annual average percentage increases with regard waterway freight and highway passengers.

With regard to telecommunications infrastructure, the number of Internet users in Hubei Province in January 2005 amounted to just 4.6%, or 2.7 million persons, of the population. Moreover, at the end of 2005, there were 12 million fixed line phone connections and 14 million mobile phone subscribers out of a total population of 60 million. This means that 43% of the population of Hubei has access to some form of telecommunications. These figures imply that for at least 57% of the population, communication in Hubei is likely to be face-to-face, and this is the way in which knowledge will be exchanged in the province. The exchange of information in Hubei will thus take longer than in an environment where telecommunications infrastructure is plentiful. Furthermore, in order to make up for the lack of telephones and Internet connections, and in order to facilitate human–human interactions and the transfer and creation of knowledge, more physical infrastructure is required, linking villages to villages, villages to towns and towns to cities. However, this interpretation may be too restrictive because a concentration of Internet availability even with reduced reliability, i.e. in universities, cannot be ruled out.

Manufacturing Industry

In terms of industry, the province of Hubei can be segmented into three regions.[16] The northern industrial region is composed of the cities of Xiangfan and Shiyan, with leading industries including electronics, car production and the manufacture of light goods. The Coastal industrial region is composed of the cities of Wuhan, Huangshi and Erzhou. The industries in this region can be broken down into the following categories—chemical and building, textile, metallurgy and engineering. The Western industrial region is composed of the cities of Yichang, Jingmen and Jingzhou. The industries in this region can be broken down into the following categories—electricity generation, light industry and electronic manufacturing. The major industries in Hubei include textiles, shipbuilding, motor vehicles and chemicals and construction materials. The focus of industrial activity in the province is centred on heavy industry, more so than in Jiangsu province. This fact may also explain why the concentration of physical infrastructure is greater in Hubei than it is in Jiangsu. Moreover, due to the fact that Hubei province is rich in mineral resources, it is the heart of the Chinese iron and steel industry. One of the most well-known steel firms, the Wuhan Iron and Steel Corporation, is present in Wuhan. There is also a synergy surrounding the activities (prospecting, construction, smelting and rolling) around this industry in Hubei Province. With regard to motor vehicle manufacture, the Dongfeng Automobile Company and the Aeolux Automotive Company are prominent in Hubei. The car industry in Hubei is forecasted to produce over 900,000 cars by the year 2010. Textile manufacturing and processing is also a prominent industry in Hubei, with a diverse range of products (silk, wool and cotton) and activities (dyeing, printing and material processing). At this point, it would be useful to note that it was much easier to set up SEZs and high-technology development zones in the Coast regions than in the inland provinces due to the legacy of the reliance of the state on heavy industry has the vehicle of economic development in the pre-reform years.

S&T Research Parks, High-Tech Zones

In Hubei Province, there are four main hi-technological development zones.[17] Firstly, there is the Wuhan East Lake New Technology Development Zone. Over three hundred foreign invested enterprises, including Xerox, Siemens, NEC, NKF and Philips, have set up operations in this zone in order to develop high-tech industries. The most prominent industries set up in this zone are software, laser and optical cable communications. Within the zone, there is an integration of knowledge creation, knowledge transfer, knowledge commercialisation and infrastructural capacity. In this regard, the zone hosts the Wuhan Post and Telecommunications Science Research Institute, the Wuhan Changfei Optical Fiber and Cable Company and the Wuhan Huaruan Software Park. Moreover, within the zone, there are twenty-three institutions of higher learning, fifty-six research institutes and twenty state-owned large- and medium-term enterprises and four nationally recognised centres of technology. The zone also houses five enterprises with revenues of over 100 million yuan. Thus, it becomes possible to identify the knowledge linkages resulting from knowledge creation giving rise to agglomeration economies—an artificial area has been created in which there is already an existing concentration of universities and institutes of research, providing skilled labour for knowledge creation to which commercial firms, offering opportunities for the transfer of foreign knowledge and skills to Chinese firms and workers, have been attracted through preferential policies and investment in physical infrastructures such as ease of access to roads, airports, railways, energy and sewage treatment facilities, with the specific purpose of the commercialisation of knowledge creation. It is specifically stated by the local government of Hubei that[18]:

In East Lake Development Zone, a number of universities and institutes, which are engaged in teaching or researching opto-electronics & information subjects, are coupled with many renowned opto-electronics & information companies, both home and abroad.

The second high-technology zone is the Xiangfan Hi-Tech Development Zone. This zone focuses on the manufacture of optical glass and is itself divided into a number of zones. The third zone is the Wuhan Economic & Technological Development Zone. This zone was set up in 1991, and in 2000, it was also designated as an export-processing zone. There are a number of physical infrastructural features associated with this zone.[19] The zone is located on the north bank of the Yangtze River. The Shanghai–Lhasa and Beijing–Zhujiang highways dissect the zone. The zone will be connected to the Beijing–Guangzhou and Beijing–Kowloon railway. Thus, an infrastructure system has been constructed with regard to road, railway, energy, telecoms, water sources and a sewage system and cargo port. In this zone, investments are concentrated in a number of sectors including automobile components, food, engineering, light industries and bioengineering. A large number of foreign companies have set up operations in the zone with countries represented including the USA, Japan, France, Sweden, Germany, the Netherlands, Belgium, Thailand, Singapore, Hong Kong, Taiwan and Chinese mainland companies. In Hubei, other zones include the Xiangfan Motor Industry Development Zone, the Yichang Huting Economic and Technological Development Zone and the Wuhan Dunkou Light Vehicle Development Zone. There are also high-technology development zones in Yichang and Xiaogan. Finally, the province houses the Wuhan Wujiashan, a high-technology development zone which was approved by the government in 2000. The zone was set up to entice Taiwanese and foreign investment in technology. Enterprises within the zone are subject to local government policies. There are a number of infrastructural features of relevance to this zone.[20] Firstly, the zone is 12 km from Wuhan city centre. Secondly, the zone is 7 km from Hankou Railway Station. Thirdly, the zone is 20 km from the Qingshan Foreign Trade Wharves. Fourthly, the zone is 18 km from the Wuhan Tianhe International Airport. Finally, the zone is within easy access of 8 major highways. In

Table 5.11 Hubei science and technology research parks statistics 2013

Development area	Number of enterprises (unit)	Number of persons engaged (person)	Total income (10,000 yuan)	Exports (10,000 US dollars)
Wuhan Donghu new technology development zone	2883	419,022	65,172,074.22	1,047,287.911
Xiangfan high-tech industrial development zone	622	138,333	20,688,463	79,835.5
Yichang High-tech industrial development zone	301	110,354	16,978,731.67	96,336.881
Xiaogan high-tech industrial development zone	345	76,737	8,346,953.066	18,210.728

Source Compiled by author using data from China's National Bureau of Statistics. China Statistical Datasheet 2014

addition to the zones of innovation already discussed, as of September 2004, there were thirty-eight development zones at the prefecture level and twenty-four at the provincial level.

Table 5.11 shows that Hubei has the technology development area with the largest number of enterprises, Wuhan Donghu New Technology Development Zone, compared to Jiangsu. Hubei also has the largest number of enterprises operating in all its high-technology zones compared to Jiangsu. However, in terms of export value, Jiangsu's export from all of its high-technology development zones is US$201 billion, but for Hubei, it is only US$12 billion. This could mean that the enterprises in the Jiangsu high-technology development zones produce more technologically valuable products or that the enterprises are simply bigger in size than those in Hubei.

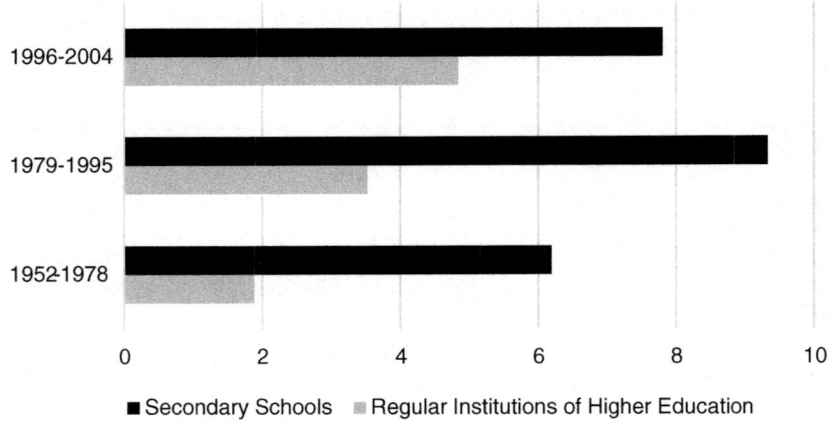

Fig. 5.28 Hubei full-time teachers weighted by provincial population—Three periods. *Source* Compiled by author using data from China's National Bureau of Statistics. China Compendium of Statistics 1949–2004. *Note* The figures in the graph represent an aggregate for each period. Enrolment measured per 10,000 persons

Education

In 2004, the number of students enrolled in regular institutions of higher education, secondary schools and universities in Hubei Province were 89,200, 4,517,200 and 1,483,000, respectively. However, as can be seen from Fig. 5.28, the largest aggregate increase in the number of full-time teachers in secondary schools occurred in the period 1979–1995. This was followed by the period 1996–2004. On the other hand, the growth of full-time teachers in regular institutions of higher education was increasing over the three periods but at a lower level compared to the growth of full-time teachers in secondary schools. The smallest aggregate increases in the numbers of full-time teachers in secondary schools and regular institutions of higher education occurred in the period 1949–1978. Nevertheless, the largest average annual percentage increase in full-time teachers employed at secondary schools was 17.37% and occurred in the period 1953–1976, the pre-reform years. Changes in the aggregate levels of teachers employed full-time can be misleading.

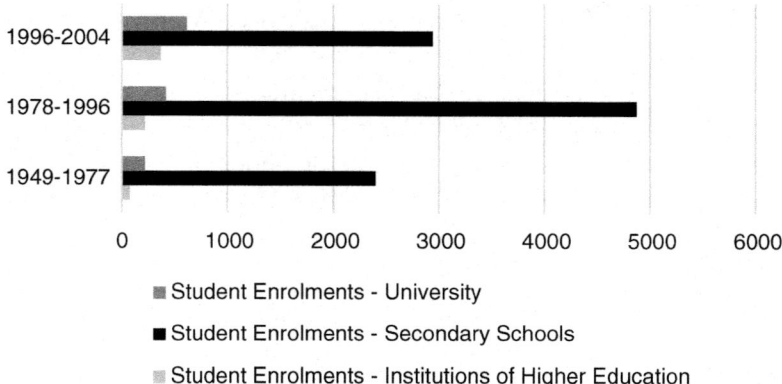

1996-2004
1978-1996
1949-1977

0   1000   2000   3000   4000   5000   6000

■ Student Enrolments - University
■ Student Enrolments - Secondary Schools
▨ Student Enrolments - Institutions of Higher Education

Fig. 5.29 Hubei student enrolments—Three periods. *Source* Compiled by author using data from China's National Bureau of Statistics. China Compendium of Statistics 1949–2004. *Note* The figures in the graph represent an aggregate for each period. Enrolment measured per 10,000 persons

Figure 5.29 shows the aggregate changes in student enrolments at secondary schools, universities and regular institutions of higher education over the three historic periods. However, in this case, although the number of students enrolled at secondary schools on an aggregate basis is largest in the period 1978–1995 than in any other period, the number of students enrolled in universities and institutions of higher education is greatest in the period 1996–2004. Nevertheless, if one looks at the annual average percentage increases in student enrolments, the picture is a different one. Indeed, in the period 1979–1995, there was an annual average percentage decrease of −1.77% in the number of students enrolled at secondary schools. Similarly, the annual average percentage increase of 23.96% for university enrolments is beaten by that in the period 1949–1978 [24.23%]. In the period 1949–1977, education was seen as the key to an innovation-led economy despite the fact that central planning dictated that economic growth was not competitively driven by companies seeking to compete with each other through innovation for an abundant consumer market.

However, innovation in this period was restricted to the military sector and to process design. Moreover, education had a distinctly political purpose, and university education, specifically, was disrupted by political upheavals such as the Great Leap Forward and more significantly during the Cultural Revolution.

The major universities in Hubei include China University of Geosciences, Huazhong Normal University, Huazhong University of Science and Technology, Hubei Institute of Education, Hubei Institute for Nationalities, Hubei Normal University, Hubei University, Wuhan University of Technology, Wuhan University and the Zhongnan University of Economics and Law.

Gansu

Gansu is one of China's Western provinces. Other provinces classified as Western provinces include Xinjiang, Tibet, Qinghai, Yunnan and Sichuan. Gansu is landlocked, although the Yellow, Wei, Tao, Bailong,

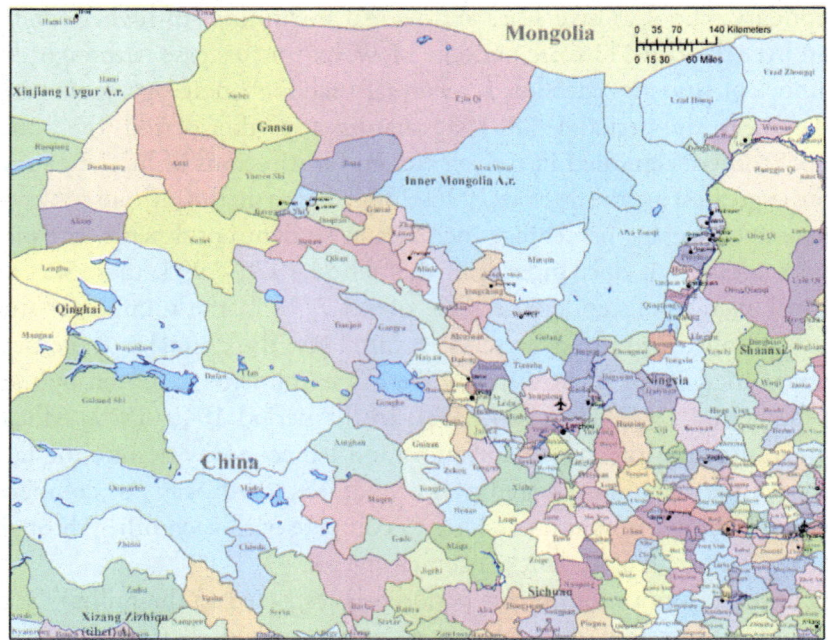

Fig. 5.30 Map of Gansu Province. *Source* http://digital-vector-maps.com

Hei and Shule Rivers pass through the province. However, water transport in the province remains an insignificant mode of transport for both commercial and non-commercial activities. Nevertheless, in landlocked Hubei, the use of water transport is more significant than in Gansu. Unlike Jiangsu, Gansu does not form any form of innovation system, such as the Yangtze River Delta, in conjunction with other provinces.

Lanzhou is the provincial capital of Gansu, although other significant towns include Jinchuan, Baiyin, Tianshui and Yumen. The province has a land area of 454,000 km^2 or approximately 4.73% of the total landmass of China. It has a population of 26.1 million persons comprising 2% of China's land mass, giving it a population density of 57 persons per sq.km in 2004. A map of the province is shown in Fig. 5.30. Figure 5.30 shows clearly that, compared to Jiangsu or Hubei, there are not many recognised urban centres (only three) in Gansu. The province comprises 80 counties, and of these twenty are government-designated minority counties. This is because Gansu is a multi-ethnic province. There are also fourteen at county city level. The eighty counties are further aggregated into five specific regions within the province.[21] These regions include Ganlin (west), Longnan (south), Longxi, Hexi (north and the biggest of the regions) and Zhonghu (middle).

The province has a number of spatial and geographical features. Firstly, it is landlocked, and its only access to water is through the Yellow River. However, waterways do not feature as a major form of transport in Gansu as it does in Hubei and Jiangsu. Secondly, a large proportion of the population specialises in agricultural production. Thirdly, the province has a low population density, and due to agricultural specialisation, the population is sparsely spread. Fourthly, the terrain of the province is hilly, and agricultural production takes place through the use of 'terraces'. Fifthly, the provinces elevation is up to 3000 m above sea level, and 15% of the land is desert with 55% either hilly or plateau in nature. Finally, the province is home to a number of China's ethnic minorities, and this in itself makes Gansu distinct from both Jiangsu and Hubei. Neither of the latter provinces have a significant minority population. With regard to intra-provincial development in the reform period, Ma et al. (2006) have found that cities in Gansu have benefited from the economic reforms, but rural areas and minority counties have not.

Infrastructure

The railway is a significant mode of transport in Gansu with Lanzhou featuring as a major transport point. It is at Lanzhou that four rail routes intersect. These include Lanzhou–Qinghai, Lanzhou–Baotao, Lanzhou–Xinjiang and Lanzhou–Longhai. One of these railway routes links Gansu with the port of Lianyungang in Jiangsu Province. The international railway which links China to Europe also runs through Gansu, and the main freight hub for this railway is found in Lanzhou. Perhaps better use of this facility could bring greater prosperity to Gansu. A new dual-track railway line has been proposed to link Gansu with Shaanxi Province, cutting travel time between the two provinces by up to three hours. These types of infrastructure linkages by reducing travel times between destinations increase the probability of face-to-face interactions and the frequency of commercial interactions and thus increase the economic density of space.

In addition to its role as a railway hub, Lanzhou is also the road hub of Gansu with five major roads arising from the city itself, linking Gansu with other provinces. Furthermore, the only airport in the province is at Lanzhou although it is some distance from the city itself. However, airlines fly to 35 destinations from the city. This is in sharp contrast to Jiangsu and Hubei each of which have a number of airports.

Other infrastructural features within Gansu include the Liujiaxia hydropower station and oil and gas pipelines passing through the province delivering oil and gas to other parts of China. The main problem with conducting a comparative case study or analysis of China's provinces is the lack of both the consistency and availability of data for the same variables. This makes a cross-sectional provincial analysis of infrastructural variables extremely difficult. This is especially true for Gansu as can be seen from the table above; four out of twelve data sets are not available. However, on the basis of the data in Table 5.12, some firm assertions can be made. These are as follows:

Table 5.12 Gansu infrastructural features

Gansu	Railway freight	Highway freight	Waterway freight	Business volume of P&T
1949–1977	60,467[a]	9891[a]	NO DATA	69,505[a]
1978–1995	**128,748**	56,105	NO DATA	319,335
1996–2004	110,076	**65,561**	NO DATA	**4,053,939**
	Export	Imports	Telephone subscribers	Length of railways
1949–1977	8735[a]	NO DATA	NO DATA	43,416
1978–1995	256,288	71,391[a]	176[a]	**35,719**
1996–2004	**462,893**	**253,216**	**1977**	17,649
	Length of highways	Railway passengers	Highway passengers	Waterway passengers
1949–1977	564,583	NO DATA	NO DATA	NO DATA
1978–1995	**609,484**	NO DATA	NO DATA	NO DATA
1996–2004	343,464	NO DATA	NO DATA	NO DATA

Source Compiled using data from China's National Bureau of Statistics. China Compendium of Statistics 1949–2004
Note Figures denoted by [a] indicates incomplete data for the period under study
Units of Measurement: Freight (10,000 tons), Length (10,000 km), Passengers (10,000 persons) Imports/Exports(USD10,000), Telephone Subscribers (10,000 subscribers), Business Volume of P&T (10000 yuan)

(a)   The aggregate growth in the length of highways and railways was more significant in the period 1978–1995 than in any other period. However, the annual average percentage changes in highway and railway length paint a very different picture. In the period 1978–1995, the length of highways only increased by an annual average of 0.13%. The largest increase in the length of highways occurred in the period 1953–1976. Railway length in the province also showed the largest annual average increase of 39.56% in the same period. This was the period associated with the 'Third Front' program, the Soviet model of heavy industrialisation, equality for all and the failed 'railways lead to prosperity' philosophy.

(b)   The number of telephone subscribers even in the period 1996–2004 is extremely low in aggregate terms. This indicates that it would be difficult for knowledge linkages to form through the exchange of ideas. Therefore, people will cling to traditional modes of communication such as writing letters by themselves or on behalf of themselves by others. Nevertheless, in the period 1997–2004, the average annual percentage increase in telephone subscribers was 30.61%. This was the highest percentage increase for all the three provinces—Hubei [19.52%] and Jiangsu [24.44%]. Furthermore, at the end of 2005, there were 5.5 million fixed line phone users compared to 4 million mobile phone users out of a provincial population of 25 million. The implication is that only 38% of the population of Gansu had access to some form of telecommunications. The telecommunications' penetration rate was 75% for Jiangsu and 43% for Hubei.

(c)   The aggregate increase in highway freight was more significant in the period 1996–2004 than in any other political period. However, when the annual average percentage changes are looked at the picture is very different. The largest annual average percentage increase in highway freight of 20.46% occurred in the period 1979–1995. The percentage increase in the period 1997–2004 was only 4.31%.

(d)   The aggregate increase in railway freight was more significant in the period 1978–1996. Nevertheless, the largest annual average percentage increase in freight of 30.44% occurred in the period 1953–1976. This is the period associated with the 'railways lead to prosperity' philosophy. The next largest percentage increase in freight traffic of 7.77% occurred in the period 1997–2004. This period is associated with the 'Western Development' Program, which was initiated in 1999.

(e)   Aggregate figures for imports, exports and business volume of post and telecommunications were more significant in the period 1996–2004. However, the annual average percentage increases in imports [40.42%] and exports [37.49%] occurred in the period 1979–2005. The largest annual average percentage increase in the business volume of post and telecommunications occurred in the period 1997–2004.

Manufacturing Industry

Industrial production in Gansu takes place either in the southern industrial region comprising Tianshui or in the central industrial region, which comprises Lanzhou, Baiyun and Jinchuan. Industries of significance in Gansu include the petrochemical industry, production of machinery especially for the petrochemical industry and the textile industry. Indeed, the major exports of Gansu are garments, machinery and petrochemical products. The nearest port to Gansu is Tianjin, and it is approximately 2000 km from the province. The export of goods manufactured in the province to overseas markets is costlier in terms of transportation costs than is the export of similar goods from the Coastal provinces. It would therefore seem sensible for export manufacturing to be located in the Coastal regions and for mineral resources to be transported from China's interior to the coast for manufacturing to be facilitated. However, the problem here lies in the fact that a combination of excessive demand and infrastructure bottlenecks means that it is often cheaper for the Coastal provinces to import raw materials and resources from countries like Australia rather than to have it transported from China's interior provinces. Some of the major enterprises in Gansu include[22]:

(a) Tianshui Great Wall Electric Group Co. Ltd—state-owned enterprise comprising five units producing different types of electrical equipment.
(b) Lanzhou Foci Herb Group—focuses on herbal pharmaceuticals.
(c) Gansu Cheezheng Industrial Group Co, Ltd—focuses on the development of Tibetan medicines.
(d) Gansu Rare Earth Group Co, Ltd—focuses on rare earths and related chemicals, 60% of goods exported to foreign countries including Japan, USA, France, Australia, Korea, Taiwan and HK.
(e) Changcheng Switchgear Factory—manufacture of transmission and distribution switchgear.
(f) Jiuquan Iron and Steel (Group) Co, Ltd—focuses on steel products—exported to Korea, Japan and the USA.

(g)   Jinchuan Group Limited—focuses on mining, chemical engineering and metallurgy.

It is also apparent that production in the province is of investment goods rather than consumption goods. However, manufacturing in Gansu takes advantage of the provinces' natural resources (herbs, metals, oil) and the industries, which have resulted from the provinces resource endowments and its central planning legacy. Petro China Co Ltd has the biggest oil refinery in western China in Lanzhou, and the development of oil and gas resources in Xinjiang has only served to enhance the development of petrochemical infrastructure in Gansu, as well as attracting a number of foreign investors.[23]

S&T Research Parks, High-Tech Zones

Only one of the fifty-three nationally designated high-technology development zones is based in Gansu, in Lanzhou. Participants in the zone focus on technologies related to chemical products, new, materials, biotechnology and mechanical and electrical products.

The zone was approved by the State Council in 1991, has an area of 29 km^2 and accommodates 1000 enterprises of which 35 are foreign invested as of 2004, including a Coca-Cola bottling plant. Furthermore, the zone had a turnover of US$1.45 billion at the end of 2004. The other state-level economic zone is the Lanzhou Economic and

Table 5.13   Gansu science and technology research park statistics 2013

Development area	Number of enterprises (unit)	Number of persons engaged (person)	Total income (10,000 yuan)	Exports (10,000 US dollars)
Lanzhou high-tech industrial development zone	600	156,211	14,007,477.1	24,989.9

Source Compiled by author using data from China's National Bureau of Statistics. China Statistical Datasheet 2014

Technological Development Zone. The Zone has 21 large and medium state-owned enterprises (SoEs), manufacturing aeronautic materials, IT & electronic products. The first major foreign enterprise to invest in the zone was Wal-Mart in 2004, and this was the fourth foreign investment in the zone.

Despite the foreign investment in Gansu and its technology park, it is clear that the concentrations of knowledge creation activities in Gansu are far fewer than in Hubei or Jiangsu. This may be due to the fact that both Jiangsu and Hubei have access to a vast potential overseas consumer market compared to Gansu. Table 5.13 shows the statistics for Lanzhou high-tech industrial development zone in Gansu. It's easy to see that while this development zone has a comparable level, if not more, enterprises to those in the high-tech development zones in either Jiangsu or Hubei. Nevertheless, the export value of goods for Lanzhou is comparably smaller to the total export value of goods in the high-tech development zones of either Jiangsu or Hubei at only US$ 249 million.

Education

The central government stipulated in 1986 in its nine-year compulsory education law that it wanted to achieve a 99% attendance rate for primary education and 85% for secondary education by the end of the twentieth century.[24] However, in Gansu Province, the objective of government policy has not been fulfilled.[25] As discussed earlier, Gansu Province is distinguished from other provinces by its topography, its large minority population and the fact that it is largely an inland agricultural province. The lack of intra-provincial employment opportunities suggests to people in Gansu that education is not a worthwhile investment because employment in the agricultural sector dominates the provincial economy. Furthermore, in terms of topography, Gansu's elevation is up to 3000 m above sea level, and 15% of the land is desert with 55% either hilly or plateau in nature. This snapshot of the province sets the background in which the Central government's education policy had to be implemented. The implementation of the government's education policy is hindered due to four reasons.[26] Firstly, rural primary schools are sparsely distributed and in mountainous areas. Secondly, there is a shortage of skilled teachers, and the conditions of schools are not as good as of those in prosperous provinces. Thirdly, provincial education budget levels are tight, and the implication is that there is a shortage of teaching resources. Fourthly, teachers in mountainous areas are not as well trained as their counterparts in more developed provinces, and therefore, resort to basic 'chalk and talk' strategies for disseminating information. Finally, provincial level financial and technological capacity to build Internet networks is limited. Due to the odds against the successful implementation of central government education policy, a national meeting to discuss rural education was held in September 2003. From this meeting, four strategies to effect government policy in rural areas were agreed.[27] Firstly, it was decided to apply technology in delivering education. Secondly, financial support to children from low-income families was to be provided. Thirdly, there was to be increased investment in education. Finally, there were to be further curriculum reforms in rural areas.

The mode for the delivery of education in rural areas following the above strategies was to be a number of VCD broadcast stations to be established throughout the province. The use of VCD technology in Gansu was seen to be more cost-effective than the use of the Internet as the latter would require a considerable initial investment which would be followed by maintenance costs. The cost of implementing and maintaining a school-based Internet network is clearly within the financial capabilities of a province such as Jiangsu, but not Gansu. The use of VCDs to promote rural education in Gansu occurred in three major steps.[28] Firstly, task objectives were set, and these objectives related to enabling schools in areas with difficult terrain to achieve the aims of central government's education policy. Secondly, VCD equipment was to be provided to schools on a consistent basis. And finally, a responsibility system was established where the principal of schools was given control of all VCD resources. Many schools use VCDs to either support teaching or to replace it completely in certain courses. Furthermore, the VCD approach serves for the training of teachers in mountainous areas who lack any formal school teacher training as the content of the VCD courses is based on the performance of 'exemplary teachers'. The use of

VCD technology in Gansu has produced a beneficial externality to rural residents who receive training on agricultural technology. Schools at the township level have interacted to develop research-teaching activities.

Lanzhou has nineteen universities and research institutes of which Lanzhou University is ranked among China's top ten universities. However, despite the well-qualified graduates produced in Gansu, many enterprises find it difficult to find suitable candidates with skills needed not only to work but also to manage effectively because there are only a small number of international companies in the province to offer such experience. Moreover, there are few opportunities Gansu graduates to be employed and thus learn management techniques through a process of knowledge transfer.[29] Therefore, in order to get the work experience to accumulate transferable skills, Gansu graduates leave the province to work in the better-developed regions of China, before returning home. The implication of this is that there is a 'brain drain' in Gansu and the returns to educational investment in the province are not equitable. Moreover, the smaller number of students going to university in Gansu and graduating, in conjunction with the 'brain drain', necessarily implies that the available pool of talent for employment in Gansu is limited, and this, therefore, necessarily acts to impede entrepreneurial activity and economic growth of the province.

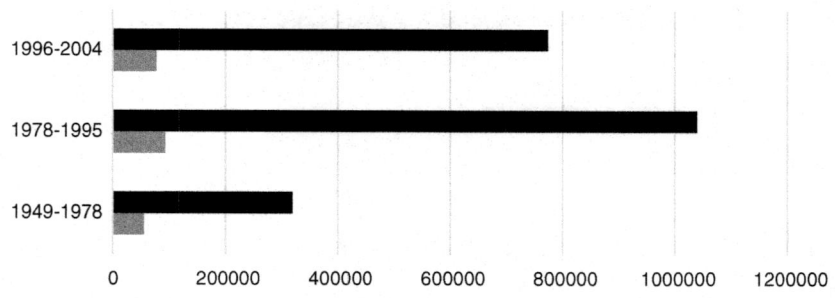

■ Full-Time Teachers Secondary Schools ▪ Full Time Teachers Regular Institutions

Fig. 5.31 Gansu full-time teachers—Three periods. *Source* Compiled by author using data from China's National Bureau of Statistics. China Compendium of Statistics 1949–2004. *Note* The figures in the graph represent an aggregate for each period

A qualitative analysis does not offer any insights into the resource and financial constraints faced by Gansu with regard to education provision and uptake. Nevertheless, it can be seen from Fig. 5.31 that the largest aggregate increase in the number of full-time teachers in secondary schools and in higher institutions occurred in the period 1978–1995. In second place was the period 1996–2004, with the lowest increase occurring in the period 1949–1977. However, when the annual average percentage changes are looked at the situation is very different. The largest annual average percentage increase in full-time teachers employed in secondary schools occurred in the period 1953–1976 [15.36%]. The second largest percentage increase occurred in the period 1997–2004. Similarly, if the annual average percentage changes in the number of full-time teachers employed at regular institutions of higher education are considered, the period 1953–1976 shows the largest increase, 10.58%. This is followed by the period 1997–2004 with an increase of 11.92%.

Figure 5.32 shows student enrolments by region and historic period. An aggregate analysis suggests that student enrolments in secondary

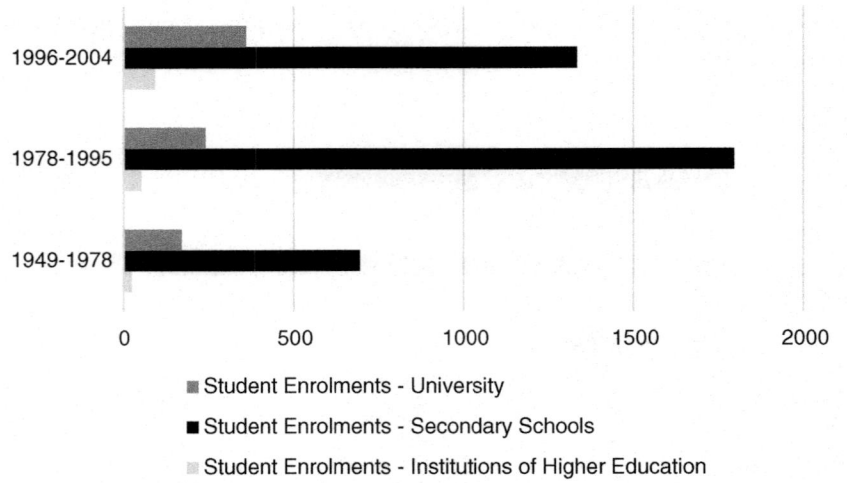

Fig. 5.32 Gansu student enrolments—Three periods. *Source* Compiled by author using data from China's National Bureau of Statistics. China Compendium of Statistics 1949–2004. *Note* The figures in the graph represent an aggregate for each period

schools show the biggest increase in the period 1979–1995 and that in universities in the period 1996–2004. However, if the annual average percentage changes are evaluated, the picture which emerges is a very different one. The largest increases in student enrolments at secondary schools [21.38%] and regular institutions of higher education [31.06%] occurred in the period 1953–1976. The annual average student enrolment at secondary schools actually decreases by −0.35% in the period 1979–1995.

With regard to the implementation of central government policy in Gansu, and more specifically the role of education as a vehicle for the formation of knowledge creation linkages in the province, it is clear that difficulties can arise in comparison with Jiangsu and Hubei. This is due to four reasons. Firstly, there is an increased cost associated with delivering education in Gansu due to its topography and minority groups. Secondly, Gansu is not as prosperous as Jiangsu or Hubei, and sources of funding for education are limited. Thirdly, the most qualified people will be least willing to work in Gansu due to the limited opportunities there. This decreases likelihood with which knowledge creation and transfer linkages can form in the province.

The inability of knowledge creation linkages to take root in Gansu is enhanced by the general unavailability of means of communication, among the population of the province, such as telephones and the Internet. Finally, in Gansu, the population tends to be sparsely distributed, and thus, the interactions necessary to form knowledge linkages are few. If these features are repeated across other provinces in western China, it is not difficult to see why disparities in income between the Coastal regions and the interior hinterland are sustained by knowledge creation as well as the utilisation of that knowledge.

Innovation in China: The Future

Having assessed three provinces, Coastal, Central and Western, in terms of the factors which may effectively contribute towards an effective regional system, it is now possible to look at the national strategy for making China a knowledge economy by 2050. The government has designated specific sectors as key areas for the focus of R&D.

These sectors include space technology, biotechnology, nanotechnology, energy technology and frontier technology. Nevertheless, Jakobson (2007) suggests that Chinese companies have focused on the development of innovative products rather than core technologies and that Chinese company's net knowledge gain has resulted from a dependence on foreign technology. However, in order to become a cutting edge knowledge-based economy, the Chinese government has designated certain areas as 'Mega Science Projects'.[30] These include quantum research, protein science, nanotechnology and developmental biology. Other areas such as advanced nuclear reactors to space have been defined as 'Mega Engineering Projects'. The Chinese government has also set objectives for the evolution of the domestic Chinese IT industry.[31] These objectives include ending the reliance on imports for IT products, the production of patented technology by Chinese IT companies, and for Chinese IT companies to play a key role in setting international standards. The focus has therefore been on supporting and creating an environment that is conducive for competitive Chinese IT companies to flourish rather than state-funded institutions, which focus on pre-existing technologies. The major IT sectors in China include telecoms, semiconductors and software. Nanotechnology is also another area in which the government has unleashed the forces of innovation. Within the Nanotechnology sector, the focus of research includes[32]:

(a) The development of the technology behind nanoelectronics and nanobiology,
(b) Reduction in the size of electronic and mechanical devices,
(c) The creation of new materials.

Nevertheless, in terms of creating an economic impact, nanotechnology research in China is still in its infancy. With regard to innovation in energy technology research, the government is focusing on the so-called clean coal technologies, hydrogen technology, fuel cell technology, nuclear fusion and reactor and distribution technologies.[33] In the Medium and Long Term S&T Plan published in 2006, biotechnology is seen as an area of frontier research, giving research in this area specific direction.[34] These directions include targeted drug discovery, manipulation of genes and protein engineering, drug design based on plants and animals, stem cell engineering and industrial biotechnology. Yu (2007) notes that the involvement of the private sector in biotechnology has been limited, while the current focus of R&D activity is focusing on gene cloning, proteomics and genomics.

Some key points have been established in this chapter. Firstly, the number of S&T personnel, Internet usage and population density decreases moving from Coastal to Western China. Secondly, government grants and bank loans as sources of funding for innovation increases moving from West to East. Thirdly, Hubei has the largest capacity compared to other provinces with regard to length of railway, highway and navigable inland waterway. It also has the largest capacity, compared to Jiangsu and Hubei with respect to the number of waterway passengers and railway freight traffic carried. With regard to Proposition 1, it is intuitive to suggest that there has been a 'brain drain' from China's interior regions to the Coastal regions. Moreover, due to their prosperity, and the decentralisation of funding for education, the Coastal provinces have been better able fund provincial education then the interior provinces have been able to. Propositions 2 and 5 are justifiable on the grounds that the economic growth of the Coastal region has made a bigger contribution to China's economic growth in the reform years. Furthermore, the exports and Internet usage of Jiangsu have been greater than comparable figures for Hubei or Gansu. Moreover, after 1980 adjusted TIFA in Jiangsu overtook that in Hubei or Gansu, although after 1995 this trend reversed. The dominance of TIFA in Jiangsu after 1980 maybe due to the creation of SEZ's and high technology development zones in the Coastal regions. The latter effect may be due to the Western Development Program. Proposition 3 is justifiable on the grounds that exports are greater in Jiangsu than Hubei or Gansu, especially in the reform years. The adjusted GIOV of Jiangsu began to diverge from Hubei and Gansu in 1972, the divergence becoming greater after 1980. This may be accounted for the emergence of primordial TVE's in the early 1970s; and the start of economic reforms after 1978. With regard to Proposition 4, it is apparent that knowledge creation seems to be more significant in the Coastal regions due to the larger number of S&T personnel and patents registered in that region. In summary, the reliance on heavy industry and natural resources increases moving from the east of China to the west. Furthermore, the population becomes less homogenous, the geographical terrain becomes more difficult, and there is a significant reduction in population density. The overall impact must be a reduction in the effectiveness of education.

Notes

1. Jakobson, L (2007), 'Introduction' in 'Innovation with Chinese Characteristics: High Tech Research in China', Jakobson et al. (2007), Palgrave.
2. www.nj.gov.cn.
3. Ibid.
4. http://www.jiangsu.net/transportation/.
5. Ibid.
6. http://www.roadtraffic-technology.com/project_printable. asp?ProjectID=3098.
7. http://www.jiangsu.net/transportation/.
8. Ibid.
9. Wei, Y.D (2002) et al., 'Widening Inter-County Inequality in Jiangsu Province, China, 1950–1995'.
10. Bramall, C (2007), 'The Industrialisation of Rural China', Oxford University Press.
11. Wei, Y.D (2002) et al., 'Widening Inter-County Inequality in Jiangsu Province, China, 1950–1995'.
12. Ibid.
13. http://www.jsdoftec.gov.cn/english/html/aboutjs.asp.
14. Ibid.
15. UCBL Information Database, http://www.ukChinabussinesslinks.com.
16. http://www.accci.com.au/keycity/hubei.htm.
17. http://www.ukChinabusinesslinks.com.
18. http://www.cnhubei.com/200502/ca677721.htm.
19. Ibid.
20. http://www.cnhubei.com/200502/ca677721.htm.

21. Ma, S et al. (2006), 'Fuzzy model of regional economic competitiveness in GIS spatial analysis: case study of Gansu, Western China', Fuzzy Optim Decis Making (2006) 5:99–111.

22. http://www.gansu.gov.cn/en/Enterprises_Detail.asp?Id=188.

23. Karnak, R & Jun, L, 'Critical Eye on Lanzhou', US-China Business Council, Sept–Oct (2005).

24. Asian Development Bank (1997), 'National Action Plan: People's Republic of China, in: Distance education for primary school Teachers; papers and proceedings of the regional seminar on distance education', Asian Development Bank.

25. Lee, J et al. (2005), 'Using VCD's to promote rural educational development in China: a case study in the Tianshui hilly areas of Gansu', Open Learning, Vol. 20, No 3, November 2005.

26. Ibid.

27. Zhou, Y and Zhang, Y (2004), 'Rural education: progress and problems' in 'China's education blue book', Yang, D(Ed).

28. Lee, J et al. (2005), 'Using VCD's to promote rural educational development in China: a case study in the Tianshui hilly areas of Gansu', Open Learning, Vol. 20, No 3, November 2005.

29. Karnak, R & Jun, L, 'Critical Eye on Lanzhou', US-China Business Council, Sept–Oct 2005.

30. Jakobson, L (2007), 'Introduction' in 'Innovation with Chinese Characteristics: High Tech Research in China', Jakobson et al. (2007), Palgrave.

31. Kroeber, A (2007), 'China's Push to Innovate in Information Technology' in 'Innovation with Chinese Characteristics: High Tech Research in China ', Jakobson et al. (2007), Palgrave.

32. Bai, C et al. (2007), 'Nanotechnology Research in China' in 'Innovation with Chinese Characteristics: High Tech Research in China', Jakobson et al. (2007), Palgrave.

33. Jiang, K. (2007), 'Energy Technology Research in China' in 'Innovation with Chinese Characteristics: High Tech Research in China', Jakobson et al. (2007), Palgrave.

34. Yu, J. (2007), 'Biotechnology Research in China' in 'Innovation with Chinese Characteristics: High Tech Research in China', Jakobson et al. (2007), Palgrave.

References

Asian Development Bank. (1997). National action plan: People's Republic of China. In *Distance education for primary school teachers; Papers and proceedings of the regional seminar on distance education*. Asian Development Bank.

Bai, C., et al. (2007). Research in China. In *Innovation with Chinese characteristics: High tech research in China*. Jakobson et al (2007), Palgrave.

Bramall, C. (2007). *The industrialisation of rural China*. Oxford: Oxford University Press.

Jakobson, L. (2007). *Introduction in innovation with Chinese characteristics: High tech research in China*. Jackobson et al (2007), Palgrave.

Jiang, K. (2007). Research in China. In *Innovation with Chinese characteristics: High tech research in China*. Jakobson et al (2007), Palgrave.

Karnak, R., & Jun, L. (2005). *Critical eye on*. US-China Business Council. Sept–Oct 2005.

Kroeber, A. (2007). China's push to innovate in information technology. In *Innovation with Chinese characteristics: High tech research in China*. Jakobson et al (2007), Palgrave.

Krugman, P. (1991). Increasing Returns and Economic Geography. *The Journal of Political Economy, 99*(3), 483–499.

Lee, J., et al. (2005). Using VCD's to promote rural educational development in China: A case study in the hilly areas of Gansu. *Open Learning, 20*(3), November 2005.

Li-Hua, R (2004), Technology and Knowledge Transfer in China, Ashgate.

Ma, S., et al. (2006). Fuzzy model of regional economic competitiveness in GIS spatial analysis: Case study of Gansu, Western China. *Fuzzy Optimization and Decision Making, 5*, 99–111.

Sutherland, D. (2005). China's science parks: Production bases or a tool for institutional reform? *Asia Pacific Business Review, 11*(1), 83–104.

Wei, Y. D., & Sunwoong, K. (2002). *Widening inter-county inequality in Jiangsu Province, China, 1950–95*.

Yu, J. (2007). *Research in China. In Innovation with Chinese characteristics: High tech research in China*. Jakobson et al (2007), Palgrave.

Zhou, Y., & Zhang, Y. (2004). *Rural education: Progress and problems in China's education blue book*. Yang, D (Ed.).

6

Tales of Two Types of Regional Integration—The UK, the EU and China

Introduction

In the 1950s and the 1960s Britain had at least two choices regarding its future economic direction. The first was the increased use of supply side associated policies to foster reduced transport costs and increased innovation and entrepreneurship. This policy choice would have been in alignment with Britain's former colonial role in which its cities and ports were uniquely linked to trade and manufacture with different parts of the world. Through the seventeenth, eighteenth and nineteenth centuries the dynamo of Britains economic growth was trade between itself and its colonies with re-exports to and imports from mainland Europe (Price 1989). The guarantor of Britain's trade supremacy was its overwhelming military power. Suppy side policies would also have fitted in with the new world order which emerged after the Second World War in which the World Bank and the IMF would support developing and economically distressed countries respectively, NATO and the UN would promote and foster world peace and GATT negotiations would stimulate increased global free trade. The second economic policy choice Britain faced in the 1950s

© The Author(s) 2017
S. Ramesh, *China's Lessons for India: Volume II*,
DOI 10.1007/978-3-319-58115-6_6

and the 1960s was to join the European Economic Community (EEC), enter into a customs unions with other European countries and eventually morph into a Single Market. The essence of the Single European Act (SEA) of 1987 would be to negate all internal barriers to trade through the enactment of the four freedoms, the 'free movement of goods, services, labour and capital', El-Agraa (2007). The SEA, from an economic perspective, was a two stage process (Pelkmans 2016). The first stage being the maximisation of integration through the enforcement of the four freedoms. The second stage was the harmonsiation or the near harmonisation of national laws and regulations to a common standard amongst the 28 countries which would eventually form the European Union (EU).

Several reasons have been put forward for the formation of the EU. One prevailing reason is that the EU was formed in order to prevent any wars from occuring in Europe again. Another reason which was put forward to justify the formation of the EU was that small countries would not survive at a time when the new economic powers of China and India would be in the ascendancy. Therefore, an economically integrated block such as the EU would stand a better chance of surviving the economic rise of China and India at a competitive level. There are other economic rationale for a bigger market. For example, in a bigger market there would be more potential customers for firms and customers would benefit from more competition between firms which would result in lower prices and more choice. Furthermore, a bigger market through efficient integration would also involve a reduction in firms costs. In the case of a single market, customs union and the EU firms costs would be lowered by the removal of tariffs on goods traded between the countries in the customs union, a harmonisation of laws and regulations associated with employment regulations and the movement of labour. Moreover, a single common currency for countries in the regional bloc would also do away with transactions costs between firms in different countries within the bloc. On the other hand regional integration between countries and within countries due to more and better infrastructure will lower firms transport costs as well as encourage entrepreneurship and innovation.

The aim of this chapter is to determine which method of regional integration is better, the one through a customs union or the one through government policy favouring greater infrastructure investment as well as greater incentives for entrepreneurship and innovation. The objective of this chapter is to use the case study methodology to compare and contrast the economic history of the United Kingdom (UK) and the EU and a reformist China. The UK formally joined the EEC, the precursor of the EU, in 1973 and China started its economic reforms in 1978, following its formal recognition as a nation state by the United States (Fraser and Murray 2002). The EU arose on the basis of regional integration through the route of a customs union, single market, a single currency and a formal union. However, China's economic rise as been based on free trade, innovation and entrepreneurship through infrastructure, knowledge creation and knowledge spillovers. In this case, China took the first economic policy choice which Britain faced in the 1950s and the 1960s, while at the same time taking advantage of the emerging post-Second World War world order and embracing GATT and eventually joining its successor, the World Trade Organisation (WTO) in December 2001 (Zeng 2013). China's supply side, market oriented reform policies would set its economy to become the second largest in the world, after the United States by 2010 (Wang 2010).

Trade Diversion, Resource Diversion and Over Competition—Market Failure

As discussed, Britain joing the EEC in 1973 and China starting its economic reforms in 1978 and embracing the post-Second World War new order would put the two countries economies on different growth trajectories. From this historical perspective a number of questions arise. Firstly, did Britain's membership of the EEC and its successor the EU result in trade diversion for Britain away from trade with the British Commonwealth and the rest of the world towards the 28 EU countries? Secondly, if this is the case did it mean that there was a restructuring of

Britain's industrial geography such that its industrial heartlands, in the north, lost competitiveness at the expense of low cost community member countries? If the answer to this is true then it would mean that the conventional answer to the loss of Britain's industrial and manufacturing capacity, the low cost advantages of the rising Asian Tiger economies would become susceptible to being labelled a half truth if not true at all. Thirdly, as Britain's membership of the EEC and subsequently the EU resulted in resource diversion from Britain to poorer countries of the EU. This could take the form of a withdrawal from Britain's circular flow of income, represented by incomes or transfer payments being sent back to other countries in the EU. Resource diversion may also be represented in the context of over-competition for limited resources. For example, if Britain spends money on the education and training of workers who may not be employed due to intense competition in the labour market due to the free movement of labour to Britain from other EU countries. Similarly, British workers may not find it so easy to learn an EU language to take advantage of the free movement of labour and to move to other EU countries to find work.

Traditional economics would suggest that increased competition, the economic fundamental of the Single Market, would result in a pareto efficient outcome or a pareto optimum. In other words, the EU's four fundamental and inseparable freedoms results in a situation such that it would not be possible to improve the welfare of a citizen of any member state by reallocating labour, capital, goods or services without negatively impairing on the welfare of the citizen of another EU member state. However, the free movement of labour can improve the welfare of the citizen of one EU member state at the expense of the welfare of another citizen of another EU member state due to over competition amongst workers for limited resources. This may lead to workers behaving irrationally compared to their near rational behaviour when fully satiated. Furthermore, such over competition and a lack of resources may exhibit itself in housing shortages, lingering domestic unemployment, long waiting times for healthcare, increased congestion on public transport and an overall fall in living standards. All of which is true in the case of Britain. So, it is evident that the Single Market does not either improve economic efficiency (unemployment nearly or at zero levels) or social welfare (no housing shortages, shorter waiting times for healthcare and no congestion on public transport). If anything, the result of the Single Market is a negative impact on social welfare. The result of the Brexit referendum in the UK in June 2016 can be viewed as an example of irrationality in which the majority were prepared, perhaps unknowingly, for the economic hardships, at least in the short-term, which may result when Britain eventually leaves the EU in return for a return of national sovereignty especially in the context of legislation and the control of immigration, the end of the free movement of labour into the UK from other EU member states.

Theories of Regional Integration

The process of integration in Europe began with the Schuman Declaration of 1950 which formed the basis for the founding of the European Coal and Steel Community (ECSC) by the 1951 Treaty of Paris (Rosamond 2000). The Treaty of Paris was signed by the founding members of the EC, France, Germany, Belgium, Netherlands, Luxembourg and Italy. As well as founding the ECSC, the Treaty also established the EC's first supranational institution, the Council of Ministers. The establishment of the ECSC had political and financial support from the United States which saw it as an effective initial step, in establishing a common market for European coal and steel, into integrating the West German economy with that of the other countries in western Europe (Ginsberg 2007). According to the latter, steel and coal production increased in the ECSC despite a negative external market environment, although the increase in steel and coal output could have been due to the economic boom in West Germany. However, while the ECSC served its purpose, the price per ton of US coal delivered to the door of European steel plants was much cheaper than that of coal produced in Europe (Bouscaren 1969). One way in which the European coal industry could be protected was through the imposition of tariffs on US coal exports to ECSC member countries. The establishment of the ECSC would eventually lead to the EEC, and more sectoral integration in the latter part of the 1950s, and the EU in the 1990s (Ginsberg 2007).

At an economic and political level it was felt that integration of the same sectors in two different community member countries would lead to spillover effects into other sectors, such as transport for example, bringing them into the integration process as well. Two of the key proponents of a theory of european integration were Haas (1961) and Lindberg (1963). The former is often linked with 'neofunctionalism' although both have diseminated a functional logic to the process of european integration in which a group of geographically connected countries sequentially form a free trade area, a customs union, a common market, monetary integration and finally political union. Entwined in this process is 'neofunctionalism' whereby national politicians will override national self-interest in the interest of the community as a whole (Haas 1961). According to the latter, at the same time supranational institutions, laws and regulations will surmount national ones, giving more power to the community as a whole over the nation state. Balassa (1961) also puts forward a sequential process of economic integration in which a community of countries moves from a free trade area (FTA), customs union (CU), common market (CM), european union to total economic integration (TEI). Such a sequential process of economic integration would involve the elimination of discrimination between firms and the factors of production such as labour belonging to different member states (Balassa 1961). Such economic discrimination between economic agents in different member states would sequentially involve the elimination of tariffs and quota's (FTA), the imposition of a common external tariff (CU), the free flow of the factors of production (CM), the harmonisation of economic policies (EU) and ultimately a single form of governance for all member countries (Nye 1968).

There are three types of regional trade agreements (Baldwin and Venables 1995). Firstly, in a *Free Trade (FTA) Area* countries in the trading block remove tariffs on goods moving from one country in the block to another but each country within the bloc is free to impose its own tariff on goods being imported from countries other than those in the block. The economic argument in favour of a free trade area is that a FTA member country would be able to benefit through comparative advantage, increased specialisation and division of labour which would result in firms production experiencing economies of scale. In other words as the firm increases output in the long run, the per unit cost of production falls. The reason for this is that if firms in a country produce the goods to which the country is best endowed to produce given a set of resources and factors of production then workers can be trained to carry out specific tasks in the production of a good. As a result over time, workers will become more and more productive, finding more efficient ways to carry out the task in less time. Theoretically, firms gain by saving on training costs and as each specialised worker increases productivity, firms will have to hire fewer and fewer workers thus saving on wage costs. Increased market size allows the firms to take more advantage of the economies of scale by selling more output and accumulating more revenues and thus profits. An increase in productivity at an aggregate level will mean that the long run aggregate supply curve will shift to the right, representing increased economic growth. The European Free Trade Area (EFTA) was formed by several western european nations, including Austria, Denmark, Norway, Portugal, Sweden, Switzerland and the United Kingdom in 1960 (USDA 1987). EFTA was formed because the constituent countries opposed supranational institutions and common external tariffs, all of which are embodied in the EC. Currently, EFTA only includes Iceland, Liechtenstein, Norway and Switzerland. In 1974 the EC and the EFTA countries signed bilateral trade agreements which removed tariffs and duties on the movement of industrial goods between EC and EFTA countries. However, EFTA became diminished in number when the United Kingdom, Denmark and Portugal joined the EU in 1973. EFTA suffered a further blow when Spain and Portugal left to join the EC in 1986.

Secondly, a **Customs Union** (CU) is a type of regional trade agreement in which countries in a trading bloc not only have tariffs removed on goods exported from one country in the bloc to another but countries within the bloc also impose the same tariffs on goods entering the bloc from countries not in the block. According to Viner (1950), two interesting trade related features of a Customs Union are trade creation and trade diversion. Trade creation occurs when low cost producers in the community replace high cost producers in importing member countries of the community. This can lead to consumers in the importing member state benefiting from lower prices. However, the high cost producers in the importing member states may go into decline and eventually go out of business. Moreover, if the costs of production by industry in an importing member state are higher than in an exporting member state then the result may be industrial decline in the high cost importing member state. On the other hand a CU may result in lower cost imports into a community member state from a non-member state, such as the Commonwealth and the rest of the world in the case of Britain, because tariffs may have made these imports more expensive than the imports from another member state. Finally, a **Single or Common Market** (CM) is a customs union plus the free movement of labour within the bloc. The European Community (EC) completed its common market by 1968 (Baldwin and Venables 1995). However, the elimination of discriminatory practices by member states against other member states did not disappear overnight and would require further community legislation later on. In the CM trade tariffs on intra-EC trade were forbidden and the free mobility of labour between EC member countries was instituted. Tariffs were removed not only on industrial products but quotas and duties on intra-EC trade were also removed to be substituted by a system of price supports and subsidies. In the context of the agricultural sector, the main focus was what became known as the Common Agricultural Policy (CAP). The main feature of the latter was the setting of minimum prices community wide on agricultural products, supported by import controls on agricultural products from outside the community and subsidies to farmers within the community. The importance of the CAP was because Germany's industrial sector was stronger than that of France, but in the context of the agricultural sector France was in a stronger position than Germany. Thus, De Gaulle, the French president at the time, was intent on protecting a strong agricultural sector at the expense of a weaker industrial sector through the negotiation of a community wide CAP, his ultimate gambit being withdrawing France from the community if negotiations failed, Pinder (1968). In contrast to the neofunctionalist spillover approach, another approach to market integration lies with increased investment in infrastructure and market oriented reforms. Figure 6.1, above depicts how increased transport infrastructure in a country as well as in a geographic

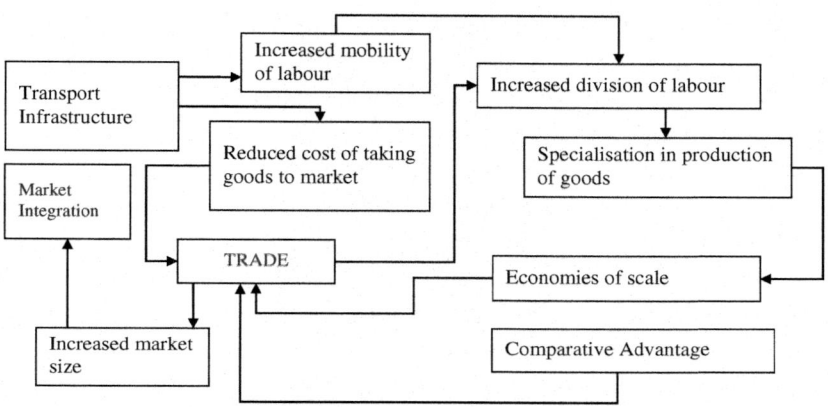

Fig. 6.1 Transport infrastructure and market integration. *Source* Author

region may lead to market integration through increased market size and increased trade. As can be seen from Fig. 6.1, increased transport infrastructure leads to not only the increased mobility of labour but also lower transport costs for producers moving goods to markets. The increased mobility of labour leads to the increased division of labour because workers can move to the regions of a country or region in which there is more demand for labour. As a result of the increased supply of workers, producers in that region will be able train workers to carry out specific tasks in the production of a good. As workers become better and better at the job, over time productivity will rise as workers find better ways to complete the tasks they have been assigned in shorter periods of time. The increasing specialisation in production by firms will mean that their production will experience economies of scale in the long run whereby the per unit costs of production falls as the firms increases output. In combination with appropriate supply side policies in order to attract foreign direct investment, a country can take advantage of its abundance in cheap labour. In conjunction with economies of scale and an abundance of cheap labour, a country can increase exports through trade, coalesce distinct internal markets and so experience market integration. At the same time to ensure that's its goods are not discriminated against, a country can join a neutral adjudicating body such as the World Trade Organisation (WTO). The purpose of the WTO is to ensure the application of universal trade rules by all countries in order to increase the consistency and transparency with which trade is conducted by member countries; and thus reduce barriers to trade (Gertler and Mihollin 2002). Moreover, according to the latter the WTO is a forum for the settlement of trade disputes between countries as well as a forum in which countries can negotiate multi-lateral trade agreements. In the case of the UK, labour migration from other EU member states should have been controlled perhaps by using the same criteria which are used to admit non-EU labour to enter into the UK. If the UK had taken a more forceful stance in negotiations with the EU at the time when the Maastricht Treaty was being discussed, the UK would probably be still in the EU today. The selection of workers based on quality, in terms of language ability and qualifications would have averted the potential for unlimited immigration into the UK.

The preceding discussion shows that there are two strategies to regional integration. The path being followed by the EU member states being one following a free trade area, a customs union, a common market, monetary integration followed by complete political integration. The fundamental weakness of the European integration project would have been the inevitable suppression of the sovereignty of individual member states by supranational institutions. One characteristic of this trend is the free movement of labour between member states. This and the acceptance of ex-Soviet states such as Poland, Romania and Bulgaria, whose level of economic and political development is more regressed than western European countries, perhaps impacted heavily in favour of the 'Leave' campaign during the UK EU referendum on the 23rd June 2016. This may have been due to the increased out migration from these countries, particularly Poland and Bulgaria, to Britain following thir accession to the EU in 2004 and 2007 respectively.

The United Kindom and Regional Integration

As discussed above, in 1960 seven western European nations formed the European Free Trade Area (EFTA). However, in 1973, Britain, Denmark and Ireland became members of the EU. Greece became the Tenth member in 1981 and in 1986, both Portugal and Spain became member states of the EU. The EU saw no further enlargement until the 1st May 2004 when Cyprus, Czech Republic, Estonia, Hungary, Latvia, Lithuania, Malta, Poland, Solvak Republic and Slovenia joined in one go. Three years later in 2007, Romania and Bulgaria were admitted as member states of the EU. By the end of 2007, the number of member countries had risen to 27, all of which ratified the Lisbon Treaty by the end of 2007, coming into effect in 2009. One political argument for EU enlargement to include the former Soviet republics and eastern European nations was perhaps to stop them falling back into the grasp of Russia. However, at an economic, political and structural level the east european countries are less advanced then more developed western European countries such as the United Kingdom. In sequential order from the least poorest to the poorest are placed Poland, Latvia, Croatia, Romania and Bulgaria. These countries remain the poorest countries in the EU in terms of real GDP per capita[1]. With Romania and Bulgaria being the poorest countries, in terms of real GDP per capita, in the European Union (Nikolova et al. 2016). Perhaps correlating with the lower level of real GDP per capita of these countries is the need to take advantage of the EU's free flow of labour by workers in these countries and migrate to economies, such as the UK, in which the standard of living is higher than in their home countries. In 2014, Poland and Romania contributed the most to the total of EU migrants to the UK[2].

Figure 6.2 shows the economic growth rates for China, the EU and the UK between 1961 and 2015. It can be seen that between 1973 and 1976 the economic growth rates of all three were around the same level. However after 1976 and 1978/1979 in particular, the trajectory of China's economic growth was at a higher level than that of either the EU or of the United Kingdom. It was in the year 1978 that China began its economic reforms, while in 1973 the UK joined the then EEC, the predecessor of the EU. However, the UK renegotiated the treaty with the EU in 1975 and held a referendum in favour of the UK remaining part of the EEC. The Single European Act (SEA)came into effect in 1987. The two main objectives of the SEA was to more efficiently facilitate the free movement of goods, services, capital and labour between member states; and the introduction of majority voting for the establishment of community wide laws (Loveland 2012).

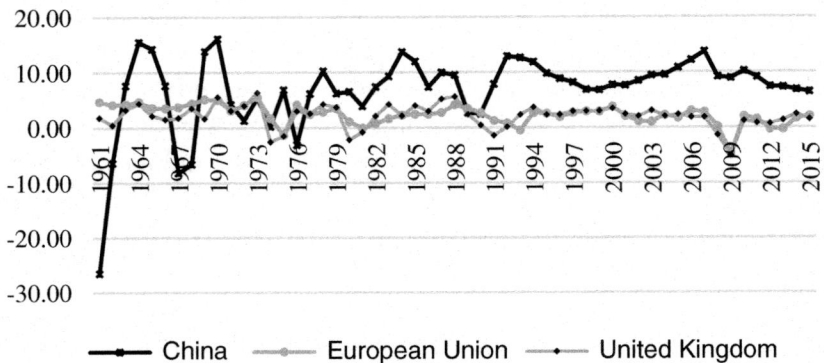

Fig. 6.2 Economic growth rates—China, EU and the UK 1961–2015. *Source* Compiled by author using data from the world bank

The aim of the SEA was to set up the single market by December 31st 1992. Around 1987/1989 the economic growth rates of China, the UK and the EU go into decline. The latter two because of a recession; and the former because of a recession and also because of the after-shocks of the Tiananmen Square incident in 1989. Nevertheless, after 1990/1991, China's economic growth rate rebounded to much higher levels than the economic growth rates of either the EU or the UK. This is because China increased the pace of its economic reforms following Deng Xiaoping's tour of Southern China. China's economic growth rate remained at much higher levels in the two decades that followed and its economic growth rate is still higher than that of either the EU or the UK even today. On the other after 1987/1989, the economic growth rates of the EU and the UK became ever more entwined while remaining at much lower levels than that of China's. The Maastricht Treaty was signed in 1992 and it came into force on 1st November 1993. The Maastricht Treaty had three objectives (Mainz 1994). Firstly, greater economic and monetary union. Secondly, facilitating the formulation of a common foreign and security policy. And lastly, more judicial and home affairs cooperation. Monetary Union envisaged the adoption of a common currency, the Euro by eligible member countries which met the Treaty's convergence criteria by 1st January 1999. By 2002, seventeen national currencies had been replaced by Euro notes and coins. The main problem with monetary union and the Eurozone is that it is

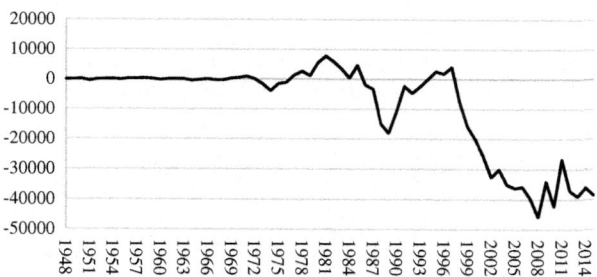

Fig. 6.3 UK trade balance (£m)—1948–2015. *Source* Compiled by author using data from the UK office for national statistics

not an Optimal Currency Area (OCA) for two reasons (Bayoumi and Eichengreen 1993). Firstly, while the SEA facilitates the free movement of labour from one member country which experiences recession to another member country which is experiencing economic growth, this has not been realised in practice. However, what has happened in practice is that workers from developing countries of the EU such as Poland, Bulgaria and Romania have migrated to more developed countries of the EU such as the UK. Secondly, the success of the Euro in the context of the OCA requires that member countries should have a joint budget, so that an expansionary fiscal policy can be applied to the economies of countries in recession, mitigating the expansion of other countries economies. The analysis indicates that China's economic reforms have been more effective at promoting higher levels of economic growth, through the integration of China's regions, than the UK's economic growth rates through integration with other EU countries.

Figure 6.3 shows the UK's trade balance, the difference between exports and imports, between 1948 and 2015. Between 1948 and 1972/1973 it can be seen that the UK's trade balance was as such that exports matched imports. In other word's the UK's trade balance, balanced between 1948 and 1972/73 when the UK trade balance went into a deficit. After 1972/1973 the UK trade balance was more volatile and showed a downward trend in favour of imports being greater than exports. The tendency towards the UK experiencing trade deficits after 1972/1973 could have been due to either the shift from the Bretton Woods fixed exchange rate regime in 1971 to a free-floating exchange rate regime. This shift would have introduced greater volatility into the UK's trade because the UK's exchange rate with other countries' currencies would have been exposed to a number of global economic and political environmental factors. However, the UK's trade deficit could have become more volatile after 1972/1973 because of the UK's entry into the European Economic Community (EEC). On the other hand, the UK's tendency towards a trade deficit after 1972/1973 could have been due to Viner's 'Trade Creation'. This would result in a trade deficit because consumption of goods produced by high cost UK producers would have been replaced by imports of goods produced by low cost producers in other EEC member countries such as Germany. China did not engage in any significant foreign trade at this time. The UK trade deficit was greatest in 1989/1990 and 1997/1998. During these periods, the global economy was experiencing a downturn. In 1989/1990 the downturn started perhaps because of a combination of the collapse of the Soviet Union and the Bank of Japan raising interest rates in mid-1989 leading to the bursting of an asset bubble, sending Japan's economy into 20 years of deflation. In 1997/1998, the downturn started perhaps as a result of the East Asian financial crisis. But the fall in the UK's trade deficit did not reach a bottom until 2008. During this time the Euro was borne and 17 EU countries became part of the Eurozone. The depth of the increase in the UK's trade deficit after 1997 could be linked with the introduction of the Euro and/or the accession of China to the WTO in 2001, after which its exports increased significantly. China's rise may have 'squeezed out' the exports of other countries including the UK.

Figure 6.4 shows the percentage change in the UK's overall and commonwealth trade balance between 1949 and 2011. It can be seen that after the establishment of the single market in 1992, in the next 20 years or more there has been only 1 year in which the UK has experienced a positive growth in the commonwealth trade balance, in 1994.

This is in contrast to previous years, in 1957, 1968, 1976, 1987 and 1990, in which the UK has experienced trade growth with the Commonwealth.

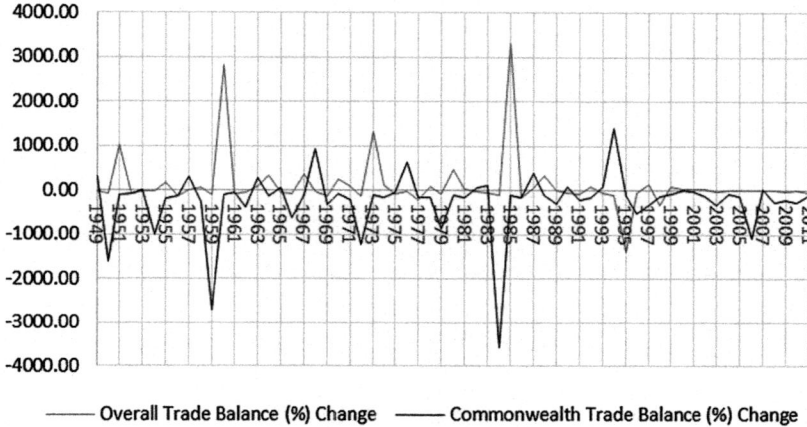

Fig. 6.4 Percentage change in UK's overall and commonwealth trade balance. *Source* Compiled by author using data from Allen (2012)*, Appendix 2, Table 2. *Note* *Contains Parliamentary information licensed under the **Open Parliament Licence v3.0**. http://www.parliament.uk/site-information/copyright/open-parliament-licence/

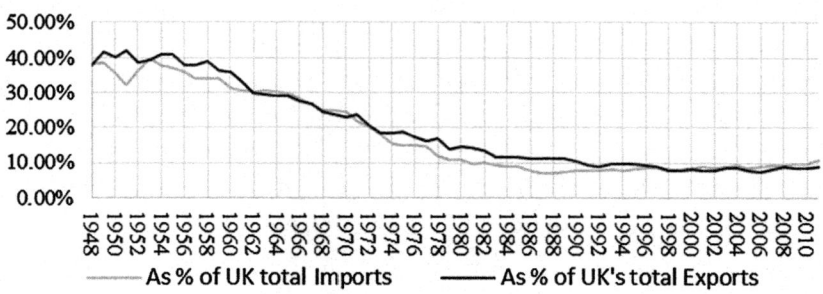

Fig. 6.5 UK's commonwealth exports and imports as % of total imports and exports. *Source* Allen (2012)*. *Note* *Contains Parliamentary information licensed under the **Open Parliament Licence v3.0**. http://www.parliament.uk/site-information/copyright/open-parliament-licence/

Figure 6.5 shows the UK's Commonwealth exports and imports as a percentage of total imports and exports. It can be seen that the UK maintains a positive balance of trade with the Commonwealth between 1948 and 1962 and between 1973 and 1997. However, between 1962 and 1972 and after 1999, the UK maintained a negative balance of trade with the Commonwealth, meaning that UK imports of Commonwealth goods were greater than UK exports to the Commonwealth. UK exports to the Commonwealth began to fall after the establishment of the SEA in 1992, and falling below imports from the Commonwealth by 1999. So, after 1999, the UK's imports from the Commonwealth as a percentage of total imports began to increase. This could have resulted because despite tariffs on imported goods from the Commonwealth, the Sterling-Euro exchange rate made it cheaper for the UK to import goods from the Commonwealth than from the EU, although the increase in imported goods from the Commonwealth after 1999 was not that significant. However, what deserves more attention in Fig. 6.5 is that UK exports to the Commonwealth as a percentage of the UK's total exports fell from 38% in 1948, 35% in 1960, 18% in 1973 and to a mere 8% in 2010. It was in 1947 that the UK granted independence to India and Ceylon and this process of decolonisation increased over the next 30 years. Yet in 1960, when the UK was one of seven countries which took part in the setting up of the EFTA, in competition to the EEC, the percentage share of its exports to the Commonwealth had not fallen by that much in comparison to its 1948 level. However, by the time the UK decided to join the EEC in 1973, while abandoning EFTA, UK exports as a percentage of total exports had fallen to 18% and over the next 37 years it would decline by 10%. In the context of Brexit and the UK government's determination to establish a 'global' role for Britain through free trade, it is difficult to see why Britain did not actively pursue trade deals with its former colonies in the years after 1948 and why Britain sought closer ties with its European neighbours. This is particularly true in the context that HM Queen Elizabeth II has been the Head of the Commonwealth for a very long time. From a political economy perspective was it a deliberate strategy by the British government to reduce the risk of trade retaliation by its former colonies for previous injustices by forging closer links with its European counterparts? Why was the Colonial Office not replaced by a Commonwealth Trade Office to foster and nurture greater trade links with Britain's former colonies? If falling trade did lead Britain into

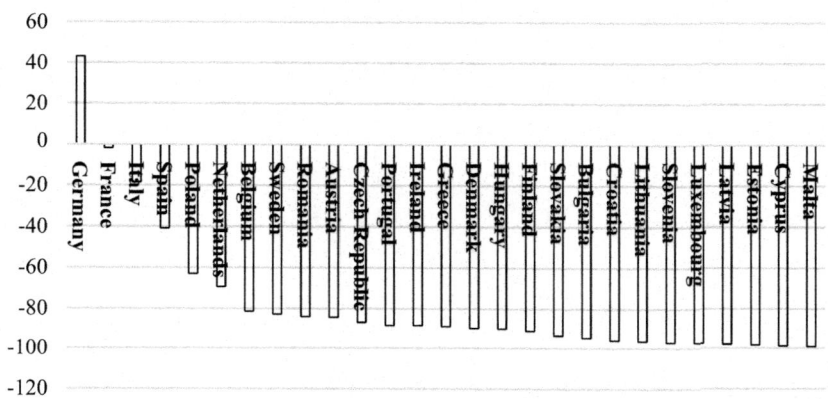

Fig. 6.6 Percentage size of EU member countries economies relative to the UK (2015). *Source* Compiled by author using data from eurostat

forging closer trade, economic and to some extent political union with the EU, could this have led to the restructuring of Britain's industrial landscape where ports and industries which had become aligned to trade with its former colonies for hundreds of years, now declined due to trade and economic links much closer to home?

Figure 6.6 above shows the percentage size of EU member countries' economies relative to the UK in terms of GDP at market prices. In this case, it is easy to see that the German economy is 42% bigger than the UK economy while the economies of other EU member states are much smaller in comparison. For example, the Polish economy is 40% smaller than the UK economy, the Romanian economy 62% smaller while the Bulgarian economy is approximately 85% smaller than the UK economy.

Clearly then even in the contemporary world there is a clear mismatch between the UK and most of the other members of the EU. Furthermore, Fig. 6.7 above shows the percentage size of EU member countries population relative to the UK in 2015. It can be seen that only the population of Germany and France is bigger than that of the UK's, 38 and 5% respectively. On the other hand, the population of other EU member countries are much smaller than that of the EU.

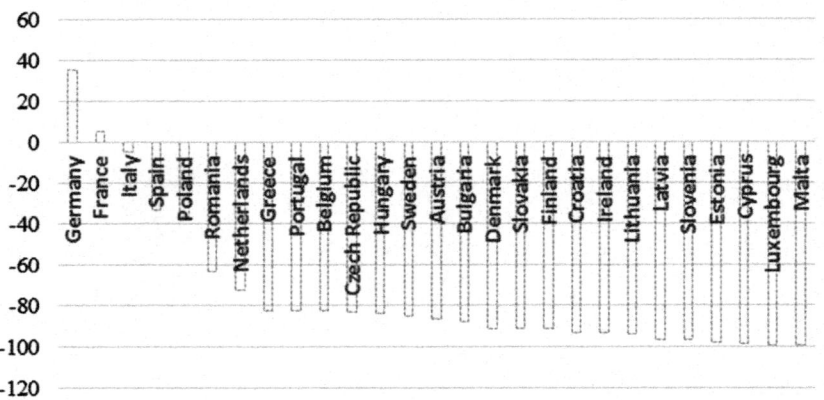

Fig. 6.7 Percent size of EU member countries population relative to the UK (2015). *Source* Compiled by author using data from the world bank

The People's Republic of China and Regional Integration

China, on the other hand, with 2.6 times the population of the EU combined, has followed an economic strategy which encompasses infrastructure investment, market oriented reforms and the application of supply side policies to facilitate economic growth. In the first 5 years of China's economic reforms since 1978, Special Economic Zones (SEZ's) were established in the Coastal region in Shenzhen, close to Hong Kong, Zhuhai and Shantou in Guangdong Province and in Xiamen in Fujian Province (Wang 2013). The establishment of the SEZ's were jointly financed by the state and by provincial government (Ge 1999). The latter suggests that the establishment of SEZ's generated a host of economic advantages for China. These included short term job creation, the generation and minimal requirement of foreign exchange reserves. The main characteristics of the SEZ's was a concentration of infrastructure accompanied by private property rights, preferential tax rates and the right of repatriation of profits made in China by foreign multinational corporations (MNC's). Private property rights recognised the ownership of equipment by MNCs as well as the ownership of accrued profits by MNC's (Wang 2013). According to the latter MNCs were set preferential tax rates in a band of 15–24%, a specific tax rate within this band depending on the level of the technological content of the MNC products. Domestic firms profits, on the other hand were taxed at a flat rate of 33% (Wang 2013). However, MNCs were in return obliged to bring to China capital equipment and technology and at the same time train Chinese workers to use the technology as well as training them to acquire managerial skills (Ge 1999). The result of this policy over subsequent years was an increase in foreign direct investment (FDI) into China, an increase in China's exports especially after its succession to the WTO in 2001, which it turn raised its economic growth rate. Empirical studies have found that joining the WTO gave Chinese exports favourable access to overseas markets (Thorbecke and Smith 2010). Increasing job opportunities resulted in the migration of millions of Chinese workers from the interior regions to the Coastal region. This is despite the fact that the country has had, until recently a rigid system of urban and rural rights for its citizens, the Hukou. The economic reforms of 1978 also tapped into the traditional entrepreneurial nature of Chinese society so evident not only in Hong Kong and Singapore but also in other parts of the world where Chinese have settled in large numbers (Harrell 1985).

Conclusion

The aim of this chapter has been to determine which method of regional integration is better, the one developing through a customs union or the one through government policy favouring greater infrastructure investment, free market supply side reforms offering incentives for entrepreneurship and innovation. The objective of this chapter has been to use the case study methodology to compare and contrast the economic history of the UK, the EU and a reformist China. A number of subsidiary questions were also raised, especially regarding the extent of the UK's trade diversion away from the Commonwealth towards the EU, resource diversion, over competition and market failure.

China's economic growth has been much higher than that of either the EU or the UK after 1973 except with one dip after 1990/1991 after which China's economic growth trajectory was much higher than that of either the EU or the UK. Even after the global financial crisis of 2008, China's economic growth was more resilient than that of either the UK or the EU, both of which experienced negative economic growth at the time followed by a week recovery. Before 1973 there was much greater variability between the economic growth rates of China, the EU and the UK. Between 1953 and 1973 when China was experiencing the Great Leap Forward and was nearing the end of the Cultural Revolution and when the UK was not a member of the EEC, China and the UK were experiencing annual average growth rates of 7.32 and 3.47% respectively. However, between 1974 and 2012, the period which encompasses China's economic reforms as well as the greater integration of the UK into the EEC and then the EU, annual average growth rates for China and the UK were 14.73 and 2.18% respectively. China's economic reforms have thus been more effective in promoting higher levels of economic growth by integrating China into the global economy while fostering greater integration of China's internal market than as the UK's strategy of greater integration with its European neighbours. Increasing trade also contributes to the economic growth of a country. The UK's trade balance became more volatile after 1973 and after the mid-1980s, the period in which the Single European Act came into effect, the UK's trade balance became negative. Thereafter, the UK's trade balance was positive only, exports being greater than imports, between 1995 and 1998. After 1998 the UK's trade balance became increasingly negative, imports greater than exports. This period encompasses the introduction of the Euro. Moreover, in the 20 year period after the establishment of the single market around 1992/1993, there has been only 1 year in which the UK experienced positive growth in trade with the Commonwealth, in 1994. This is in contrast to this happening in numerous previous years, in 1957, 1968, 1976, 1987 and 1990. More interestingly, UK exports to the Commonwealth as a percentage share of the UK's total exports fell from 38% in 1948 to 35% in 1960 then to 18% in 1973 and just 8% in 2010. A number of question arise from this trend. Firstly, was it this trend which triggered the UK's European integration strategy? Secondly, why did Britain not try to maintain and grow links with its former colonies? It is surprising that it did do so having invited Commonwealth citizens to the UK to fill job vacancies which could not be filled domestically due to a shortage of labour, after the late 1940s. Nevertheless, many Commonwealth citizens had even fought on the side of the UK during World War 2.

The results of the analysis provides evidence that between 1948 and 2010, the percentage share of the UK's total exports to the Commonwealth fell by approximately 30%; and that China's integration strategy through infrastructure investment and free market reforms offering incentives for entrepreneurship and innovation has increased China's economic growth at a rate much higher than that of the UK following a customs union integration strategy. Evidence for resource diversion, over competition and market failure in the UK economy may be provided by the UK's 'Leave' campaign victory in the Brexit referendum of the 23rd June 2016 in which the majority voted to the leave the EU because of housing shortages, long NHS waiting lists and competition of jobs. However, this can be interpreted as being a subjective view. But it represents an area where further quantitative and qualitative research is needed.

Notes

1. Eurostat.
2. UK Office of National Statistics.

References

Allen, G. (2012). *UK-commonwealth trade statistics, SNEP6497*. House of Commons Library: Economic Policy and Statistics Section.

Balassa, B. (1961). The theory of economic integration. *Kyklos, 14*(1), 1–17.

Baldwin, R., & Venables, A. (1995). Regional economic integration. *Handbook of international economics, 3*, 1597–1644.

Bayoumi, T., & Eichengreen, B. (1993). Shocking aspects of European monetary unification. In F. Torres & F. Giavazzi (Eds.), *Adjustment and growth in the European monetary union* (pp. 193–229). New York: Cambridge University Press.

Bouscaren, A. (1969). *European economic community migrations*. New York: Springer Science & Business Media.

El-Agraa, A. (2007). *The European union: Economics and policies* (8th ed). Cambridge: Cambridge University Press.

Fraser, T.G., & Murray, D. (2002). *America and the world since 1945*. Macmillan: Palgrave Macmillan.

Ge, W. (1999). Special economic zones and the opening of the chinese economy: Some lessons for economic liberalisation. *World Development, 27*(7), 1267–1285.

Gertler, N., & Mihollin, E. (2002). Public participation and access to justice in the world trade organisation. In C. Bruch (Ed.), *The new 'public': The globalisation of public participation*. Washington DC: Environmental Law Institute.

Ginsberg, R. (2007). *Demystifying the European union: The enduring logic of regional integration*. Plymouth, UK: Rowman & Littlefield Publishers.

Haas, E. (1961). International integration: The European and the universal process. *International Organisation, 15*(3), 366–392.

Harrell, S. (1985). Why do the Chinese work so hard?: Reflections on an entrepreneurial ethic. *Modern China, 11*(2), 203–226.

Lindberg, L. N. (1963). *The political dynamics of European economic integration*. Stanford: Stanford University Press.

Loveland, I. (2012). *Constitutional law, administrative law and human rights: A critical introduction* (6th ed). UK: Oxford University Press.

Mainz, D. (1994). The maastricht treaty and the design of a European federal state. *Temple Int'L & Comp. L.* J, 8.

Nikolova, M., Roman, M., & Zimmermann, K. (2016). Left behind but doing good? Civic engagement in two post-socialist countries. *Journal of Comparative Economics*. doi:10.1016/j.jce.2016.04.006.

Nye, J. (1968). Comparative regional integration: Concept and measurement. *International Organisation, 22*(4), 855–880.

Pelkmans, J. (2016). Why the single market remains the EU's core business. *West European Politics, 39*(5), 1095–1113.

Price, J. (1989). What did merchants do? Reflections on British overseas trade, 1660–1790. *The Journal of Economic History, 49*(2).

Rosamond, B. (2000). *Theories of economic integration*. New York: St Martin's Press.

Thorbecke, W., & Smith, G. (2010). How would an appreciation of the ren-
minbi and other East Asian currencies affect China's Exports? *Review of International Economics, 18*(1), 95–108.

USDA. (1987). 1987 Fact book of u.s agriculture, miscellaneous publication
No. 1063. United States Department of Agriculture.

Viner, J. (1950). *The customs union issue.* New York: Carnegie Endowment for
International Peace.

Wang, H. (2010). *The Chinese dream: The rise of the world's largest middle class
and what it means to you.* Bestseller Press.

Wang, J. (2013). *The economic impact of special economic zones: Evidence from
Chinese municipalities, 101,* 133–147.

Zeng, J. (2013). *State-led privatisation in China: The politics of economic reform.*
UK: Routledge.

7

Conclusion

The economic reforms in China which began in 1978 have stimulated innovation and entrepreneurship which has facilitated knowledge spillovers in the wider economy due to the Chinese economics capacity for institutional flexibility. The roots of this lie in the institutional vacuum in which the command economy of the People's Republic of China found itself in 1949. This institutional vacuum allowed Chinese policymakers to experiment to find a 'balanced' path for sustainable economic growth and prosperity. However, the Great Leap Forward led to famine and starvation. The Cultural Revolution aimed for ideological purity but led to the degradation of economic growth and economic development. Finally, the Chinese Communist Party was able to unburden the economy from the shackles of central planning and to unleash the wheels of prosperity, by introducing free market reforms on an evolutionary basis in 1978 towards achieving a socialist market economy. The economic reforms fostered strong institutional links between government, universities and research institutes and entrepreneurs. This allowed knowledge spillovers to facilitate sustained economic growth. However, China's market integration was uneven, and economic growth resulted in increasing income disparities between China's Coastal region

© The Author(s) 2017
S. Ramesh, *China's Lessons for India: Volume II*,
DOI 10.1007/978-3-319-58115-6_7

and its Central and Western regions. The rising prosperity of China's Coastal region and its much higher contribution to China's economic growth than its other regions was cemented by the embedding of knowledge creation in China's Coastal region. Although China's market integration due to the economic reforms has been unbalanced, this market integration has contributed more to China's economic growth than has been the contribution to Britain's economic growth through its market integration with the other EU countries through a customs union, a single market and a formal union. Moreover, India's economic growth has been hindered by the economy's institutional rigidity which resulted from the colonial past, being cemented by the adoption of a rigid centrally planned, license economy after independence in 1947. India's ancient caste system has also contributed towards the economy's institutional rigidity. It is this institutional rigidity which has constrained India's innovation, entrepreneurship and knowledge spillovers to the wider economy preventing high levels of sustained economic growth which characterised the Chinese economy until recent times.

The time has now approached where because sufficient evidence has been gathered and the analysis presented robust that the research questions set out in Chap. 4, Vol. 2 can be answered.

'How Have infrastructure, knowledge creation and knowledge spillovers contributed to the economic growth of China?'

From 1949 to 1977, government policy placed great emphasis on the misplaced judgement that the railways, central planning and heavy industry would bring prosperity to China. For example, in the period 1953–1977, Gansu registered the largest percentage increases in the length of railways, the number of railway passengers and railway freight. In the same period, Hubei registered the largest percentage increases in the number of waterway and highway passengers, as well as waterway and highway freight transported. The importance of the interior of China in this period is further exhibited by the high and almost equal percentage increases in the levels of adjusted TIFA in Hubei and Gansu compared to Jiangsu. Nevertheless, after 1980, the percentage increases in adjusted TIFA in Jiangsu overtook that of both Hubei and Gansu. This is clear evidence of the impact of the economic reforms, which began in 1978. However, after 1995, the percentage increases in adjusted TIFA of Gansu overtook that of both Jiangsu and Hubei. These may be an indication of an emerging Western Development Plan. The results discussed suggest that in the pre-reform period, the government invested in railway infrastructure for the purposes of supporting heavy industry in northern China, closely following the Soviet model of development. Light manufacturing industry, which was to have great significance in the years following 1978, did not have any place in the central command economy of the years 1949–1977. However, small-scale rural enterprises, the predecessors of TVEs, which specialised in the manufacture of light goods began to be established in Jiangsu from the early 1970s, while SoEs remained the central plan 'backbone' of the interior hinterland. It is notable that it was in 1972 that the Gross Input Output Value of Jiangsu and Gansu began to diverge. The results discussed relate to Proposition 3 which is discussed in Chap. 4, Vol. 1.

Knowledge creation has sustained income disparities between the Coastal regions of China and its interior since 1978. Patent data does to an extent confirm this statement. For example, in the period 1985–2005, more patents were granted, [Fig. 4.9, Chap. 4, Vol. 1], on a year by year basis in Jiangsu compared to Hubei or Gansu. Moreover, the trend in innovation is greater amongst industrial and mineral enterprises; enterprises are more significant in the Coastal regions than in the interior regions. However, other results conflict with this view. For example, the rate of increase in telephone subscribers and teachers employed in secondary schools was more notable in Gansu after 1978 than in Hubei or Jiangsu. The same thing can be said about university enrolments. However, despite Gansu's predominant growth rates with regard to these factors, Jiangsu has a larger aggregate balance with respect to each of them. Other results can be used to reinforce this point. For example, in 2001, Jiangsu had the largest number of full-time teachers, graduates, the number of new products, scientists and engineers as well as the number of natural science topics under research. Moreover, Jiangsu has the greatest source of funds for innovation, whether bank loans, enterprise funds or government grants. In this respect, entrepreneurship seems to be predominant in Jiangsu because it has the greatest number of LMEs than either Hubei or Gansu. Nevertheless, the paradox is that Gansu has more LMEs than Hubei. This is a paradox because Gansu is less developed than is Hubei. Aspects of Proposition 4 and Proposition 1, discussed previously in Chap. 4, Vol. 1, have been relevant here. Knowledge spillovers have in the main been facilitated through FDI and government reforms which have incentivised entrepreneurship due to the horizontal integration of the activities of research institutes with commercial enterprises. Entrepreneurship has been the conduit of knowledge spillovers.

The post-1978 economic reforms have created deepening income disparities between China's Coastal regions and its interior hinterland. Nevertheless, the government instituted the Western Development Plan and the Eleventh Five-Year Plan in order to address this problem. These initiatives have been less than successful in reversing the tide of the increasing disparities in income between China's Interior and Coastal provinces. The two volumes of this series, China's Lessons for India, can now be concluded by answering the research questions which were stated in Chap. 4, Vol. 1.

'From a political historical perspective, how have the post-1978 economic reforms contributed to building soft and hard infrastructure in China?'

The emphasis of post-1978 economic policies focused on the development of SEZs and Open Coastal areas in the 1980s and the high-technology development zone's and science and technology parks in the 1990s. Indeed, China's development strategy and development model were a combination of 'islands of Capitalism in an ocean of central planning' diffused with national reforms focusing on R&D and education. Here, the 'islands of Capitalism' refer to the SEZs and other development zones. The role of infrastructure focused around the development of these areas. In the period 1979–1995, percentage increases in waterway and highway freight were greatest in Jiangsu as well as the percentage increases in the length of highways and highway passengers. It is possible to suggest that the changes in the length of highways in Jiangsu, at this time, maybe be attributable to the development of SEZs. The development of highways in Jiangsu followed the same pattern in the period 1997–2004. However, in the same period, Gansu showed the largest increase with respect to highway freight. But with respect to percentage changes in the number of railway and highway passengers, Hubei registered bigger increases than Jiangsu. Nevertheless, where as the aggregate length of railways in the period 1949–1977 is significant in Jiangsu, there is an overall decrease in the period 1995–2004. The same can be said for railway stock in Hubei and Gansu but the decline in railway stock is more indicative in Jiangsu. This decline may be accounted for by the requirement of sectors to produce at a rate of return; and the dependence of the interior of China on heavy industry. On the other hand, the development of Coastal industry focused on the manufacture of light goods with a high-technology content, as well as cost-effective access to international markets. Thus, in the Coastal provinces, there was less reliance on the railways, while the preponderance of natural resources in China's interior required more use of the railways.

The integration and concentration of physical infrastructure and soft infrastructure investment in one geographical area [SEZs and NHTIDZs] facilitated in the formation and maximisation of agglomeration economies, which arise due to physical and knowledge transfer linkages. In 1979, three special economic zones (SEZ) were set up in Guangdong and in Fujian province. It had been hoped that foreign investors would treat these SEZs as export processing zones. However, this did not happen and as a result further policy changes were made. In 1984, fourteen Coastal cities and Hainan Island were designated as open areas. Hainan Island was designated a special economic zone in 1988. In addition to these changes, in 1985, a number of wider areas were selected to receive foreign investment and priority investment. These areas included the Changjiang River Delta, the Pearl River Delta and the Minnan Delta Economic Region. The reason behind the designation of the delta Coastal areas of China as priority recipients of FDI was the failure of the SEZs to attract minimum investment and joint ventures to receive maximum foreign investment.[1] High-tech enterprise zones [NHTIDZ's] were the second generation SEZs with a technological export orientation. They were set up as a backdrop to the 'Open Door' policy. Enterprises in the high-tech zones were engaged in R&D, sales and industrial management and concentrated in high-tech zones because of the preferential policies applied to firms in these zones which operated without any form of state control. In 1985, preferential policies were applied in the first high-tech zone set up in Shenzhen; in 1988, the Zhongguancun high-tech centre was set up in Beijing, taking advantage of the proximity of some of the best research and teaching institutions in China. The setting up of high-tech zones had been an important feature of the Torch Program. Indeed, it was because of the Torch Program that high-tech zones were set up all over China. However, in order to ensure consistency in the way that each high-tech zone was set up and administered on a daily basis, a policy document was issued in 1991. According to Jing (2000), the high-tech zones were set up in such a way that 50% were set up in Central provincial cities, 25% in Coastal cities and the remaining in the industrial cities. The spatial density of such zones decreases moving from China's coast to its interior hinterland. Moreover, those zones in the Coastal regions contributed much more significantly to China's economic growth than the inland ones. For example, in 2004, Suzhou High-Tech DZ contributed US$ 1 billion to China's economy. There was also a tendency to situate S&T parks in areas where universities and research facilities tended to concentrate. Furthermore, universities set up sites in the Coastal region; and firms in the Coastal region networked with firms in the interior hinterland.

The role of education within Chinese society changed during the reform period. Before the reforms, there was much emphasis on ensuring that the masses were politically educated with an emphasis on vocational education to suit the needs of central planning and heavy industry. During this period, there was no need for fostering creative thinking in students. The only requirement of education was to produce workers who would fulfil the requirements of the respective Five-year plan. However, after 1978, the emphasis of educational policy was on quality, choice and creativity. This approach was underlined in the Eleventh

Five-Year Plan with the slogan of 'endogenous innovation and harmony'. China's educational reforms have been more effective in the Coastal regions such as Jiangsu because of the provinces' ability to better fund provincial education due to its increased prosperity. However, interior provinces such as Gansu suffer from lack of resources, difficult terrain, a non-homogeneous population and a 'brain drain' to the Coastal regions. These factors reduce the effectiveness of education in these regions. There is thus a need for China to establish a consistent and coherent national education system with common standards, adequate central government educational funding for the poorer provinces and an increased drive by the central government in making the Internet available to all for educational purposes. The growing importance of the Internet for the Chinese knowledge economy was established in Chap. 2, Vol. 2. If China follows such a path, then China can break from the mould cast by the 1978 reforms and ensure that a national innovation system is created and enhanced in the context of the Triple Helix Model. At present regional innovation systems may exist in China, but an effective national innovation system is dysfunctional.

'In China's case, why has manufacturing concentrated in the coastal regions leaving the periphery to play a minor role in national economic growth?'

In China's case, manufacturing has concentrated in the Coastal regions leaving the periphery interior Central and Western regions to play a minor role in national economic growth for three reasons. Firstly, government policy and economic reforms after 1978 facilitated the formation of three regions of economic growth centred on the Coastal regions—the Pearl River Delta, the Yangtze River Delta and the Bohai Sea Rim. Secondly, due to government economic policy and the subsequent formation of the SEZs and NHTIDZs, it was possible for China to combine its comparative advantage in cheap labour to manufacture low technology goods in the first phase of post-reform development and then in the second phase to produce high-technology goods. In doing so, foreign capital was more efficiently utilised. Thirdly, there was preponderance for the industry in the interior of China to specialise in heavy industry and machinery, while Coastal provinces such as Jiangsu had already begun to develop small-scale rural enterprises specialising in the manufacture of light goods as early as the 1970s.

How can India learn from China's experience?

Specifically, India should focus on facilitating economic growth through a combination of infrastructure investment, facilitating innovation, facilitating entrepreneurship at the microeconomic level; as well as facilitating dynamism, adaptability and flexibility in the evolution of institutions over time. In general, India should:

(a) Do more to promote entrepreneurship, especially amongst lower castes and females.
(b) Repeal draconian labour laws which make it expensive for firms and entrepreneurs to hire workers.
(c) Set up a small-scale venture capital fund for entrepreneurs. This will enable small-scale (rural and urban) entrepreneurs to acquire the finances required to start a business.
(d) Promote and strengthen equality legislation and do more to empower women so that they can side-step the constraints of discrimination and contribute towards the country's economic growth.
(e) Increase government funding for R&D at universities and research institutes, so that innovative projects can be undertaken. This will strengthen the links between centers of research and firms so that knowledge can be more easily commercialised in the context of products and services.
(f) Implement high-technology zones and incubators for start-ups at universities in order to facilitate horizontal linkages between centres of research and commercial firms.
(g) Incentivise researchers by strengthening intellectual property rights so that researchers will be able to profit from innovation.

(h) Designate Mumbai, Chennai and Kolkata to become open coastal cities with preferential economic and business policies for both domestic firms and overseas firms. These policies could include lower corporate tax rates, the right to repatriate profits to other countries and private property rights.

(i) Implement special economic zones in Tamil Nadu, Maharashtra and Gujarat close to ports with government-funded infrastructure and preferential policies to attract foreign MNCs to engage in manufacturing. The preferential policies could include those discussed in (h). In return, the MNCs should be obliged to bring to India, advanced technology and advanced management skills.

(j) Improve all types of physical infrastructure within India as well as infrastructure connecting India to its surrounding countries, especially China, in the long term. This will improve trade between India's states as well as improve India's trade with neighbouring countries by lowering transport costs and integrating markets within India and with India and its neighbouring countries, thus expanding markets.

The main findings of Vols. 1 and 2 of this book series would suggest the following. Firstly, the Indian government should instigate policies which focus on the evolution and development of more efficient institutions. Secondly, the Indian government should instigate policies which form a better link between research institutions and firms. Thirdly, the Indian government should better ensure that the primary purpose of infrastructure is not only to lower firms' transport costs but also that it is efficient and integrates markets within India as well as with India and its neighbours. Infrastructure development would tend to more effective, based on China's experience, when it is dense and near the Coastal region. It is for this reason that the three Coastal cities of Mumbai, Chennai and Kolkata should be classed as open cities with a preferential economic and business environment for domestic and overseas firms so that they are incentivised to invest in manufacturing in these cities. The need for more workers in these areas will attract more and more of the rural unemployed and underemployed. Their rising incomes in conjunction with the market integrating effects of dense local infrastructure and not so dense nationwide infrastructure will more effectively promote national economic growth. These are China's economic lessons for India. However, although this book series has not analysed the economic implications of corruption and tax collection, the government of India could also implement measures to tackle corruption, as it did recently with changes in the value of cash denomination, and to improve the efficiency of the tax collection system. Moreover, reforms could also be introduced so that banks accounts are mandatory for salary payment.

Note

1. Tracy, N. (1997). 'The South East: The Cutting Edge of China's Economic Reform', in 'China's New Spatial Economy: Heading Towards 2020', Linge, L (Eds).

Index

Printed by Printforce, the Netherlands